The Lord of the Rings
and Philosophy

Popular Culture and Philosophy™

Series Editor: William Irwin

The Lord of the Rings and Philosophy

One Book to Rule Them All

Edited by
GREGORY BASSHAM
and
ERIC BRONSON

OPEN COURT
Chicago and La Salle, Illinois

Volume 5 in the series, Popular Culture and Philosophy™

**To order books from Open Court, call toll free 1-800-815-2280,
or visit our website at www.opencourtbooks.com**.

Open Court Publishing Company is a division of Carus Publishing
Company.

Copyright ©2003 by Carus Publishing Company

First printing 2003

Printed and bound in the United States of America

Library of Congress Cataloging-in-Publication Data

The Lord of the rings and philosophy : one book to rule them all /
edited by Gregory Bassham and Eric Bronson.
     p. cm. — (Popular culture and philosophy ; v. 5)
    Includes bibliographical references and index.
    ISBN 0-8126-9545-3 (pbk.)
    1. Tolkien, J. R. R. (John Ronald Reuel), 1892-1973. Lord of the
rings. 2. Tolkien, J. R. R. (John Ronald Reuel), 1892-1973—Philosophy.
3. Fantasy fiction, English—History and criticism. 4. Middle Earth
(Imaginary place) 5. Philosophy in literature. I. Bassham, Gregory,
1959- II. Bronson, Eric, 1971- III. Title. IV. Series.
PR6039.032L6356 2003
823'.912—dc22
                                 2003015450

To the entwives—wherever they may roam

Contents

Acknowledgments

Every book is a journey, and it is a pleasure to say "Thag you very buch" to the many good people who made this one so stimulating and enjoyable.

First, our thanks to the contributors. Eighteen months is too short a time to work with such excellent and admirable authors.

Second, to Bill Irwin, the fearless series editor: thanks for your unflagging support and encouragement, your wise council, and the excellent pipe-weed.

Third, to David Ramsay Steele, Carolyn Madia Gray, and the fine production and marketing staff at Open Court: We don't know half of you half as well as we should like, but we admire your energy and professionalism, and we are grateful for all you have done to make this book a success.

Thanks are also due to Steve Colby, Jeremy Sauers, Jonathan DeCarlo, John Davenport, Brian Pavlac, Rachel Bronson and John and Casley Rose Matthews, for providing helpful feedback on drafts of the essays. A special word of appreciation to Abby Myers, our editorial assistant, who read and commented on the entire manuscript, tracked down quotes, and helped out in various and sundry ways.

Eric is most appreciative for the logistical support received from Arthur Blumenthal and Phil Krebs at Berkeley College. As always, Greg's greatest debt is to his wife, Mia, and son, Dylan, for their love, patience, and understanding.

Abbreviations

References to Tolkien's most frequently cited works occur in parentheses throughout the book, followed by the page numbers. The following abbreviations are used:

H   *The Hobbit: or, There and Back Again.* New York: Del Ray/Ballantine Books, 2001.

FR   *The Fellowship of the Ring.* New York: Del Ray/Ballantine Books, 2001.

TT   *The Two Towers.* New York: Del Ray/Ballantine Books, 2001.

RK   *The Return of the King.* New York: Del Ray/Ballantine Books, 2001.

S   *The Silmarillion*, edited by Christopher Tolkien. Boston: Houghton Mifflin, 1977.

L   *The Letters of J.R.R. Tolkien*, edited by Humphrey Carpenter. Boston: Houghton Mifflin, 1981.

Introduction:
The Wisdom of Middle-earth

J.R.R. Tolkien's *The Lord of the Rings* has been a publishing and literary phenomenon for half a century. Since its publication in 1954–55, Tolkien's fantasy epic has sold more than fifty million copies, and has been voted the greatest book of the twentieth century in several recent readers' polls.

With Peter Jackson's blockbuster film version of the great Quest, Tolkien's magical tale of cheerful hobbits, snarling orcs, and short-tempered wizards garnered millions of new fans. The day before New Line Cinema released *The Lord of the Rings: The Two Towers* nationwide, *The New York Post* ran a full-page article with a front-page teaser: "*Lord of the Rings* for Dummies." Toy stores are crammed with Aragorn action figures, Legolas trading cards, and other *Lord of the Rings* paraphernalia. The movie's theme of pursuing a magical ring was used as the theme for the 2002 NBA playoffs, and even parodied in Comedy Central's notorious *South Park*.

But not all Tolkien devotees are happy about this sudden surge in popularity. After *The Two Towers* was released, websites were awash with anger over the sometimes substantial variations between the book and the movie. As debates erupted over the Internet (sometimes in elvish), the old empire struck back. On the official *Lord of the Rings* website, one old-timer disgustedly called a *Rings* neophyte a "complete idiot" for not knowing that a wizard's power comes from his staff.

To satisfy everyone, it appears that we need more than a "*Lord of the Rings* for Dummies." We need a "*Lord of the Rings* for Smart People."

With this in mind, we've assembled a distinguished cast of seventeen erudite philosophers and other academics, (all of them devoted *Lord of the Rings* fans) and asked them to help out with some of the deeper philosophical questions raised by the books and movies. Can power ever be wielded for good, or is it always corrupting? Should death be seen as a "gift"? Can golden rings and dragon's treasures ever bring us true happiness? If an ent fell in the forest, and no one was around to hear, would it make any sound?

Tolkien himself, of course, was an Oxford professor of Anglo-Saxon, not a professional philosopher. He was, however, a leading scholar in his field and a close friend of leading British intellectuals such as C.S. Lewis, Owen Barfield, Charles Williams, Neville Coghill, and Hugo Dyson. Moreover, as a devout Roman Catholic, he was deeply interested in such perennial philosophical and theological issues as good versus evil, fate versus free-will, mind and body, life after death, and environmental stewardship. All these philosophical issues, and more, are introduced in Tolkien's writings and explored in this collection.

This is not to say, of course, that Tolkien explicitly thought about or intended all the various ideas and theories discussed in this volume. Our main goal is to highlight the philosophical significance of *The Lord of the Rings*, not to tease out any hidden philosophical meaning or message.

We hope this book will not only help you understand many of the deeper issues that inform *The Lord of the Rings*, but also spark an interest in the enduring questions of philosophy. In his letters, Tolkien remarks that one of his goals in writing *The Lord of the Rings* was "the elucidation of truth, and the encouragement of good morals in this real world" (*Letters*, p. 194). Like Tolkien, we believe that fiction—and popular culture in general—can serve as an effective medium for eliciting and presenting philosophical ideas. This appeal to popular culture goes back at least to Socrates, the first great philosopher in Western civilization. To encourage people to think about their lives and beliefs, Socrates often used examples from art, sports, music—whatever his interlocutors knew about and were interested in. In a similar way, we believe that today's popular culture can help to get people excited about the great questions of philosophy.

So light your hobbit pipe and warm your toes with a generous nip of elvish cordial. As the philosopher-wizard Gandalf says, "If you have walked all these days with closed ears and mind asleep, wake up now!"

PART I

The Ring

1

The Rings of Tolkien and Plato: Lessons in Power, Choice, and Morality

ERIC KATZ

If a mortal being—a human or a hobbit, for example—possesses a Ring of Power, would he choose a moral life? When we ask this question, we might be concerned about the physical abilities and limitations of the possessor of the Ring. We might wonder whether a mere hobbit, such as Sam Gamgee, could wield the powers of the Ring in the same manner that Aragorn, a human nobleman could. Would the Ring provide different kinds of power to different kinds of beings, so that some strong willed individuals—such as Aragorn—would have the power to control the minds and actions of others, while weaker-willed individuals—Gollum comes to mind—would only use the Ring as a means of escape and evasion?

Although these are interesting questions about the way the Rings of Power are physically used, in this essay I am not primarily concerned with the *physical* aspects of the use of the Ring; I am rather concerned with the *moral* aspects. Does the use of a Ring of Power entail any moral or ethical limits? Is there a morally right or morally wrong way to use a Ring? These questions become even more important when we consider not just any Ring of Power, but the One Ring of Sauron, for the possessor of the One Ring can wield almost unlimited power, and a being who possesses such power would seem to have little reason to concern himself with the dictates of morality.

In *The Lord of the Rings*, J.R.R. Tolkien presents us with several clear examples of the relationship between personal choice, power, and morality. Indeed, the story of the One Ring, and Frodo's quest to destroy it, can be seen as a modern representation of a problem in ethical thinking originally posed by the ancient Greek philosopher Plato in his classic dialogue, the *Republic*. Plato was also concerned with the relationship between power and morality. He tells us the story of Gyges, who finds a ring of magical power. The ring causes its wearer to be invisible. Gyges uses the ring to enter the palace, seduce the queen, and kill the king. Plato's question to us is whether or not one should be a moral person even if one has the power to be immoral with impunity. Does immense power destroy the need to be a moral person?

It is interesting to view Tolkien's tales of the rings as a variation of this old Platonic moral problem. Sauron's One Ring is similar to the ring of Gyges in that it gives its possessor the power to act beyond normal limits.[1] The characters who seek to use the One Ring believe that many of their desires can be satisfied, without regard to the interests or needs of any other creature. The story of Sauron's Ring is a representation of the idea that unlimited power cannot co-exist with morality; the Ring represents the idea that absolute power is in conflict with behavior that respects the wishes and needs of others. But the use of Tolkien's Ring is a matter of personal choice. One does not have to follow the example of Plato's villain, Gyges; all beings are capable of rejecting the use of a Ring of Power.

Tolkien's characters react to the possibility of possessing the vast power of the One Ring in different ways. Gollum is utterly destroyed by his desire for the Ring. Boromir is seduced by the

---

[1] Both rings render their wearers invisible. The One Ring, however, has many powers that Gyges's ring does not. In particular, the One Ring gives power to a possessor according to his or her stature (FR, p. 411); is morally corrupting; prevents or slows aging and decay (FR, p. 285; L, p. 152); sharpens hearing, dims sight, and enables a wearer to understand unknown languages (TT, pp. 388–89); permits a wearer to see, and to be seen by, things in the invisible world (FR, p. 249), and enables a sufficiently powerful wearer to perceive all that is done by means of the lesser Rings, and to see and govern the thoughts of those who wield them (S, p. 288). Interestingly, the Ring affects different individuals and races differently. Dwarves, for example, are apparently immune from some of the ordinary effects of the Ring (S, p. 283).

thought of wielding unlimited power for the good of Gondor, but Galadriel rejects the use of the Ring altogether. Sam and Frodo each use the Ring in a limited way and thus avoid its worst effects; but while Frodo succumbs to its power, Sam, like Galadriel, ultimately rejects it. Tom Bombadil appears to transcend the Ring's power entirely. These characters and their relationship to the use of the One Ring thus reveal to us several different answers to the question posed by Plato. We can make the personal choice to reject unlimited power and to act by the principles of morality.

Let's examine the arguments and the stories in more detail.

Plato's Challenge of Immorality

Plato's long dialogue, the *Republic*, is concerned with one central issue: the justification of the morally good life. "Why be moral?" is the crucial question that must be answered. The participants in the main section of the dialogue (Books II–X) are Socrates, who defends the importance of the moral life, and Glaucon and Adimantus, who play devil's advocate and defend the life of immorality. Plato sets himself an imposing task, for Glaucon and Adimantus present the strongest possible case for the life of immorality—can we justify choosing a moral life even when the immoral life is more rewarding? If an immoral life leads to wealth, power, and fame while a morally virtuous life leads to poverty, powerlessness, and abuse, then why be moral?

It is during this argument that Glaucon recounts the story of the shepherd Gyges and his discovery of a magical ring that makes the bearer invisible. As we have seen, Gyges uses the ring for evil purposes—he seduces the queen of the kingdom, slays the king, and becomes himself the ruler of the land. For Glaucon, this is what all men would do. He imagines that there are two such rings of invisibility, one possessed by a just or moral man, and one by an unjust or immoral man. Even the just man would succumb to the power offered by this ring. "No one could be found . . . of such adamantine temper as to persevere in justice and endure to refrain his hands from the possessions of others . . . though he might with impunity take what he wished . . . and in all other things conduct himself among mankind as the equal of a god" (*Republic* II, 360b–c).

For Glaucon, people are morally good only because they cannot act with impunity—they fear punishment for their evil actions. For any person, the best possible world would be one in which the individual could act without any fear of being punished, acting with unlimited power to satisfy his own desires regardless of the evil effects on others. The worst possible world, in contrast, would be one in which the individual would be abused by others with no power to respond. Morality is thus a compromise between these two possible extremes: the rational people in a community agree to limit their own selfish behavior and not harm others. We agree not to abuse other people and in turn society protects us from potential abusers. Glaucon argues that there is thus nothing really good about the morally good life. If we had the power to act as we choose without fear of punishment we would not be morally good. The question "Why be moral?" is thus answered with the cynical response of the immoralist: the moral life is the life chosen by the weak.

Plato seeks to refute this cynical conclusion and justify the value of the moral life. The argument is long, but the essential point of Plato's response is simple: the immoral life is a worse life than a morally virtuous life because ultimately the immoral life corrupts the soul of the immoralist. The immoral life leads to a fundamental unhappiness: mental anguish, the loss of friends and loved ones, and emotional bankruptcy. All the power in the world cannot compensate for the psychological emptiness of an immoral life. The moral person, in contrast, lives a life of integrity and personal fulfillment, even if he or she is limited in power, wealth, and fame. The moral person is at peace with himself.

For Plato, then, the moral person rejects the use of a Ring of Power. The moral person prefers to live a life of inner peace and integrity, a life guided by moral principles, not a life of power and the mere satisfaction of self-interest. Using the story of a magical ring that gives its possessor unlimited power, Plato is able to illustrate and answer one of the basic questions of philosophy: how should I live my life?

The Temptation of the One Ring

With this ancient challenge to the moral life as background, we can see how Tolkien's characters demonstrate various responses to the question posed by Plato: would a just person be corrupted by the possibility of almost unlimited power? Through these different responses, Tolkien shows us—not by philosophical argument, but by the thoughts and actions of "living" characters—why we should be moral beings, why we should live a virtuous life. But Tolkien's stories about the One Ring actually improve and augment Plato's argument, for Tolkien's Ring explicitly corrupts the souls of its possessors. The use of the One Ring corrupts the desires, interests, and beliefs of those who wield it. Plato *argues* that such corruption will occur, but Tolkien *shows* us this corruption through the thoughts and actions of his characters. Moreover, Tolkien also shows us the difficulties involved in living a life of virtue: there are burdens to be undertaken and sacrifices that must be made to fulfill the requirements of morality.

The character that most obviously illustrates Plato's argument that the unjust life leads to nothing but unhappiness is Gollum, who is invariably described as a miserable creature, afraid of everything, friendless, homeless, constantly seeking his "precious" Ring. Gollum is the mortal being who possessed the Ring for the longest period of time and he seems almost completely corrupted by the desire for it—every action he takes in the book, even guiding Frodo and Sam on their journey into Mordor, is designed to regain the Ring. It is during the long journey through the barren lands surrounding Mordor that we see the true disintegration of Gollum's personality, all caused by the desire of the Ring. Gollum constantly talks to himself, for his soul is split in two: one part is Sméagol, the hobbit he was before the Ring came into his possession, and one half is Gollum, the creature whose only desire is to possess the Ring again. The only reason that Gollum cooperates with Frodo and Sam is that the two halves (what Sam calls "Slinker and Stinker") have made a truce: "neither wanted the Enemy to get the Ring" (TT, p. 274). Frodo recognizes the immense power that the thought of the Ring has on Gollum's mind. Earlier, he made Gollum swear on the Ring that he would be a faithful guide (TT, p. 250), but soon after, near the Black Gate of Mordor, Gollum was in "great distress" at the thought that Frodo would lose the Ring:

> "Don't take the Precious to Him! . . . Keep it, nice master, and be kind to Sméagol. Don't let Him have it. Or go away, go to nice

places, and give it back to little Sméagol. . . . Sméagol will keep it
safe; he will do lots of good, especially to nice hobbits." (TT, p.
273)

This outburst by Gollum prompts Frodo to get to the heart of
the matter, to describe to Gollum the peril he faces, the danger
of losing his soul. Gollum swore a promise by what he calls the
Precious. The Ring will not only hold Gollum to this promise,
but will seek a way to twist it to Gollum's own undoing.
"Already you are being twisted," Frodo tells Gollum (TT, p. 276).
And then, with a strange prescience of the climax of the story,
Frodo states that if the need arises, he would himself put on the
Ring and command Gollum to cast himself into the fire.

Gollum is thus a clear example of the corruption of the soul
and the loss of a meaningful life caused by the overwhelming
desire for the Ring of Power. But Gollum is not a complete
example of the problem posed by Plato, for we do not see the
moment when he makes the choice to use the Ring. For Plato,
as well as for Tolkien, the crucial moment in each character's
story is the moment in which they are tempted to use the Ring.
It is that moment of choice that determines a character's fate,
that moment of choice that bears a remarkable similarity to
Plato's story of the shepherd Gyges and his decision to use the
ring of invisibility. Gollum's moment of choice occurred long
before the opening pages of *The Lord of the Rings*—even long
before the beginning of *The Hobbit*. Although Gandalf recounts
the story—how Sméagol kills his friend Déagol to gain possession of the Ring (FR, p. 58)—we do not live through Sméagol's
original moral crisis and decision. In Gollum instead we see
merely the final result of the life led in the pursuit of power, a
life of misery and corruption.

Boromir is the character who most closely fits the model of
Glaucon's moral argument concerning the shepherd Gyges—the
virtuous man corrupted by the temptation of power. Tolkien
depicts Boromir as a man of action—noble, good-hearted, and
brave—who is bewildered by the complexities of the plan to
destroy the One Ring. During the Council of Elrond, Boromir
asks why those assembled should not think that the Ring "has
come into our hands to serve us in the very hour of need . . . .
Wielding it the Free Lords of the Free may surely defeat the
Enemy . . . . Let the Ring be your weapon . . . Take it and go

forth to victory!" (FR, p. 300) Boromir wants to use the One Ring for good purposes. He sees nothing wrong with using the Ring to satisfy the desires of the free peoples of Middle-earth (and of himself) to defeat the evil of Sauron.

Boromir's idea to use the Ring is rejected by Elrond—and the rest of the members of the Council—in terms that evoke Plato's argument in the *Republic*: "We cannot use the Ruling Ring . . . . It . . . is altogether evil . . . . The very desire of it corrupts the heart" (FR, p. 300). Using the power of evil ultimately destroys the soul ("corrupts the heart").

Boromir seems to be persuaded, and throughout the journey south with the Fellowship he does not talk about wielding the Ring for the forces of good. But in the climax to *The Fellowship of the Ring*, Boromir is overcome by the temptation to use the Ring in the war against Mordor. He secretly follows Frodo into the woods near Amon Hen in order to convince him to bring the Ring to Gondor. Yet Boromir's words betray him, as he begins to envision himself as a great warrior in command of the Ring and of all the forces against Mordor. First, he argues that the Ring will save his people, but it soon becomes clear to Frodo that there are more selfish motives at work. "It is not yours save by unhappy chance," Boromir says. "It might have been mine. It should be mine. Give it to me!" (FR, p. 449) Boromir attempts to take the Ring by force, but Frodo slips the Ring onto his finger, turns invisible, and escapes.

Boromir redeems his heroic nature by defending Merry and Pippin against the attacking orcs, and as he dies he confesses to Aragorn that he attempted to take the Ring from Frodo. The corruption caused by the Ring is thus not permanent, but perhaps only because Boromir ultimately had so little contact with the *Ring*. Nevertheless, Boromir is a perfect example of the immoralist's challenge that Glaucon proposes in Plato's dialogue: Boromir is the just man who finds a Ring of Power and is unable to resist the temptation to act with impunity, as if he were a god. The desire for the power of the Ring so corrupts his soul that he accuses Frodo of being an evil ally of the Dark Lord. The ethical lesson is clear: a Ring of Power corrupts even the person who is brave, strong, and virtuous.

Who can avoid corruption? Before the temptation and death of Boromir, Tolkien has shown us the temptation of Galadriel, the Lady of Lothlórien. Galadriel is one of the most powerful elves of Middle-earth, and Frodo offers to give her the One Ring. Frodo's motives for the offer are complex: he is afraid of the journey ahead and worried that he may not be able to accomplish his task, but he also has just realized that the destruction of the Ring will lead to the end of the elvish presence on Middle-earth. Perhaps if Galadriel accepts the Ring, the evil of Mordor can be defeated and the elves saved. "You are wise and fearless and fair, Lady Galadriel," says Frodo. "I will give you the One Ring, if you ask for it. It is too great a matter for me" (FR, p. 410).

At first Galadriel laughs, for Frodo is tempting her with the greatest temptation imaginable, and she sees the irony in her powerlessness, for if she really wanted the Ring, she could simply take it from Frodo by force. But to take the Ring by force would be to act in an evil way; it would show that the Ring had already corrupted her. "I do not deny that my heart has greatly desired to ask what you offer," she tells Frodo. Galadriel has pondered for many long years what she might do if the Ring should fall into her hands. "The evil that was devised long ago works on in many ways . . . . Would not that have been a noble deed to set to the credit of his Ring, if I had taken it by force or fear from my guest?"

Now she has no need to take it by force. Frodo is freely offering it to her. So Galadriel continues:

> "You will give me the Ring freely! In place of the Dark Lord you will set up a Queen. And I shall not be dark, but beautiful and terrible as the Morning and the Night! Fair as the Sea and the Sun and the Snow upon the Mountain! Dreadful as the Storm and the Lightning! Stronger than the foundations of the earth. All shall love me and despair!" (FR, p. 410)

At this point Galadriel lifts up her hand, and from the elvish Ring that she wears comes forth a great light. "She stood before Frodo, seeming tall beyond measurement, and beautiful beyond enduring, terrible and worshipful" (FR, p. 410). It is here that Frodo—and we the readers—see what Galadriel might be if she were to accept the Ring. A being of beauty and power, impossible not to love and not to fear. But Galadriel passes the "test" that Frodo unwittingly presents to her, for she refuses to take the One Ring:

Then she let her hand fall . . . . she was shrunken: a slender elf-woman, clad in simple white, whose gentle voice was soft and sad.

"I pass the test," she said. "I will diminish, and go into the West, and remain Galadriel." (FR, pp. 410–11)

Galadriel refuses the One Ring. She remains true to her principles, to her integrity as an individual, to herself—she will "remain Galadriel." Through her, Tolkien shows us that a strong and virtuous person can refuse the temptation of immense power, even at a great personal cost; for Galadriel knows that by refusing to accept the power of the Ring she will be helpless to maintain the elvish presence in Middle-earth. Galadriel thus represents one answer to the immoralist's challenge of Plato. She refuses to let the possibility of power corrupt her soul.

Boromir and Galadriel demonstrate two different responses to the problem posed by Plato concerning the relationship between power, personal choice, and morality. With these two characters, unlike Gollum, we see the actual moment of choice. But although the responses of Boromir and Galadriel are different, one aspect of their choices is the same: neither ever physically possesses the Ring. What of the characters that do choose to use the Ring? Do their actions help us understand the relationship between power, corruption, and morality? Here we must turn to Tom Bombadil, Frodo, and Sam.

The Use of the Ring

Perhaps the most interesting being that uses the One Ring is Tom Bombadil, the Master of the Old Forest. Bombadil is, unfortunately, cut from the movie version of *The Fellowship of the Ring*, but readers of the book will remember the arduous journey of the four hobbits through the Old Forest, and their eventual rescue (two rescues, actually) by Bombadil, a being who appears to have complete command over all the living things of the Forest. Who is Bombadil? No clear explanation is ever given in *The Lord of the Rings*. He is not a wizard, nor an elf, nor a mortal man. His wife, Goldberry, describes him to Frodo quite simply: "He is, as you have seen him . . . . He is the Master of wood, water, and hill" (FR, p. 140). And Tom describes himself as "Eldest . . . here before the river and the trees." He remembers the first raindrop and the first acorn, made paths before the Big People and saw the little People arriving. "He knew the dark under the stars when it was fearless—before the Dark Lord came from Outside" (FR, pp. 148–49). Tom is called "Iarwain Ben-adar" by Elrond during the Council, a name that means "oldest and fatherless" (FR, p. 297).

Whoever he is, he is surely one of the most powerful and benign characters that the hobbits meet in their journey across Middle-earth. In the midst of their conversations together, Tom asks to see the "precious Ring." Frodo, "to his own astonishment," draws out the Ring from its hiding place and simply hands it over to Tom. Tom laughs as he holds the Ring, looks through it with one eye, offfering the hobbits "a vision, both comical and alarming, of his bright blue eye gleaming through a circle of gold." But then the most extraordinary event occurs: Tom puts on the Ring and does not disappear. It has no power over him, and he gains no power from it. He does a quick magic trick with the Ring, spinning it in the air and causing it to momentarily vanish, so that when Frodo gets the Ring back he is a bit perturbed. Is it the real Ring? Frodo puts the Ring on, and vanishes from sight—but not from the sight of Tom. Tom sees Frodo even as he tries to leave while wearing the Ring. He calls out: "Come Frodo, there! Where be you a-going? Old Tom Bombadil's not as blind as that yet" (FR, p. 151).

Thus Bombadil appears to be more powerful than the Ring— or at least totally unaffected by its corruption. But at the Council of Elrond Gandalf explains that Tom "is his own master. But he cannot alter the Ring itself, nor break its power over others" (FR, p. 298). If we consider the way the power of the Ring affects an individual's moral character, then Bombadil is an anomaly. He is not corrupted by the Ring, nor does he seem to desire it. At best, he is curious to see it and to see how it affects the Ring-bearer, Frodo. Bombadil does not need the Ring—he is his own master.

So far, we have seen that the two characters that reject completely the power of the One Ring, Galadriel and Bombadil, are not mortal beings. Is Tolkien telling us that only immortal or divine beings can resist the power of the Ring, that mere mortals—humans like ourselves, such as Boromir—have to succumb to the temptation and corruption of the power of the Ring? To answer this question, we must examine how two hobbits— Frodo and Sam—deal with the possession of the Ring.

Frodo, of course, is the Ring-bearer, the central figure and hero of *The Lord of the Rings*. He possesses the Ring more than any other character during the events depicted in the trilogy, and he uses the Ring more than any other character. Is he corrupted by the use of the Ring? To a certain extent, yes. Frodo's use of the Ring becomes ever more conflicted as his journey progresses, so that ultimately he is "captured" by the power of the Ring and is unable to destroy it. Although Frodo is tempted to put on the Ring when he first encounters the Black Riders early in his journey, the first time that Frodo uses the Ring, as we have seen, is in the House of Tom Bombadil. His motivation, in that first use, is relatively innocent: he is "perhaps a trifle annoyed" with Bombadil for treating the "perilously important" Ring in so lighthearted and carefree a manner, and so he decides to make sure the Ring is still his, for Bombadil could have switched rings during his brief magical trick (FR, p. 151). Frodo clearly has confused emotions. Tolkien presents us with two tempered descriptions of Frodo's pleasure in using the Ring. When he first put on the Ring and saw that Merry was astonished that he had disappeared, "Frodo was delighted (in a way)." Then, when Tom directed Frodo to stop the game, "Frodo laughed (trying to feel pleased), and taking off the Ring he came and sat down again" (FR, p. 151). Tolkien does not explain why Frodo was not completely delighted and pleased. Is it because of the evil power of the Ring? A virtuous individual knows that the use of the Ring is wrong, so when one uses it one is filled with the conflicting emotions of power, satisfaction, and guilt. Frodo is thus already being affected by the Ring.

Frodo dons the Ring two other times in the early pages of *The Fellowship of the Ring*, once by "accident" in the inn at Bree, and once at the battle with the Black Riders near the summit of Weathertop. Clearly, Frodo does not consciously decide to put on the Ring while singing his song at Butterbur's inn. So Frodo can only be blamed here for being careless, but this is a carelessness that is probably being caused by the force of the Ring. Then on Weathertop, we see that the Ring answers to the commands of others. As the Black Riders approached Aragorn and the hobbits, Frodo's "terror was swallowed up in a sudden temptation to put on the Ring." Although he had the same desire when he was trapped in the Barrow earlier, this time the desire is different: "he longed to yield. Not with the hope of escape, or of doing anything, either good or bad: he simply felt that he must take the Ring and put it on his finger." And of course he does yield, for "resistance became unbearable" (FR, p. 221). The Black Riders, the Nazgûl who wear the nine Rings given to the human race of men, have exerted their collective wills to force him to put on the Ring. So here we see that Frodo does choose to put on the Ring—unlike the accident at Bree—but his choice is not a free choice; it is a result of compulsion, the psychological power of other ring-bearers on the bearer of the One Ring.

The next time Frodo puts on the Ring it is a free choice without any hint of compulsion: he dons the Ring in order to escape from Boromir and to separate himself from the rest of the Company. Yet as he runs away he climbs to the top of Amon Hen and sits on the ancient stone throne of the kings, where he surveys the lands around him, aided by the power of the Ring. This moment is filled with danger, for Sauron senses that someone is wearing the Ring, and the Eye of the Dark Lord begins to search him out. Frodo is filled with dread and a deep psychological conflict: he resists the Eye, crying out to himself "never" but perhaps he is saying "I come to you." "He could not tell." Then he hears another voice urging him to take off the Ring. These two "powers" contend within him. Writhing and tormented, for a moment he is exactly balanced between them.

> Suddenly he was aware of himself again. Frodo, neither the Voice nor the Eye: free to choose, and with one remaining instant in which to do so. He took the Ring off his finger. (FR, p. 451)

Just as with Galadriel's test, Frodo finds the power within himself to resist the force of the Ring. He overrides the power of the Ring when he becomes himself again. But he has used the Ring as a matter of conscious choice to escape danger and to gather knowledge. The Ring is having more and more of an effect on him; he is closer to becoming a wielder of the Ring, not simply its bearer.

Ultimately the force of the Ring overpowers even Frodo. Throughout the long journey into the heart of Mordor, we are constantly told of the physical and psychological weight of the

Ring. The closer Frodo gets to Mount Doom, the more resistant the Ring is to his will and the harder it is for Frodo to go on. But when he reaches the Cracks of Doom, he is unable to perform his mission. Sam witnesses the scene as Frodo stands before the fire and proclaims: "I have come . . . But I do not choose now to do what I came to do. I will not do this deed. The Ring is mine!" Then Frodo puts the Ring on his finger and vanishes (RK, p. 239). It is thus left to Gollum to wrestle with the invisible Frodo, and in a desperate attempt to grab the Ring for himself, he accidentally destroys it in the fires of Mount Doom. Gollum bites off Frodo's finger, holds the Ring aloft and in his joy loses his footing and falls into the fire. The Ring is destroyed and Frodo is saved.

While Frodo is slowly eaten away by the corruption of the Ring, his companion Sam defeats the Ring's power in the short time that he is the Ring-bearer. Sam takes the Ring at the end of *The Two Towers*, for he believes Frodo to be dead and the task has fallen upon him to complete the mission of the Fellowship to destroy the Ring. But he discovers that Frodo is alive and has been captured by orcs, and he therefore abandons the overall mission in an attempt to save his master.

> "They must understand that—Elrond and the Council, and the great Lords and Ladies with all their wisdom. Their plans have gone wrong. I can't be their Ring-bearer. Not without Mr. Frodo." (TT, p. 390)

Sam must remain true to himself, and the central mission in his life is to protect Frodo.

Sam, though, is stymied in his attempt to follow the orcs into the Tower of Cirith Ungol, and eventually he stands alone on the high path that leads into Mordor. It is here that Sam encounters his fundamental moral decision. He feels the power of the Ring, even though he is not wearing it, for "as it [the Ring] drew near the great furnaces where, in the deeps of time, it had been shaped and forged, the Ring's power grew, and it became more fell, untameable save by some mighty will" (RK, p. 185).

Sam now feels himself "enlarged, as if he were robed in a huge distorted shadow of himself, a vast and ominous threat halted upon the walls of Mordor" (RK, p. 185). The Ring tempts him, "gnawing at his will and reason," and he sees a vision of himself as "Samwise the Strong, Hero of the Age, striding with a flaming sword across the darkened land, and armies flocking to his call as he marched to the overthrow of Barad-dûr."

> And then all the clouds rolled away, and the white sun shone, and at his command the vale of Gorgoroth became a garden of flowers and trees and brought forth fruit. He had only to put on the Ring and claim it for his own, and all this could be. (RK, p. 186)

But Sam is equal to his test, and he knows that it is not for him to bear the Ring and challenge the Dark Lord. Tolkien explains that two things keep Sam safe from the seductive power of the Ring: his love for Frodo and his own sense of self. First and foremost was Sam's love of his master, Frodo, but there was also Sam's "still unconquered . . . plain hobbit-sense." Sam knows that he is not big enough to bear such a burden, "even if such visions were not a mere cheat to betray him."

> The one small garden of a free gardener was all his need and due, not a garden swollen to a realm; his own hands to use, not the hands of others to command. (RK, p. 186)

Deep down in his heart, Sam knows who he is. As Galadriel knew to remain Galadriel and to reject the Ring, Sam knows that he can never be other than the plain commonsense hobbit, Samwise Gamgee, the small and caring gardener of the Shire. Fortified by his love for Frodo, he remains true to himself and rejects the power of the Ring. In Sam's rejection of the One Ring during his most extreme crisis we learn that the virtuous and strong-willed person can turn away from a life of evil, a life of almost unlimited power, by focusing on his or her true self.

It is clear that Tolkien is demonstrating to us the progressive forces of corruption of the possession and use of the One Ring, for even Frodo, the hero of the book, succumbs to its corruption in his failure to destroy the Ring. He begins with innocent and accidental uses of the Ring's power, but eventually gives over to its seductive power by making conscious and deliberate decisions to wear the Ring, and even, at last, not to destroy it.

And as in Plato's argument, the key feature of the corruption caused by the Ring is the corruption of the soul, the "heart," or the personality of the wielder of the Ring. To resist the Ring is to remain oneself, to be the person you are without any extraordinary powers. All who come in contact with the Ring (except, it appears, Bombadil) lose themselves (at least momentarily) in the desire to be greater than they are.

Personal Choice, Power, and Morality

Why be moral? What kind of life should I choose? What kind of person should I become? These are the fundamental questions of ethics, or moral philosophy. In Tolkien's tale of the One Ring of Power we find the answer to the challenge to the moral life first proposed by Plato almost 2,400 years ago. Faced with the ability to satisfy one's desires without limit and without consequences, can a person choose the path of virtue and renounce immense power? For Plato, the answer was yes, for the moral person can realize that a life of immoral power will corrupt the heart and soul. Power without love, friendship, and personal fulfillment will lead to unhappiness, a fundamental unhappiness that is beyond relief.

In Tolkien's characters we see vindication of this Platonic vision of the importance and meaning of the moral life. All of the characters who encounter the Ring are given a choice; all are tempted to wield the Ring, and some find within themselves the power to reject it. Indeed it is the one character without a choice—Gollum, for his choice was made long before the events of *The Lord of the Rings* begin—that perhaps most exemplifies the fundamental unhappiness that is the result of the ceaseless quest for power without a moral life. The moment of choice is essential—the moment when a rational being must decide what kind of life he will lead.

Plato returns to the idea of choice at the conclusion of the *Republic*. There he calls the selection of one's fundamental character "the supreme hazard for a man" and one that must be guided "with his eyes fixed on the nature of his soul" (*Republic* X, 618b–e). Tolkien also has his characters fix their gaze on the nature of their souls. For Galadriel, Bombadil, and Sam, the characters who most clearly reject the Ring, who remain uncorrupted by its seduction of unlimited power, their strength comes from their awareness of their own being, who they are and what they can accomplish. These characters know their own limits. Why be moral? Plato asks. And Tolkien answers, "to be yourself." What kind of life should I choose? A life that is in accord with my abilities. If you need a Ring of Power to live your life, you have chosen the wrong life.

2

The Cracks of Doom: The Threat of Emerging Technologies and Tolkien's Rings of Power

THEODORE SCHICK

The Rings of Power forged by Sauron and the elves are the most powerful technology in Middle-earth. Some, like science-fiction writer Isaac Asimov, take the Rings to be a symbol of industrial technology. He writes:

> One day, [my wife] Janet and I were driving along the New Jersey Turnpike, and we passed a section given over to oil refineries. It was a blasted region in which nothing was growing and which was filled with ugly, pipelike structures, which refineries must have. Waste oil was leaking at the top of tall chimneys and the smell of petroleum products filled the air.
>
> Janet looked at the prospect with troubled eyes and said, "There's Mordor."
>
> And, of course, it was. And that was what had to be in Tolkien's mind. The ring was industrial technology, which uprooted the green land and replaced it with ugly structures under a pall of chemical pollution.[1]

Tolkien explicitly rejects any such interpretation, however. In the Foreword to *The Lord of the Rings*, he says of his work, "As

---

[1] Isaac Asimov, "Concerning Tolkien," in *Magic: The Final Fantasy Collection* (New York: HarperPrism, 1996), p. 155.

for any inner meaning or 'message', it has in the intention of the author none. It is neither allegorical nor topical" (FR, p. x).

Although Tolkien denies that *The Lord of the Rings* is allegorical, he admits that it is applicable, that is, that it can be applied to our earthly situation (L, p. 262). In a letter to Rhona Beare, for example, he says:

> If I were to 'philosophize' this myth, or at least the Ring of Sauron, I should say it was a mythical way of representing the truth that *potency* (or perhaps rather *potentiality*) if it is to be exercised, and produce results, has to be externalized and so as it were passes, to a greater or less degree, out of one's direct control. (L, p. 279)

In this chapter I explore just how applicable Tolkien's solution is to the problem of externalization that we face, namely, what should we do with those technologies that threaten to destroy us? Should we adopt the solution proposed by the Council of Elrond and destroy them? Or should we follow the advice of Boromir and try to use them to our advantage?

Scientists tell us that we're on the brink of developing technologies that will give us powers exceeding those that the Rings of Power give their possessors, namely, nanotechnology, genetics, and robotics. Recognizing the danger inherent in these technologies, some, like Bill Joy, Chief Scientist for Sun Microsystems, argue that we should throw them back into the fire, or at least not forge them in the first place, for they have the potential to destroy the human race.[2] Others, like Eric Drexler, the first to systematically explore the possibility of nanotechnology, maintain that if developed and used prudently, these technologies can eliminate poverty, eradicate disease, and grant us immortality.[3] To see what light *The Lord of the Rings* throws on these alternatives, we'll need to know more about the nature and purpose of the Rings.

---

[2] Bill Joy, "Why the Future Doesn't Need Us," *Wired* (April 2000). <http://www.wirednes.com/wired/archie/8.04/Joy_pr.html>.
[3] Eric Drexler, *The Engines of Creation* (Garden City: Anchor Press/Doubleday, 1986).

The Rings of Power

In the Second Age of Middle-earth, elven jewel-smiths led by Celebrimbor and aided by Sauron, forged a number of Rings of Power (S, pp. 287–88). The most important of these Rings are mentioned in the verse from which the inscription on Sauron's ring comes: there are three rings for the elven-kings, seven for the dwarf-lords, nine for Mortal Men, and one for the Dark Lord of Mordor, "One Ring to rule them all."

Although the elven jewel-smiths used knowledge gained from Sauron to make the Rings, Elrond informs us that the three elven rings—Vilya, worn by Elrond; Nenya, worn by Galadriel; and Narya the Great, worn by Gandalf (RK, pp. 337, 339)—"were not made by Sauron, nor did he ever touch them" (FR, p. 301). Similarly, the elves never handled Sauron's Ring. It was forged in secret in the Mountain of Fire (Mount Doom) by Sauron himself. Sauron did have a hand in forging the Rings of the dwarves and humans, however, and as a result, they had a power to corrupt that the elven Rings did not.

Although the Rings created by Sauron were designed to give their possessors wealth or dominion over others, that was not the purpose of the elven Rings. According to Elrond, "Those who made them did not desire strength or domination or hoarded wealth, but understanding, making, and healing, to preserve all things unstained" (FR, p. 301). This motive is peculiar to the elves of Middle-earth and derives from their decision not to return to the West at the end of the First Age.

The elves were the first rational incarnate creatures created by Ilúvatar (the supreme God of Middle-earth) and thus are sometimes referred to as "Firstborn." Humans were created sometime later and have thus acquired the appellation "Followers." The most significant difference between these two races is that elves are immortal while humans are mortal. Tolkien explains:

> The doom of the Elves is to be immortal, to love the beauty of the world, to bring it to full flower with their gifts of delicacy and perfection, to last while it lasts, never leaving it even when 'slain', but returning—and yet, when the Followers come, to teach them, and make way for them, to 'fade' as the Followers grow and absorb the life from which both proceed. (L, p. 147)

Immortality is a burden to the elves because, as inhabitants of Middle-earth, they are changeless beings in an ever-changing world. All that they hold dear is destined to fade away, including themselves.

The First Age of Middle-earth ended with the overthrow of the first enemy, Morgoth, and the desolation of the Western lands of Middle-earth. The elves living in Middle-earth at the time were strongly counseled by the Gods to take up residence in Eressëa, an island west of Middle-earth but in sight of Valinor, the original home of the elves. Some elves, however, chose to stay in Middle-earth, for they desired "the peace and bliss and perfect memory of 'The West' [their original home in Valinor], and yet to remain on the ordinary earth where their prestige as the highest people, above wild Elves, dwarves, and Men, was greater than at the bottom of the hierarchy of Valinor" (L, p. 151).

The elves that stayed—the Delaying Elves—decided that it was better to rule in Middle-earth than serve in Valinor. They longed for the West, however, and Sauron used this desire to gain their confidence and create the Rings.

In the First Age of Middle-earth, Sauron became the chief captain and servant of Morgoth. After Morgoth was defeated, Sauron was commanded by the Valar to return to Valinor to receive his judgment, but he stayed in Middle-earth and became "a reincarnation of Evil, and a thing lusting for Complete Power—and so consumed ever more fiercely with hate (especially of gods and Elves)" (L, p. 151). To try to bring the elves under his power, he put on a fair appearance and offered his knowledge to help the elves rebuild Middle-earth. He was not admitted to Linden, home of Gil-galad and Elrond, for they distrusted him, even though they didn't know who he was. But the elves of Eregion were more desirous of improving their lot. Consequently, they succumbed to Sauron's entreaty:

> "But wherefore should Middle-earth remain for ever desolate and dark, whereas the Elves could make it as fair as Eressëa, nay even as Valinor? And since you have not returned thither, as you might, I perceive that you love this Middle-earth, as do I. Is it not then our task to labour together for its enrichment, and for the raising of all the Elven-kindreds that wander here untaught to the height

of that power and knowledge which those have who are beyond the Sea?" (S, p. 287)

The prospect of remaking Middle-earth in the image of Valinor proved to be irresistible to the elves of Eregion. They admitted Sauron into their realm and let him share his knowledge with the jewel-smiths of Eregion, and thus the Rings came into being.

The chief power of all the rings of power, explains Tolkien, was "the prevention or slowing of *decay* (i.e. 'change' viewed as a regrettable thing)." This appealed to the more or less Elvish motive of preserving what is desired or loved, or its semblance. However the rings also "enhanced the natural powers of a possessor—thus approaching 'magic', a motive easily corruptible into evil, a lust for domination" (L, p. 152).

Nowhere was the power of preservation more evident than at the Mound of Amroth in Lothlórien. When the Fellowship reached it,

> The others cast themselves down upon the fragrant grass, but Frodo stood awhile still lost in wonder. It seemed to him that he had stepped through a high window that looked on a vanished world. . . . No blemish or sickness or deformity could be seen in anything that grew upon the earth. (FR, p. 393)

The healing effect of the Ring technology stands in stark contrast to the effects of many other technologies, including Asimov's industrial technology mentioned at the outset. Such technology often has the effect of destroying the countryside or depleting non-renewable natural resources. However, the technology of the elven Rings cannot simply be identified with industrial technology, because the primary purpose of the Rings is to heal and preserve. Industrial technology, on the other hand, serves mainly to produce labor- or time-saving devices. Similarly, the One Ring cannot be identified with the atomic bomb, because it too has none of the Rings' healing or preservative powers. So there's reason to take Tolkien at his word and view *The Lord of the Rings* as an examination of the dangers of placing power in external objects, which, of course, is the danger inherent in all technology.

The Threat of Emerging Technologies

Some of the technologies that we are currently forging will give us unprecedented power to heal and preserve things. But they will also give us the power to destroy the earth and all of its inhabitants. Unlike nuclear technology, they can be created and wielded by small groups of individuals. Consequently, Bill Joy believes they pose a greater threat to mankind than any we have ever faced:

> The 21st century technologies—genetics, nanotechnology, and robotics (GNR)—are so powerful that they can spawn whole new classes of accidents and abuses. Most dangerously, for the first time, these accidents and abuses are widely within the reach of individuals or small groups. They will not require large facilities or rare raw materials. Knowledge alone will enable the use of them.
>
> Thus we have the possibility not just of weapons of mass destruction but of knowledge-enabled mass destruction (KMD), this destructiveness hugely amplified by the power of self-replication.
>
> I think it is no exaggeration to say that we are on the cusp of the further perfection of extreme evil, an evil whose possibility spreads well beyond that which weapons of mass destruction bequeathed to the nation-states, on to a surprising and terrible empowerment of extreme individuals.[4]

Like the Rings, these new technologies can easily fall into the wrong hands, and because there is such a great potential for accident and abuse, Joy believes that the most prudent course of action is to not develop them in the first place. So he favors a ban on all research into these technologies. There are some things, he claims, that we are better off not knowing. To get a sense of the peril and potential of these new technologies, let's examine one of them—nanotechnology—in more detail.

Nanotechnology, according to Thomas Theis, Director of Physical Sciences at IBM's Thomas J. Watson Research Center, is "the capability to design and control the structure of an object

---

[4] Joy, "Why the Future Doesn't Need Us," *op. cit.*

on all length scales from the atomic to the macroscopic."[5] The size of atoms and molecules is measured in nanometers—billionths of a meter. Thus nanotechnology is the attempt to build devices by directly manipulating the atoms and molecules out of which they are made. This sort of molecular engineering is something that living organisms do every day. The ribosomes in our cells, for example, make proteins by fishing amino acid molecules out of protoplasm and knitting them together in long chains. Eric Drexler reasoned that, in principle, there's no reason we couldn't make machines that function like ribosomes. Instead of knitting together amino acids to make proteins, however, he envisioned universal assemblers that could knit together any sort of atom or molecule to create any sort of structure. Since the properties of a thing are determined by the nature and arrangement of its atoms, universal assemblers will essentially give us the ability to create anything that it's physically possible to create. Drexler explains:

> Because assemblers will let us place atoms in almost any reasonable arrangement, they will let us build almost anything that the laws of nature allow to exist. In particular, they will let us build almost anything we can design including more assemblers. . . .With assemblers we will be able to remake our world or destroy it.[6]

The elves created the Rings because they wanted to remake their world. Nanotechnology promises to give us the same power.

Universal assemblers would make matter replicators of the sort found on the TV series, *Star Trek*, a reality. Theoretically, we could put the design specifications of any object into an assembler-driven replicator, and as long as it was supplied with enough of the right sort of atoms, the replicator would produce it. With enough carbon atoms to work with, for example, such a replicator could create a diamond of any size. But it wouldn't

---

[5] Thomas Theis, "Information Technology Based on a Mature Nanotechnology: Some Societal Implications." *Societal Implications of Nanoscience and Nanotechnology.* National Science Foundation (March 2001), p. 60. <http://www.wtec.org/loyola/nano/NSET.Societal.Implications/nanosi.pdf>.
[6] Drexler, *Engines of Creation*, p. 14.

be limited to just replicating inanimate objects. It could create any possible object, living or non-living, sentient or non-sentient. Thus, genetic engineering and robotics would be greatly enhanced by the advent of universal assemblers.

Like the Ring technology, nanotechnology also promises to eliminate poverty, disease, and old age. With the ability to create any kind of object, no one should have to do without the luxuries of life, much less the necessities. And with the ability to manipulate individual atoms and molecules, no one should have to endure a damaged body. Injury and aging are the result of cellular damage that, in turn, is the result of atoms and molecules becoming displaced. Properly programmed assemblers should be able to repair any sort of cellular damage by putting the displaced atoms back into their original configuration. Once such cell repair machines become available, no one should have to suffer the ravages of old age. As Drexler notes, "With cell repair machines . . . the potential for life extension becomes clear. They will be able to repair cells so long as their distinctive structures remain intact, and will be able to replace cells that have been destroyed."[7] The Rings also grant their wearers extended life, but that life is not a particularly vigorous one. As Bilbo relates to Gandalf:

> "I am old, Gandalf. I don't look it, but I am beginning to feel it in my heart of hearts. *Well-preserved* indeed!" he snorted. "Why, I feel all thin, sort of *stretched*, if you know what I mean: like butter that has been scraped over too much bread." (FR, p. 34)

Whether such weariness is the result of any artificially induced immortality or just that induced by the Rings, only time will tell.

The Rings also have the ability to enhance the powers of their possessors, and all the Rings, with the exception of the elven Rings, had the power to make their wearers invisible. Remarkably enough, the United States government has just given MIT fifty million dollars to use nanotechnology to develop materials that will give soldiers those powers. The goal of the newly developed "Institute for Soldier Nanotechnologies" (ISN)

---

[7] Ibid., p. 145.

is to "create lightweight molecular materials to equip the foot soldier of the future with uniforms and gear that can heal them, shield them, and protect them against chemical and biological warfare."[8] Not only should nanotechnology be able to produce an armor that is stronger than *mithril*, it should also be able to give its wearer super-human powers. Ned Thomas, Director of the ISN, asks us to "imagine the psychological impact upon a foe when encountering squads of seemingly invincible warriors protected by armor and endowed with super-human capabilities, such as the ability to leap over a twenty-foot wall."[9]

Nanotechnology may also allow the creation of a functioning invisibility cloak similar to the car-cloaking technology featured in the recent James Bond flick, *Die Another Day*. Such a cloak would "interweave existing organic polymers that change the way they reflect light in response to mechanical strains or applied electric fields. . . . these could be combined with a micromechanical sensor array and used to reproduce the light that would pass through if the soldier was not there, creating an effect approaching invisibility."[10] The new technologies thus seem to put almost all of the powers of the Rings within our grasp.

Although the potential benefits of nanotechnology are great, so are the risks. Chief among them are the risks to human, plant, and animal life. Universal assemblers will be able to reproduce themselves—to self-replicate. But a self-replicating assembler could be much more dangerous than any existing virus or bacteria, for it could consume the earth's organic material in a matter of days. Drexler describes some of the dangers inherent in self-replicating assemblers:

> "Plants" with "leaves" no more efficient than today's solar cells could out-compete real plants, crowding the biosphere with an inedible foliage. Tough, omnivorous "bacteria" could out compete real bacteria. They could spread like blowing pollen,

---

[8] Ken Campbell, "Army Selects MIT for $50 million Institute to Use Nanomaterials to Clothe, Equip Soldiers," *MIT News* (March 14, 2002). <http://web.mit.edu/newsoffice/nr/2002/isn.html>.

[9] Ibid.

[10] Eugenie Samuel, "U.S. Army Seeks Nanotech Suits." *New Scientist* (March 4, 2002). <http://www.gyre.org/news/cache/1935>.

replicate swiftly, and reduce the biosphere to dust in a matter of days.[11]

This scenario has come to be known as the "grey goo" problem because, if left unchecked, rogue assemblers could transform the surface of the planet into a grey goo, a mass of self-replicating nanobots.

The destruction of all living things is only one of the dangers posed by nanotechnology. Since an assembler can manufacture anything that it is physically possible to produce, it can manufacture any sort of weapon; biological, chemical, or nuclear. Armed with a sufficiently fast replicator, anyone could amass enough firepower or lethal agents to destroy whatever he or she wanted.

Possible Solutions

What can be done to prevent such disasters? Drexler has suggested a number of strategies. One is to contain the replicators behind impenetrable walls or in laboratories in outer space. Another is to build counters into the replicators that only allow them to replicate a limited number of times. A more desperate measure is to try to destroy all the records of how the first assemblers were made so no one else could develop them. Finally we could try to build nanobots designed to destroy dangerous replicators, much like white blood cells destroy dangerous bacteria and viruses.[12]

Joy finds these proposals naïve, for he believes that they will either be ineffective or create replicators as dangerous as the ones they are intended to destroy. Consequently, he contends that our only hope is to forego further research into these technologies. He writes:

> These possibilities are all thus either undesirable or unachievable or both. The only realistic alternative I see is relinquishment: to limit development of the technologies that are too dangerous by limiting our pursuit of certain kinds of knowledge.[13]

---

[11] Drexler, *Engines of Creation*, p. 172.
[12] *Ibid.*, pp. 182–87
[13] Joy, "Why the Future Doesn't Need Us," *op. cit.*

If we don't limit our pursuit of knowledge, Joy foresees a technological arms race far more dangerous than the nuclear arms race ever was.

Enforcing a ban on research into nanotechnology, genetics, and robotics would require a verification regime of unprecedented proportions. Since such research can be conducted in one's basement, the only way to prevent it would be to give the government almost unlimited surveillance powers. Relinquishing research into these technologies, then, would require relinquishing a great deal of privacy and freedom. Joy realizes this, but is apparently willing to make the sacrifice for the sake of preventing greater harm.

Would the sacrifice of personal liberty be worth it? Or is Joy's solution just as undesirable and unachievable as he claims Drexler's is? Even if the government had a camera in every room—as it did in Orwell's *1984*—it would still probably not be able to prevent research into these technologies because, unlike nuclear research, it does not require centralized control or massive amounts of machinery. And even if we could effectively stop research in America, there's much less of a possibility of stopping it world wide. Rogue states and terrorist organizations know full well the potential power of these technologies. They would not relinquish research on the basis of any recommendation from the United States or the United Nations. And if they developed those technologies before we did, the United States and the United Nations might cease to exist.

What's more, relinquishing these technologies would mean that we would not be able to reap any of their benefits. Those suffering from illness or poverty or old age would never be able to avail themselves of the most effective means of dealing with those problems. Foregoing such goods for the sake of a hypothetical harm would be extremely difficult to do.

There is no doubt that these technologies could destroy us. But so could many other technologies, such as nuclear technology. Yet nuclear technology is no longer the threat it used to be. The threat of nuclear war is still with us, but the threat posed by the widespread use of nuclear power has been greatly diminished. When nuclear power was first developed, many pundits thought that it would soon become our dominant power source. But it never achieved that status because various individuals banded together to oppose its proliferation. The anti-nuclear movement, the environmental movement, and the Union of Concerned Scientists, for example, played an important role in restricting the use of nuclear power. The pundits didn't foresee this opposition because it was a grass roots effort, not one mounted by established institutions.

The case of the nuclear power industry shows that technology doesn't develop in isolation; it develops in a social context that may affect its utilization in unforeseen ways. Once the public becomes better informed about these technologies, grass roots efforts may serve to tame them in much the same way that they tamed nuclear technology. One of the central themes of *The Lord of the Rings* is that history can be profoundly affected by "unforeseen and unforeseeable acts of will" (L, p. 160). Even Sauron with his vast intelligence network could not foresee the effect the Fellowship would have on his plans. Bill Joy, with his much more limited resources, can't be considered to have a clearer view of the future.

In the Third Age of Middle-earth, the elves had lost the knowledge of how to create the Rings. Only Sauron could have forged any new Rings. Destroying the One Ring insured that no new ones would ever be made. This situation is vastly different from the one we face. The knowledge of nanotechnology, genetic engineering, and robotics is spread throughout the world, and although shutting down one set of laboratories might slow their development, it certainly would not stop it. There is no single device we could destroy that would eliminate the threat posed by these technologies. Thus our situation may not be as analogous to that of Middle-earth as it would first appear. If there were other enemies like Sauron with the capability of creating additional Rings of Power, would the Council of Elrond have voted to destroy the One Ring? If dwarves and humans and hobbits had active research programs into Ring technology, would the elves have decided to destroy the most powerful Ring? Perhaps. But they might also have decided to initiate their own research program to see whether there was some way to modify the Ring so that it would retain its powers and be free of Sauron's evil influence.

3

"My Precious": Tolkien's Fetishized Ring

ALISON MILBANK

One of the most dramatic scenes in the first *Lord of the Rings* film, *The Fellowship of the Ring,* is the Council at Rivendell at which elf and dwarf nearly come to blows, while in a golden glow worthy of a Glassner jewelry advertisement, the Ring shines serenely on, untouched and untouchable. The focus shifts so that the combatants fade to soft-focus, and the ring in close-up fills the whole screen. We are all drawn to the Ring: readers, filmmakers, and a number of contributors to this volume. Although the Ring is a feature borrowed from ancient Germanic and Nordic myth, I shall argue that we are all in thrall to the Ring because of its contemporary relevance to the way we perceive, lust after, and use the "rings" or commodities of our own society. For me Tolkien's text is not an escapist fantasy but a challenging work that "reads" us as fetishists and offers us an alternative model for our relations with the world of things by means of sacrifice and gift.

Stockings, Rings, and Erotic Control

To explain what I mean by fetishism let us return to that cinematic frame of the chastely glowing ring. Like any close-up shot the effect is to separate the object from its context, so that it seems to exist alone. In that sense, every photographic or filmic close-up operates fetishistically in the sense employed by the psychologist Sigmund Freud. For the fetishist the stocking, the glove, the fur or the individual body part becomes the focus of sexual desire in so far as it is fixed and separated off from any relation with the whole person or body. In his 1927 essay, "Fetishism," Freud attributes this desire for fixity to a refusal to fully accept that one's mother is not all-powerful—or, in Freudian terms, does not have the phallus. In pursuing and possessing an object that stands for his mother, the fetishist is able to own and control this maternal sexual power he both fears and loves. For a deep terror of the female genitals underlies such behavior and the fetish provides a safe substitute for the risky self-giving of the sexual act.[1]

It is interesting that the One Ring of Power, which I want to suggest is viewed fetishistically, is twice gained as a result of literal separation from the owner's body, once by Isildur hacking off Sauron's finger, and again by Gollum biting off Frodo's finger. Separation marks the Ring from its creation, since it is forged by Sauron in secret, and is deliberately hidden from the makers of the other nineteen Rings of Power. Even these beneficent Rings, however, have something fetishistic about them because they were made in order to prevent the loss and decay of beautiful things. In aiming to create preventatives against loss, the elves share the fetishist's desire to fix the object of sexual arousal, so that it is untouched by age, decay, or mortality. We are told explicitly in Tolkien's myth collection, *The Silmarillion,* that the Noldor elves won't give up living in Middle-earth and yet they want also to have the bliss of those across the Sea in the Blessed Realm (S, p. 287).

There is, of course, an element of fetishism in much sexual behavior, but usually the stocking merely articulates a boundary of difference and is a means to arousal because it creates a distinction between flesh and clothing that draws attention to the naked leg above the stocking-top. For the lover, the stocking recapitulates the pursuit and uncovering of the desired body; for the fetishist, possession of the stocking is an end in itself. In the

---

[1] For more on Freud's impact on feminist philosophy, see Teresa Brennan's, "Psychoanalytic Feminism," in Alison M. Jaggar and Iris Marion Young, eds., *A Companion to Feminist Philosophy* (Malden, Massachusetts: Blackwell, 1998), pp. 272–79.

same manner we see the Ring's owners becoming transfixed by the Ring, rather than using it as a means to their desires. Chillingly, each owner, from the great Isildur to the hobbit Bilbo Baggins, comes to find it "Precious," and impossible to give up. They become as Smaug the dragon, hoarding treasure for its own sake and meeting threat of its removal with violence. Once Gollum becomes the Ring's possessor he finds himself drawn to underground places, and it is deep in the Misty Mountains that he loses it to Bilbo.

Critics have often noticed the lack of sexual activity in *The Lord of the Rings*. This, I believe, can be explained through the corrosive power of the Ring, which takes the focus away from the romantic quest and subsumes to itself the power of the erotic. Only with the destruction of the Ring can the characters truly love, marry and have children. And those who have borne the Ring for any length of time do not marry at all. While not wishing to send readers off on a genital-spotting expedition through Middle-earth, it is noticeable that Tolkien offers a most convincing Freudian *vagina dentata* (teethed vagina) in the ancient and disgustingly gustatory spider Shelob. She represents an ancient maternal power that swallows up masculine identity and autonomy. According to Freud, her castrating hold is precisely what the sexual fetishist fears, and seeks to control by his possession of the fetishized object. She must be faced up to and outwitted before the Ring can be restored to the true maternal source of the fiery "Cracks of Doom." Appropriately, it is the equally ancient and yet empowering woman, Galadriel, who earlier renounced the temptation to be the all-powerful female principle, a "She-who-must-be-obeyed," who provides the light by which Shelob may be overcome. If men in the novel must give up fetishism, women must stand down from their frozen idealization, as Arwen does when she renounces immortality to marry Aragorn.

Paradoxically, although the fetish is intended as a means of erotic control—and a means of warding off the castrating female—its importance as the only possible means to erotic pleasure and the self-identity of the fetishist renders him in its thrall as if it were a god, in the manner of the totemic religious practice from which Freud took his original concept. This process is most graphically exemplified in the transmutation of the river-hobbit Sméagol into the craven Gollum. Possession of the Ring by murder of his friend leads to his self-division and alienation, so that he now speaks of himself in the third person, in babytalk— "Don't hurt us! Don't let them hurt us, precious!"— while the Ring is now personified and looked to as a source of aid and protection. Like early Native American totemists, Gollum has figuratively placed his soul inside the fetish for safe-keeping. Without the Ring, therefore, he is literally torn in two, and, as he replies to Faramir, "no name, no business, no Precious, nothing. Only empty" (TT, p. 335).

In his enthrallment Gollum gives the reader insight into the secret of the mighty Sauron himself. When he forged the Ring, Sauron actually placed some of his power inside, to his great cost when it was lost. Now having lost his physical body he lives a wraithlike existence, akin to that of his slaves, the Nazgûl, with his power transferred to the Ring. Indeed, he is now present mainly as an agent of unceasing surveillance, as a giant and lidless eye, which Frodo glimpses in Galadriel's mirror: "the Eye was rimmed with fire, but was itself glazed, yellow as a cat's, watchful and intent, and the black slit of its pupil opened on a pit, a window into nothing" (FR, p. 409). Like Gollum, Sauron is empty and there is no purpose in his will for power apart from the desire for the Ring itself. Rather, Sauron is completely nihilistic and seeks to reduce Middle-earth to ashes, to render everything as null as himself.

Rings and Things

It is central to Tolkien's conception that it is not just the depraved who fetishize the Ring but anyone who has to do with it, and even those who, like Boromir, merely see it occasionally. One can infer from this that Middle-earth is already a fallen world, enmeshed in evil. That this evil makes its effect through fetishism, however, marks the onset of a relatively recent form of alienation, particular to a modern capitalist economy. Fifty years before Freud's essay on fetishism the term was employed as a central concept in German philosopher Karl Marx's great critique of industrial capitalist economy. His groundbreaking book *Capital* describes the disconnected and phantasmal nature of our relations with the things we produce. As Marx observes, once a piece of wood is made into a table, it is still just a table, but once in the market "as soon as it steps forth as a commodity it is changed into something transcendent. It not only stands with its feet on the ground, but in relation to all other commodities, it stands on its head and evolves out of its wooden brain grotesque ideas."[2] Any television advertisement showing a nubile woman caressing a car's bodywork provides evidence of our tendency to treat commodities as if they had a life of their own.

Marx went on to argue that in the modern market economy we lose relations between makers and consumers, and are estranged even from the objects of our own labor. Relationships between things are substituted for those between people, and these commodities acquire an idolatrous character as fetishes: they are totally of our own creation but we fail to recognize this. In our own lives this can take the form of a lifestyle constructed by means of designer labels, and of the near impossibility of finding out information about the producers of our clothes and our food.

I am not trying to suggest that *The Lord of the Rings* is a Marxist text and that Tolkien hoped for the Peoples' Republic of the Shire, but certainly by means of the Ring the novel provides a thoroughgoing critique of our dragonish tendencies to hoarding, idolatry, and alienation, the radicalism of which is revealed when put alongside these psychological and economic analyses. Moreover, Tolkien was a devout Catholic and the papal encyclicals on social teaching in the twentieth century were as critical of capitalism as they were of state socialism. And while secular writers may offer insight into Tolkien's critique, it can be claimed that for an adequate response to the problem of fetishism a religious dimension is important.

For Tolkien, all created things are good, as he states in the myth of creation that opens his *Silmarillion*. And it is evident from Tolkien's various Indexes to the third volume of *The Lord of the Rings* that the world of objects is important to him, for he gives an entire section to the category, "Things" (RK, pp. 488–490). Looking down the list of items one finds an unusual combination of those one would expect, such as rings, weapons, flowers, and books, and the unexpected, such as a

---

[2] Karl Marx, *Capital: A Critique of Political Economy*, translated by Samuel Moore and Edward Aveling (New York: Modern Library, 1936), Volume 1, p. 82.

postal system, battles, meetings, dates, and languages. The reason for the inclusion of such immaterial concepts lies in Tolkien's adoption of a much more ancient usage of the word, "thing." The *Oxford English Dictionary* gives as its earliest example of the usual modern meaning of "thing" as inanimate object, a reference from 1689.[3] Prior to that, a thing meant a matter, an event, even, in Anglo-Saxon and Old Norse and German, a Parliament, as Heidegger emphasizes in his essay on the Thing, "a gathering, and specifically a gathering to deliberate on a matter under discussion, a contested matter."[4] It is from a matter brought forward for important deliberation, an event or experience, that our modern understanding of "thing" evolves as something separate from ourselves, and an object of our perception. In origin, however, there is something inherently communal in a thing as a matter between people in a meeting-place. "Thinging gathers," as Heidegger puts it.[5] Today, when we are not in thrall to fetishized objects, we go to the opposite extreme and treat things as inert and of no account. Indeed, the object of desire in the December shop-window quickly loses all aura on the January sale rack.

Tolkien's theology so validates making and creativity that the most important objects in his fictional world are good. The relatively rare bad objects are inevitably dominatory or destructive in character, as, for instance, the Grond, the nasty battering ram named from Morgoth's mace, with an iron wolf-shaped head. Furthermore, there are not very many things in *The Lord of the Rings*, and the "Things" appendix is much shorter than that for people/creatures or places. After leaving the relatively thing-filled Shire, there are few objects, and most of these are "things" in the Middle English sense of the equipment one takes on a journey. The items taken by the Fellowship are few: food, cooking utensils, water bottles, pipes and pipe-weed, gray elven cloaks, and weapons. The world has been pared down to the few things necessary for sustenance and protection. Thus, the paucity of items renders them doubly precious, as, for example,

---

[3] *The Oxford English Dictionary upon Historical Principles*, 13 volumes (London: Oxford University Press, 1961), Volume 11, p. 309.
[4] Martin Heidegger, *What Is a Thing?*, translated by W.B. Barton, Jr., and Vera Deutsch (South Bend: Gateway, 1967), p. 174.
[5] *Ibid.*, p. 174.

the rope Sam suddenly remembers he brought from the Lórien boat:

> "Rope!" cried Sam, talking wildly to himself in his excitement and relief. "Well, if I don't deserve to be hung on the end of one as a warning to numbskulls! You're nowt but a ninnyhammer, Sam Gamgee: that's what the Gaffer said to me often enough, it being a word of his. Rope!"
>
> "Stop chattering!" cried Frodo, now recovered enough to feel both amused and annoyed. "Never mind your Gaffer! Are you trying to tell yourself you've got some rope in your pocket? If so, out with it!"
>
> "Yes, Mr. Frodo, in my pack and all. Carried it hundreds of miles, and I'd clean forgotten it!" (TT, p. 237)

There is a distinctly comic tone to this scene with Sam dancing with delight over the rope while Frodo clings to a cliff-face, and the homely language contrasting with the extremity of the situation. This in no way detracts from the magical quality of the rope, indicated by its silken texture and silvery sheen. As it dangles down it evokes other salvific ropes, such as the line let down by the Biblical Rahab for Joshua's spies that then became the sign to spare her when Jericho was attacked.[6]

With or without literary parallels, the rope has a fullness of presence in this scene. It is prompt when needed, beautiful and useful. Sam accords the rope full appreciation: "It looks a bit thin, but it's tough; and soft as milk to the hand. Packs close too, and as light as light. Wonderful folk to be sure" (TT, p. 238)! Sam refers here to the elvish makers of his rope and he begins to undo the fetishism of things by restoring the relation of object to maker, and the fixed object to potency and use.

Gift-giving and Ring-bearing

It is also important for the full presence of Sam's rope that it was given to him as a gift by the elves of Lórien. Indeed, practically every good object in the whole novel turns out to be a gift, beginning in the very first chapter with Bilbo's birthday party at

---

[6] Joshua 2:15–18.

which, according to hobbit custom, he gives rather than receives birthday presents. Gandalf too provides a gift in the form of fire-works, which in their spectacular self-destruction are a very pure form of gift-giving. Many of the company's weapons are gifts, the very food they eat comes from Rivendell, or Gollum's rabbit hunting (in the closest he gets to human community), or from the *lembas* of the Lórien elves. Galadriel and Celeborn are primarily gift-givers, whether by sight of the seeing-pool of prophecy or in the magic objects they give Sam and Frodo—the box of super-potent fertilizer and seed and the phial of light.

In granting gifts, Galadriel and Celeborn imitate the actions of the kings in the Norse and Anglo-Saxon sources from which Tolkien derived his Rings of Power. In one such source, the poem *Beowulf,* on which Tolkien was an important authority, the king, Hrothgar, is called a "ring giver" and he showers Beowulf with presents after Beowulf has killed the monster Grendel.[7] Rings are gifts that bind the wearer to the giver in these ancient tales. And if one receives gold objects as gifts from the true owner, no harm ensues to the wearer.

A prominent example in Norse mythology is the ring, Draupnir, made by the dwarves Brokk and Eitri for the god Odin, which produced eight new rings every ninth night. It was this ring that the desolated Odin placed on the pyre of his son, Baldur, after the latter's death from the mistletoe dart, and which the son returned to his father as a keepsake via Hermod, who visited him in Hel.[8] This enriching ring, marked by gift and sac-rifice, is not usually mentioned as an influence on *The Lord of the Rings*, even though it is the only ring in the early sources that is voluntarily renounced. More frequently discussed by Tolkien critics is the dragon Fafnir's ring that was taken by his slayer, Sigurd, which led to his downfall and that of the whole house of the Volsungs.[9]

What these Northern stories of rings show is that a ring stolen curses its possessor, whereas a ring given cements rela-

---

[7] *Beowulf and Judith*, edited by Elliott Van Kirk Dobbie (New York: Columbia University Press, 1953), p. 38.

[8] See Snorri Sturluson, *The Prose Edda* (London: Everyman, 1998), p. 116.

[9] Arthur Morgan, "Medieval, Victorian, and Modern: Tolkien, Wagner, and the Ring," in Rosemary Gray, ed., *A Tribute to J.R.R. Tolkien* (Pretoria: University of South Africa Press, 1992), pp. 16–28.

tionships, even beyond the grave. Both positive and negative connotations can be found in *Beowulf,* in which the hero first receives rings from Hrothgar, later becomes a ring-giver himself, and only dies when he seeks gold rings for his people from a dragon's lair. Similarly, the elven rings in Tolkien are beneficent, concentrating the powers and unity of their bearers, Galadriel, Elrond and Gandalf, all of whom were given the rings by others, which frees them from the trace of fetishism involved in the original forging, as does their willingness to sacrifice the power of their rings for the common good.

Letting Things Go

In order to benefit from these gifts, the protagonists of *The Lord of the Rings* have first to give up their possessions, their homes and families. The Quest of the Fellowship charts an attempt to deal with the fetishism of the object, and to restore relations with people and with things. The only way this may be secured is through acts of self-sacrifice, and by the destruction of the fetishized Ring. Unlike most quests, in which a beloved object is gained, the Fellowship is inaugurated to return the Ring to its place of origin, and thereby to reverse the fetishizing process that cuts it off from context, origin and materiality. The whole process is presented in comic mode in the opening of the novel when Bilbo, who had not been candid in his account of how he acquired the Ring from Gollum, sets about a potlatch scale sacrifice of everything and every object in his life. He throws a lavish party and gives away what remains of his dragon gold to make up for his Sigurd-like possession of it; he gives away his home and its contents, his hobbit existence itself, and goes off like some Indian holy man. Frodo then follows the same path and makes the sacrifice of giving up his happy life in the Shire to bear the Ring. Like the Ring he becomes separate, and is unable to return and be accepted by his own community. He is also badly wounded by the Morgul-knife of the Black Rider. So Frodo does not merely sacrifice the Ring but himself, as he indicates to Sam as they leave for the Grey Havens, "When things are in danger: someone has to give them up, lose them, so that others may keep them" (RK, p. 338). Note that it is not just people that are in danger but "things," the whole phenomenal cosmos, and it is *all that* that he must give up.

Frodo, who gave his life, is then himself given passage to the Undying Lands by Arwen to show that giving up is the means of restoration. And in order to show that an unfetishized life is possible, we are earlier given the example of Tom Bombadil and Goldberry, who are notably also the exemplars of romantic fulfilment in the story. They were left out of the films, and are often something of an embarrassment to critics as being extraneous to the epic form of the novel. In my view Tom and Goldberry's difference is deliberate and is important to the novel's purposes in offering a challenge to the fetishism rife in Middle-earth. For Tom Bombadil is the unfallen "master of wood, water and hill" precisely because he does not own them. Rather he receives everything as a gift and is himself a gift-giver, who is first seen bringing water-lilies to Goldberry. That a gift-economy is being opposed to fetishism is made quite plain by Tom's behavior with the Ring. To Frodo's disapproval he treats it with scant respect, throws it up in the air, and can see through its invisibility magic. He treats it, in fact, like a very pretty ring and nothing more.

Bombadil nicely illustrates the distinction Tolkien draws between magic and enchantment in his essay "On Fairy-stories": magic "is *power* in this world, domination of things or wills," whereas enchantment "does not seek delusion, nor bewitchment and domination; it seeks shared enrichment, partners in making and delight, not slaves."[10] There is something cheerfully fictive and enchanted about Bombadil (signaled to us by his talking in verse), and this tells us that we too can transform our world into one of enchantment in which we see things as they really are: rings as pretty pieces of shining metal, and men and women as utterly real and yet utterly mysterious. In contrast to Tom's singing that rescues the hobbits from entrapment, the honeyed tones of Saruman are merely tricks of dominatory magic that fixate their audience so that they do not see what is really going on.

The novel ends, very simply, with Sam's return home from the Grey Havens. His hobbit home is a scene of simple objects appropriately arranged that deliberately recreates the yellow

---

[10] J.R.R. Tolkien, "On Fairy-stories," in *The Tolkien Reader* (New York: Ballantine, 1966), p. 53.

light, fire and waiting woman of Bombadil's house. The great
and onerous quest ends with the restoration of the objectified
world, which is now freed from fetishism for use:

> And he went on, and there was yellow light, and fire within; and
> the evening meal was ready, and he was expected. And Rose
> drew him in, and set him in his chair, and put little Elanor upon
> his lap.
> He drew a deep breath. "Well, I'm back," he said. (RK, p. 340)

The objects of fire, food, light, and shelter unite here to signify human warmth and community. By making Sam function
as a chair for his little daughter in a family trinity, the text
affirms the familial relation of objects to persons. Chairs are
only chairs; they have no magical qualities, but they allow
human connection—"Thinging gathers." The fetishized Ring is
now replaced by the family circle. There is a triumphant
emphasis on the word "and" in these two final sentences. Its
repetition sets up a rhythm of connections between the different things in the scene that asserts their unity in combining to
bless human life.

Now that objects are returned to full participation they can
signify themselves. Galadriel's phial caught the light of the star
Eärendil, and its magic came from participation in the source of
light that Eärendil redeemed by rescuing it from fetishization by
warring groups and returning it to its origin. Thanks to all that
has gone before to redeem the object in *The Lord of the Rings*,
any light can now have that same quality, when it serves human
need and is valued for its utility and its beauty. Hobbits in the
story seem to have been invented precisely in order to appreciate this ordinary domestic world of objects, just as the proper
end of the ents is to love trees. In one sense, the whole complex
nest of invented languages and creatures, histories and mythologies exists in order that, like Sam, we can see the ordinary world
in an unfetishized manner. This is the "recovery" of vision that
Tolkien himself states is the purpose of the fantasy or fairy-tale.
And that he means the recovery of a right relation to objects as
intrinsic to this recovery is seen in the following passage:

> And actually fairy-stories deal largely, or (the better ones) mainly,
> with simple or fundamental things, untouched by Fantasy, but

these simplicities are made all the more luminous by their setting. For the story-maker who allows himself to be "free with" Nature can be her lover not her slave. It was in fairy-stories that I first divined the potency of the words, and the wonder of the things, such as stone and wood, and iron; tree and grass; house and fire; bread and wine.[11]

Tolkien calls this love "wonder," as a faculty of vision that accords full presence to that which one sees and is challenged by in its otherness. We learn to see things as if for the first time. This wonder is very far indeed from fetish worship because it celebrates the connections that fetishism denies. Treebeard's word for "hill" exemplifies this relationality:

> "*A-lalla-lalla-rumba-kamanda-lind-or-burúmë*. Excuse me: that is part of my name for it; I do not know what the word is in the out-side languages: you know, the thing we are on, where I stand and look out on fine mornings, and think about the Sun, and the grass beyond the wood, and the horses, and the clouds, and the unfold-ing of the world." (TT, p. 66)

In his sign for "hill" Treebeard reconnects the object with the world of phenomena, and of thoughts, and with himself. In ent language an object is signified by the range of its *connections* by which it achieves its true identity, not by separation, as in hill being defined by those things it is not: "hill" not "rill." Individuality thus comes from the multitude and variety of inter-connections. Again, "Thinging gathers."

The Lord of the Rings, then, is an ethical text that teaches us to give up dominatory and fixed perceptions in order to receive the world back as gift. The novel itself offers an inexhaustible plenitude of things, but they are not self-referential. For the elves, their songs and their gifts originate outside Middle-earth itself in a Blessed Realm just glimpsed by the reader before Frodo disappears forever. This realm is the source of the "light and high beauty" (RK, p. 211) that Sam perceives in the sky above the dreadful plain of Gorgoroth. The wonder and abun-

---

[11] *Ibid.*, p. 59.

dance of all the things that constitute Middle-earth have a divine origin, so that, as we leave the novel, we are somewhat melancholy. For we are unable to remain fetishistically fixated by the details of the story, but left rather with a craving for something more: a hunger for breaking our own unnatural attachment to things, a hunger for transcendence itself.

PART II

The Quest for Happiness

4

Tolkien's Six Keys to Happiness

GREGORY BASSHAM

Rivendell. Hobbiton. Lothlórien. The very names conjure up images of peace, beauty, and contentment. Many readers of *The Lord of the Rings* (myself included) believe that they would be happy living in such places, and Tolkien certainly presents these communities as exceptionally happy places in which to live. Of course, Tolkien's invented world is very different from our own. There are no traffic jams, annoying telemarketers, or bad reality-TV shows in Middle-earth. Nor, apparently, are there any divorces, mudslinging political campaigns, or psychoactive drugs other than beer. Still, Middle-earth is similar enough to our own world that useful comparisons and lessons can be drawn. In this essay, I ask what the inhabitants of Rivendell, Hobbiton, and Lothlórien—Tolkien's hobbits and elves—might teach us about the secrets of true happiness and fulfillment. To my mind, six important lessons stand out.

1. Delight in Simple Things

Hobbits are merry, good-natured folk who delight in simple pleasures: eating and drinking, pipe-smoking, gardening, wearing brightly colored clothing, attending parties, giving and receiving presents, making simple jests, and gathering at village pubs with friends and neighbors. They live uncomplicated, rustic lives in "close friendship with the earth" (FR, p. 2), dislike complex machinery, have no real government, and enjoy singing simple, comical songs about hot baths and shinbone-munching trolls.

The elves, though much wiser and more sophisticated than hobbits, also primarily delight in simple things: telling tales, singing songs, making beautiful things, preparing simple but delicious food, watching the stars, and communing with nature. Tolkien saw a connection between happiness and a capacity to delight in simple, everyday pleasures. And this is a connection many philosophers have noted as well.

The Greek philosopher Epicurus (c. 341–270 B.C.) pointed out one obvious reason for favoring simple, "natural" pleasures over artificial or "superfluous" ones: they tend to be more frequent and easy to obtain.[1] People who find satisfaction in watching sunsets, going for long walks in the woods, and spending quality time with family and friends can usually find many opportunities to enjoy these experiences. In contrast, those who seek happiness in the more elusive pleasures of wealth, power, prestige, or fame often come up empty handed.

There is a deeper reason why happiness is often associated with simpler lifestyles and a capacity to delight in simple pleasures. In his 1993 book *The Pursuit of Happiness*, psychologist David G. Myers summarized the results of thousands of recent scientific studies of happiness and well-being. He found that the most important factors that contribute to lasting happiness are:

- fit and healthy bodies
- positive self-esteem
- feelings of control over our lives and our time
- optimism
- outgoingness
- challenging and meaningful work
- adequate opportunities for rest and leisure
- intimate and supportive relationships
- a focus beyond the self
- a spiritual commitment that entails hope, a sense of purpose, and communal support and service.[2]

---

[1] Epicurus, "Letter to Menoeceus," in Whitney J. Oates, ed., *The Stoic and Epicurean Philosophers* (New York: Modern Library, 1957), p. 32.

[2] David G. Myers, *The Pursuit of Happiness* (New York: Avon, 1993), p. 206;

If these are indeed the keys to enduring happiness, it is not hard to see why Americans, on average, are no happier today than they were in the 1950s (despite the fact that average buying power has more than doubled).[3] In fact, the kinds of fast-paced, stress-filled lives many of us lead today may make it harder for us to achieve happiness, because we're too busy to focus on the things that most reliably produce it. A century and a half ago, Henry David Thoreau, the great American apostle of simplicity, wrote:

> Our life is frittered away by detail . . . [M]en labor under a mistake. The better part of a man is soon plowed into the soil for compost. By a seeming fate, commonly called necessity, they are employed, as it says in an old book, laying up treasures which moth and rust will corrupt and thieves break through and steal. It is a fool's life, as they will find when they get to the end of it, if not before. . . . Simplify, simplify. . . . a man is rich in proportion to the number of things which he can afford to let alone.[4]

For more than two years, Thoreau lived a simple, mostly solitary life in the Concord woods, because, he said, he "wished to live deliberately, to front only the essential facts of life, and see if I could not learn what it had to teach, and not, when I came to die, discover that I had not lived."[5] Had Thoreau built his famous cabin on Bywater rather than on Walden Pond, no doubt he would have found the Shire and its inhabitants much to his liking.

2. Make Light of Your Troubles

The Society of Friends, popularly known as the Quakers, is a Protestant sect that arose in mid-seventeenth-century England

---

and David G. Myers, "Research-Based Suggestions for a Happier Life," online at www.davidmyers.org/happiness/research.html.
[3] Myers, *The Pursuit of Happiness*, p. 41.
[4] Henry David Thoreau, *Walden*, in Walter R. Harding, ed., *The Selected Works of Thoreau* (Boston: Houghton Mifflin, 1975), pp. 305, 247, 298.
[5] *Ibid.*, p. 304.

and quickly became established in the American colonies. For generations, devout Quakers have memorized a list of twelve rules for living known as "The Quaker Dozen." Among the rules are precepts such as "work hard," "love your family," "show kindness," "have charity in your heart," and the very hobbit-like admonition to "make light of your troubles."[6]

Tolkien comments frequently on the hobbits' ability to "make light of their troubles." Gandalf remarks on the hobbits' "amazing power of recovery" (TT, p. 220) and cautions Théoden that "hobbits will sit on the edge of ruin and discuss the pleasures of the table, or the small doings of their fathers, grandfathers, and great-grandfathers, and remoter cousins to the ninth degree, if you encourage them with undue patience" (TT, p. 178). Separated from Pippin, Merry finds himself missing his friend's "unquenchable cheerfulness" (RK, p. 41). And after Merry and Pippin's harrowing escape from the orcs, no could have guessed from their light-hearted talk that they "had suffered cruelly, and been in dire peril" (TT, p. 58).

Making light of troubles also means finding hope and beauty in even the most dire circumstances. Of the four hobbits in the Fellowship of the Ring, only Sam remains absolutely undaunted and uncomplaining to the very end of the Quest. And in one memorable passage Tolkien makes clear that Sam's optimism and strength have deeper roots than simply personal devotion or native pluck:

> Then at last, to keep himself awake, he crawled from the hiding-place and looked out. . . . There, peeping among the cloud-wrack above a dark tor high up in the mountains, Sam saw a white star twinkle for a while. The beauty of it smote his heart, as he looked up out of the forsaken land, and hope returned to him. For like a shaft, clear and cold, the thought pierced him that in the end the Dark Shadow was only a small and passing thing: there was light and high beauty for ever beyond its reach. (RK, p. 211)

---

[6] Olive Ireland Theen, "Grandfather's Quaker Dozen," in William Nichols, ed., *A New Treasury of Words to Live By* (New York: Simon and Schuster, 1959), p. 218.

The hobbits' ability to remain cheerful and unbowed in the face of hardship and suffering is one of their most endearing qualities. It is also, of course, a virtue much praised by philosophers. Many religious philosophers, like St. Augustine, urge us to rejoice and be glad, because life is short, sufferings are temporary, and our true home is in heaven, where our reward will be great.[7] Many secular philosophers, like the famous Stoic Marcus Aurelius, exhort us to be courageous and serene, because all human strivings are insignificant from the standpoint of eternity, and there is no memory or pain in the oblivion of the grave.[8] But whatever our point of view on these ultimate issues, we can both admire the inner strength and appreciate the wisdom of those who make light of their troubles, for by so doing they brighten not only their own lives but the lives of those around them.

3. Get Personal

Hobbits are a clannish and highly sociable people. Their dwellings are often spacious, and inhabited by large, extended families (FR, p. 8). They tend to be honest, loyal, courteous, well-mannered, moderate, generous, hospitable, and are so peaceable that most don't lock their doors at night (FR, p. 111) and "no hobbit has ever killed another on purpose in the Shire" (RK, p. 310). Indeed, so close-knit, orderly, and mutually supportive are the hobbits of the Shire that they have no need for anything more than the most minimal government and police force (FR, p. 10). They do have "Shirriffs," but their job mainly involves "walking round the country and seeing folk, and hearing the news," and ascertaining where the good beer can be found (RK, p. 305).

One of the hobbits' most striking traits is their remarkable capacity for friendship. At the Council of Elrond, Sam, Merry, and Pippin insist on accompanying Frodo on his Quest, heedless of

---

[7] See St. Augustine, *City of God*, translated by Marcus Dods (New York: Modern Library, 1950), pp. 676–680; John Henry Newman, "Equanimity," in *Parochial and Plain Sermons* (San Francisco: Ignatius Press, 1987), pp. 988–996.

[8] See Marcus Aurelius, *Meditations*, in *The Stoic and Epicurean Philosophers*, pp. 522–23; Epicurus, "Letter to Monoeceus," pp. 30–31.

the obvious dangers. When the Fellowship is attacked by orcs at Parth Galen, Frodo chooses to go on alone, wishing to spare his friends from almost certain torment and death in the dungeons of Barad-dûr. And of course without the unwavering friendship and devotion of Sam, Frodo's Quest and the hopes of all the Free Peoples would have failed.

The importance of belonging to other people—of forming close, supportive attachments—is something many philosophers have noted as well. Aristotle, for instance, devotes nearly a fifth of his *Nicomachean Ethics,* his great work on human excellence and fulfillment, to a discussion of the good of friendship. Friendship, he says, is indispensable for a happy and fulfilled human life, for it holds families and communities together, stimulates to noble actions, provides refuge and consolation when misfortunes strike, and offers guidance to the young and assistance to the elderly.[9] Indeed, in Aristotle's view, friendship is "the greatest of external goods,"[10] "for without friends no one would choose to live, though he had all other goods."[11]

Aristotle's insights about the importance of close relationships are strongly supported by contemporary social psychology. Studies show that people with intimate, supportive relationships tend to be both happier and healthier than those who lack such relationships.[12] Studies show, for example, that

- The happiest university students are those who feel satisfied with their love life.
- Those who enjoy close relationships cope better with various stresses, including bereavement, job loss, and illness.
- College alumni who preferred a high income and occupational success to having very close friends and a close marriage were twice as likely as their former classmates to describe themselves as "fairly" or "very" unhappy.
- People report greater well-being if their friends and families support their goals by frequently expressing interest and offering help and encouragement.

---

[9] Aristotle, *Nichomachean Ethics,* 1155a10–25.
[10] *Ibid.,* 1169b10.
[11] *Ibid.,* 1155a5.
[12] Myers, *The Pursuit of Happiness,* Chapters 8 and 9.

- Asked, "What is necessary for your happiness?" most people mention—before anything else—satisfying close relationships with family, friends, or romantic partners.[13]

No doubt if some hobbit-Aristotle had written his or her own
Nicomachean Ethics, the goods of friendship and connectedness
would have featured at least as prominently as they do in
Aristotle's version.

4. Cultivate Good Character

In a draft letter to Peter Hastings, Tolkien remarks that one of
his aims in writing *The Lord of the Rings* was "the encouragement of good morals" (L, p. 194). One way Tolkien tries to do
this is by the traditional literary, moralistic, and prophetic device
of linking happiness with good moral character.

With very few exceptions, happy characters in *The Lord of
the Rings* are good and come to good ends, whereas unhappy
characters are bad and come to bad ends. Think, for example,
of Sam, Aragorn, Faramir,[14] and Gandalf among the good characters, and Gollum, Saruman, Wormtongue, and Denethor
among the bad. This pattern is not invariant: Aragorn's mother,
Gilraen, for example, suffers a premature and unhappy death
(RK, p. 376). But for the most part, Tolkien's Middle-earth is a
conventional fairy-tale world in which the good guys slay the
dragon and win the princess and the bad guys bite the dust.[15]

But is this fairy-tale world anything like *our* world? Isn't ours
a world in which "nice guys finish last" and a great many
Sharkeys and Pimples wind up with most of the good beer and
pipe-weed? Well, "not so hasty," as Treebeard would say.

It is clear that, in this life at least, some happy people are not
good and some good people are not happy. This shows, in

---

[13] *Ibid.*, pp. 149–150.

[14] For many viewers, one of the most disappointing aspects of the Peter
Jackson film version is the way in which Faramir is portrayed as a morally conflicted character. Readers who have seen the films but not read the books
should be aware that in the books Faramir is unambiguously good.

[15] Or at least this is true of the period covered in *The Lord of the Rings*, the
end of the Third Age. The picture that emerges in *The Silmarillion* is distinctly
darker and more tragic.

philosophers' lingo, that goodness is neither a "necessary" nor a "sufficient" condition for being happy. Nevertheless, as many philosophers and psychologists have noted, there is a strong causal connection between goodness and happiness.[16]

Flip back to page 50 in this chapter and look again at the factors researchers have found to be most strongly associated with lasting happiness. Notice that among these are "intimate and supportive relationships" and "a focus beyond the self." Clearly, if you are a complete jerk, your chances of achieving these things will be practically nil. Humans, by nature, need to feel loved, respected, trusted, and appreciated. We need to feel as if we're contributing to something larger than ourselves, that the world will be just a little bit better for our having lived. As Rabbi Harold Kushner, author of the best-selling book, *When Bad Things Happen to Good People*, remarks,

> Human beings have a *need* to be good. . . . Our human nature is such that we need to be helpful, thoughtful, and generous as much as we need to eat, sleep, and exercise. When we eat too much and exercise too little, we feel out of sorts. Even our personalities are affected. And when we become selfish and deceitful, it has the same effect. We become out of touch with our real selves; we forget what it feels like to feel good. . . . [O]nly a life of goodness and honesty leaves us feeling spiritually healthy and human.[17]

Hobbits didn't need psychologists to tell them these truths; they knew them in their bones. And so do we, really. Sometimes we just need to be reminded.

5. Cherish and Create Beauty

Happiness and goodness are strongly linked in *The Lord of the Rings*. So too are happiness and beauty. Rivendell and Lothlórien (not to mention Eressëa, Númenor, and Gondolin) are places of light and great beauty. Mordor, Orthanc, and Minas Morgul, in contrast, are dark, barren, and ugly. Unhappy

---

[16] For a discussion of this issue, see Chapter 1 of this volume.

[17] Kushner, *When All You've Ever Wanted Isn't Enough*, pp. 180–81, 183.

characters in the novel tend to be physically ugly (Sauron, Gollum, and the orcs), whereas happy characters tend to be strikingly beautiful (Arwen and Galadriel) or at least pleasant in appearance (Frodo and Faramir). Moreover, happy peoples in Tolkien's writings are almost invariably described as artistic and creative. This is true of the elves, the immortals of Valinor, the Dúnedain of Númenor, and the mighty builders of Gondor in its prime. Even the rustic hobbits, we are told, have "long and skilful fingers" and can make many "useful and comely things" (FR, p. 2). In contrast, the orcs live in dark, ugly dwellings, wear filthy garments, eat vile food, and try to destroy beauty wherever they encounter it.

Tolkien is right: we need beauty in our lives. In our schools, workplaces, and neighborhoods, ugliness enervates and depresses, while beauty inspires and refreshes.

Tolkien is right, too, in seeing a connection between creativity and happiness. Often our happiest moments are periods of unselfconscious absorption that psychologist Mihaly Csikszentmihalyi calls "flow."[18] Such experiences, Csikszentmihalyi found, are particularly common in artists, dancers, writers, and others engaged in creative tasks. Creative people, says psychologist Abraham Maslow, are "all there, totally immersed, fascinated and absorbed in the present, in the current situation, in the here-now, with the matter-in-hand."[19]

Why is it that humans (and hobbits and elves) have such a need for beauty and creativity in their lives? For Tolkien, as a Christian, the deepest explanation was theological: "we make in our measure and in our derivative mode, because we are made: and not only made, but made in the image and likeness of a Maker."[20] The Christian God creates the world, and as a creator, he is, in a real sense, an artist. According to this conception, all humans made in His likeness are also artists. We find happiness in beauty and creativity because we have our source in, and are ultimately oriented towards, Beauty and Creativity itself.

---

[18] Myers, *The Pursuit of Happiness*, pp. 132–33.

[19] Quoted in *ibid.*, p. 133.

[20] J.R.R Tolkien, "On Fairy-stories," in *The Tolkien Reader* (New York: Ballantine, 1966), p. 55.

6. Rediscover Wonder

One of the happiest characters in *The Lord of the Rings* is undoubtedly Tom Bombadil. Completely absorbed in the natural history of the little realm he shares with Goldberry, fearing nothing, lacking nothing, Tom is a veritable fountain of jollity and mirth. Tolkien never tells us who or what Bombadil is. But in his letters Tolkien does explain that Bombadil has taken a kind of "vow of poverty" (L, p. 179). He has renounced all control, has "no desire of possession or domination" (L, p. 192), and takes delight in things for themselves, "because they are 'other' and wholly independent of the enquiring mind" (L, p. 192; italics omitted). So free of desire is Bombadil that the One Ring of Power itself has no hold on him.

The elves have a similar, but lesser, capacity to become absorbed in "the other." They are, as Treebeard observes, "less interested in themselves than Men are, and better at getting inside other things" (TT, p. 70). As immortals, elves dwelling in Middle-earth are grieved by the flow of time (FR, p. 437) but do not easily succumb to *ennui,* or boredom. Unlike humans, who have a "quick satiety with good" (L, p. 344), elves have an almost endless appetite for poetry, songs, gazing at the stars, and walking in sunlit forests. Whereas humans see a beautiful sunset and say "ho-hum," the elves see it with ever-fresh wonder and delight.

Here Tolkien is saying to us: Learn from the elves. Cultivate wonder, delight, freshness of vision. As poet and naturalist Diane Ackerman writes:

> The world we take for granted wobbles with mysteries and sensory delights . . . Come to the window and look at all the marvels bustling through one slender moment: Lens-shaped clouds signaling high winds aloft. Roof shingles overlapping like pigeon feathers. A magnolia tree's buds already burgeoning with fuzzy flower pods . . . Such is the texture of life, the feel of being alive on this particular planet . . . When we pause to sense [such things], we become wonder-struck and experience a richly satisfying frame of mind that—for lack of a better word—we call joy.[21]

---

[21] Diane Ackerman, "Come to the Window and Look," *Parade Magazine,* January 13, 2002, p. 4.

Frodo has a sensory reawakening of this sort when he arrives in Cerin Amroth, the heart of the ancient realm of Lothlórien. While his companions lie on the grass,

> Frodo stood awhile still lost in wonder. It seemed to him that he had stepped through a high window that looked on a vanished world. . . . He saw no colour but those he knew, gold and white and blue and green, but they were fresh and poignant, as if he had at that moment first perceived them and made for them names new and wonderful. (FR, p. 393)

And later, as he climbed a rope ladder up a tree, Frodo

> laid his hand upon the tree beside the ladder: never before had he been so suddenly and so keenly aware of the feel and texture of a tree's skin and of the life within it. He felt a delight in wood and the touch of it, neither as forester nor as carpenter; it was the delight of the living tree itself. (FR, p. 394)

In his neglected essay, "On Fairy-stories," Tolkien calls this regaining of freshness of vision "recovery." Recovery, in Tolkien's sense, involves regaining a "clear view," cleaning our windows so to speak, "so that the things seen clearly may be freed from the drab blur of triteness and familiarity."[22] It is thus a "return and renewal of health,"[23] a healing of a spiritual blindness. And this healing, Tolkien believed, is one thing that fairy-tales and works of fantasy like *The Lord of the Rings* can do. By juxtaposing the enchanted with the familiar, the magical with the mundane, such works allow us to see the world with fresh eyes. Having encountered ents and towering mallorns, we forever see elms and beeches differently. The blue ocean and silver moon suddenly appear wondrous and strange. The green earth again becomes "a mighty matter of legend" (TT, p. 29). We pierce what C.S. Lewis calls "the veil of familiarity" and begin to see the world as elves see it: as miraculous and charged with the grandeur of Ilúvatar the Creator.

---

[22] Tolkien, "On Fairy-stories," p. 57.
[23] *Ibid.*

Tolkien: Fantasist and Philosopher

In the Foreword to the second edition of *The Lord of the Rings*, Tolkien remarks that his prime motive in writing the book "was the desire of a tale-teller to try his hand at a really long story that would hold the attention of readers, amuse them, delight them, and at times maybe excite them or deeply move them" (FR, p. ix). He certainly succeeds in this. But he also does much more. Through his portrayal of happy hobbits and elves and the strong, healthy communities they build, he becomes our philosophical guide, pointing us to ways of living and thinking and perceiving that can help us to lead richer, more joy-filled lives.[24]

---

[24] My thanks to Joe Kraus, Tod Bassham, John Davenport, Abby Myers, Leanne Bush, Bill Irwin, David Ramsay Steele, and especially Eric Bronson for helpful comments on earlier drafts of this chapter.

5

The Quests of Sam and Gollum for the Happy Life

JORGE J.E. GRACIA

Tolkien's heroes and anti-heroes are extraordinary beings. Think of Gandalf the Grey and Saruman the White, the good and bad wizards who wield enormous magical powers; of Aragorn, a man greater than life and a king of old; and of the Dark Lord Sauron the Great, the very embodiment of evil. Even those who, like Bilbo and Frodo, are not quite extraordinary in themselves, are vested with unusual qualities by their heroic quests. As narrated in *The Hobbit*, Bilbo goes on to defeat Smaug, an evil dragon with plenty of resources and cunning. Frodo engages in the most difficult task that anyone could possibly undertake: the destruction of the Ring of Power coveted by Sauron. And at the end of the story the ultimate reward of both Bilbo and Frodo is to sail, in the company of Gandalf, on a ship into the Uttermost West (RK, p. 339). These are beings whose lives transcend ordinary bounds, and it is for this reason that it is difficult for us to learn anything from them that can directly apply to our lives. Yes, we accompany them in their quests, observe their difficulties, desires, and temptations, and approve or condemn their actions. But we do this only at a distance, for we are too removed from the reality in which they exist to understand fully what they are about, or to empathize with their successes and failures.

Not everyone in Tolkien's *The Lord of the Rings* has the same heroic stature, however. There are many characters that are closer to our size, and it is from them that we can more easily learn something suitable to our situation. They are good and bad in ordinary senses we can grasp, and their search for a happy life, whether successful or in vain, is also within our limited understanding. They are not wizards, kings, or mighty warriors; they are ordinary beings who succeed and fail, just like us, and who have to make do with ordinary resources. In particular, I have in mind two characters who are cut very much from our mold. They play key roles in Tolkien's epic, but their roles are not heroic, and their qualities are made of a stuff to which we can relate. They are Sam Gamgee and Sméagol (also known as Gollum because of the peculiar noises he makes with his throat).

Of the two, Gollum is the more fascinating character. In director Peter Jackson's New Line Cinema movies, Gollum is brought to life as an ugly but humane computer generated character, whose own psychology drives much of the plot. He represents the good gone bad, something which is always intriguing for those of us who are struggling to stay with the first. Sam represents the good that stays good even under temptation. Both Sam and Gollum want the same thing: to be happy. Both work hard at it. But only one of them succeeds: Sam reaches his goal and Gollum ends in disaster. Why? This is the momentous philosophical question, because it concerns the nature of the good life, the life of happiness. We need to answer it, because in answering it we can perhaps also learn something important about how to achieve happiness for ourselves.

Two of a Kind

Sam and Gollum present us with significant and useful contrasts and similarities because they share the same nature. If it is true that happiness depends on one's nature, the kind of being one is—as Aristotle claimed—then it would not be very helpful to compare the happiness of beings that are naturally different. It would not make sense, for example, to compare how elves and wizards are happy, for it is quite possible that what makes them so are quite different things. But Sam and Gollum are both hobbits. The first came from the Shire and the second is descended from a branch of hobbit-kind "akin to the fathers of the fathers of the Stoors" (FR, p. 57).

But not only do they have the same hobbit nature, they also have a similar culture. True, Gollum has forgotten much of it as a result of his solitary lifestyle, and the Stoors lived a wilder and more primitive life than the hobbits from the Shire (L, p. 290), but the culture of both has the same roots. As Gandalf explains to Frodo when he is recounting the story of the original encounter between Bilbo and Gollum: "There was a great deal in the background of their minds and memories that was very similar. They understood one another remarkably well, very much better than a hobbit would understand, say, a Dwarf, or an Orc, or even an Elf" (FR, p. 59). When Bilbo runs into Gollum in the caves of the Misty Mountains, they both know how to engage in a game that was going to prove tragic for Gollum, the Riddle-game (H, pp. 73–80). Indeed, they both know the same riddles, and it is Bilbo who breaks the rules of the game by asking a question rather than posing a riddle when he runs out of ideas. Bilbo is pressed to challenge Gollum in order to escape: "What have I got in my pocket?" (H, p. 78) Gollum's mistake, which he realizes when it is already too late, is to accept the question and to try to answer it. "Not a fair question. It cheated first, it did. It broke the rules" (FR, p. 63). Like the philosopher Ludwig Wittgenstein, Gollum should have said that the question was not allowed by the rules, and therefore he was entitled to reject it. But once he accepted the question and tried to answer it, even though he demanded three guesses, which is unusual, he was bound by his promise. Gollum, like all hobbits, attaches great weight to riddle contests.

We are also told that he used to like tales, as Sam and other hobbits do (TT, p. 364; FR, p. 70). And Gollum, on at least one occasion, withstood great pain, "as a hobbit might" (FR, p. 60). So Sam and Gollum have much in common, and this is why it makes sense for us to ask how they can be happy and whether we can follow a similar path.

The Pursuit of Happiness

Let us begin with an assumption that does not seem far-fetched, namely, that we all want to be happy. It is not far-fetched because a good number of philosophers, beginning perhaps with Aristotle, have in fact pointed out that this is exactly what we all want. When it comes to living well, Aristotle writes, "the general run of men and people of superior refinement say that it is happiness, and identify living well and faring well with being happy . . ."[1] True, if we ask ordinary persons what their aims in life are, what they ultimately desire, not all are likely to say happiness. Some might say that they want power, others that it is fame, others pleasure, still others money, and a few, I am sure, will say that they want to be virtuous. There might even be some who speak about a desire to serve God, to conquer the world, to advance science, or to know as much as there is to know. But if we prod them further, I think they will come around to Aristotle's conclusion, namely, that what they really want is to be happy. Their disagreement is not about this ultimate end, but rather about what it means to be happy and how one gets to be so.

So let us assume that Sam and Gollum both want to be happy. What we need to know, then, is what they think this consists in, how they think they can get there, and whether in fact they do. Moreover, whether they reach their goal or not, we need to know why they succeed or fail. Here we shall find the moral of the story and what we hope to learn from this tale.

We know that Sam ends up happy, and Gollum ends up not just in misery but in destruction. Indeed, it is one of the interesting facts about Tolkien's tale that, even though he undergoes all kinds of travails, Sam is not unhappy. At times, Sam is troubled, worried, hungry, exhausted, afraid, sad, frustrated, and even in pain. But Tolkien never tells us that he is unhappy or that he is ever seriously tempted to turn back from the Quest that brought him into difficulties. Just the contrary. He is single minded and steadfast. And even in the greatest crisis he faces, when he thinks Frodo is dead and he is all alone, rather than considering cutting his losses and running, his main thought is to complete the task he and Frodo had undertaken, to "*see it through*" (TT, p. 386).

The situation with Gollum is just the reverse. He seems to be in a permanent state of unhappiness. He suffers, like Sam, from all sorts of difficulties, but the source of his misery is not these. He is dissatisfied, vulnerable, and unable to find peace and relief in life (RK, p. 238). Gandalf describes him to Frodo as

---

[1] *Nichomachean Ethics*, translated by W. D. Ross, in Richard McKeon, ed., *The Basic Works of Aristotle* (New York: Random House, 1941), p. 937, 1095a17–20.

"altogether wretched," and this even when he had the Ring, which for him was the ultimate object of desire. He lives a lonely, sneaky, miserable life, which arouses pity mixed with horror in Bilbo when he first encounters him. It is a life constituted of "endless unmarked days without light or hope of betterment . . ." (H, p. 87).

So what is it that Sam and Gollum consider their overall aim, the goal that they think will bring them happiness? Consider Gollum first: What does he want? The answer is unambiguous: the Ring of Power, his Precious. "We wants it, we wants it, we wants it!" he repeats to himself in a kind of frenzy (TT, p. 268), an expression of his insatiable desire and lust for it. And what does the Ring provide? One thing is escape from Him, Sauron, who had subjected Gollum to torture in Mordor, and who also wants the Ring (FR, p. 64). "He'll eat us, if he gets it, eat all the world" (TT, p. 273). Regaining the Ring would give Gollum strength to fight Ringwraiths, and thus presumably security; prestige and fame, which being Lord Sméagol, Gollum the Great, and *The* Gollum would bring; and food, particularly fresh fish from the sea, juicy and sweet (TT, p. 268). But above all he just wants to have the Ring, for without it he feels lost. Life without the Ring is nothing. Close to his destruction, he confesses that "when Precious goes" he will "die, yes, into the dust" (RK, p. 237).

And what does Sam want? He wants neither to be a wizard nor a warrior. Originally, before he and Frodo set out on their quest, he wanted adventure and to see elves and exotic creatures like Oliphaunts (FR, p. 70; TT, p. 283). But more deeply, what he really wants is to be back in the Shire, the place he cares for more than any other. This is what he is "hoping for all the time" (TT, p. 363), for then he can see Rosie again, and share a life with her and his friends. The Shire is never very far from his mind, and is the only place where he would like to be. When Lady Galadriel looks into his innermost desires, they are revealed to consist in "flying back home to the Shire to a nice little hole—with a bit of garden . . ." (FR, p. 401).

A most important difference between the desires of Gollum and Sam, then, is that Gollum wishes for the possession of his Precious by himself, alone, whereas Sam's desires involve others: Frodo, Rosie, and his friends in the Shire. There is a social dimension to the happiness of Sam that is completely lacking in the happiness that Gollum pursues. Sam's happiness includes others of his kind, but Gollum's happiness excludes everyone. Gollum hides in an isolated place at the roots of the Misty Mountains, at the bottom of a tunnel, in a solitary island of rock in a cold lake frequented only by occasional goblins, which he eats when he gets the opportunity by catching them by surprise. His very survival depends on the destruction of others and his enjoyment of solitude, since he was "driven away, alone, and crept down, down, into the dark under the mountains" (H, p. 73). He lives away from his land, time, and kin. After finding the Ring, he became unpopular and was finally expelled from the community on orders from his own grandmother. So "He wandered in loneliness" (FR, p. 59), having as his only companion the thing he coveted and hid because of the fear that someone else would take it away from him.

By contrast, Sam is always giving. We should not be surprised at his attitude toward the master he loves, but his generosity does not stop with him. His loving nature is revealed when Sam realizes the power of the seed-box Lady Galadriel had given him at Lothlórien. Instead of keeping it for his garden, as even Frodo suggests, he uses it for the restoration of the whole Shire to its former splendor after it had been devastated by Saruman and his minions (RK, p. 330). His thought is always for others.

There are consequences to the desires of Gollum and Sam. Gollum's condition deteriorates. He becomes dark and slimy. His eyes enlarge and become pale and luminous to allow him to see in the dark and catch the blind fish that live in the lake. He talks to himself and sometimes makes no distinction between himself and his precious Ring. The confusion about who he is goes even deeper, for at times there seem to be two halves of one person, conversing with each other. One is Sméagol, the remnants of the old hobbit, where there is still some good left; the other is Gollum, the slave of the Ring who will do anything to have it and keep it and is consumed with wickedness. Sam calls these two halves Slinker and Stinker (TT, p. 274). Neither name is flattering, for Sam dislikes and is suspicious of both, but the Sméagol half is not altogether lost to evil and treachery. He wants to save his "nice master," Frodo, and when Faramir says that Gollum is wicked, Frodo responds: "No, not altogether wicked" (TT, p. 338). Indeed, when Gollum uses

"I" to refer to himself, this "seem[s] usually to be a sign, on its rare appearances, that some remnants of the old truth and sincerity were for the moment on top" (TT, p. 280).

The consequences of Sam's desires are of a different sort. He is slowly transformed from a rather immature and simple hobbit in search of adventure into a resourceful servant, a loyal companion, a fierce guardian, and a loving friend. There is also an important difference between how Sam and Gollum pursue their respective goals. Because Gollum's mind is set on recovering the Ring which in his view was first stolen by Bilbo, he puts no conditions on this task. He engages in whatever activity he thinks will bring about the desired effect. And treachery against Frodo and Sam is never far from his mind. Director Peter Jackson emphasizes this point by choosing to end *The Lord of the Rings: The Two Towers* with Gollum's treacherous plans rather than Tolkien's ending in Shelob's cave.

The case with Sam is very different. He also has an ultimate goal—to live in the Shire with those he loves. But this goal is mediated by another goal that he puts in between: helping Frodo destroy the Ring. He never considers leaving Frodo alone and going back to his dear country. Indeed, although he is not particularly smart, he outwits Frodo in order to accompany him when Frodo decides to abandon the other members of the Fellowship (FR, p. 456). Why? Because his first and foremost attachment is not to an object, but to a person. His goal is not possession, but fellowship. He loves Frodo. And this love translates into loyalty, unlike Gollum's distorted "love" for Déagol and weak feeling for Frodo, which both end up in betrayal.

Like Gollum, Sam also has two halves between which he feels "torn." But the two halves in question have to do with his relation to the two people he loves most, Rosie and Frodo. And when Frodo tells him that he is "as happy as anyone can be," this refers to the fact that Sam is engaged in the life of the Shire, surrounded by his family and friends (RK, p. 338).

Sam's happiness is not unmixed with sadness. He, like his friends Merry and Pippin, is "sorrowful" at Frodo's parting. But, like them, he has "great comfort in his friends" on his way back from the Grey Havens (RK, p. 340). Upon his return, "Rose drew him in, and set him in his chair, and put little Elanor upon his lap. He drew a deep breath. 'Well, I'm back,' he said" (RK, p. 340). These lines close Tolkien's story, because Sam, like

Aragorn, is a wanderer who has returned to his land, and his return is the end of his quest, a quest for happiness which is answered with the fellowship of family and friends.

Gollum also loves something. He loves the Ring, but the Ring is the only thing he loves. The Ring is "the only thing he had ever cared for, his precious" (H, p. 87). And this is not a person; it is merely a thing, even if it is magical and possessed of extra-ordinary powers. Indeed, Gollum's desire for the Ring makes him betray the love he was supposed to have for his friend Déagol, whom he murders in order to steal the Ring (FR, p. 58). His misunderstanding of love is clear in the encounter in which he repeatedly calls Déagol his love, even while he is strangling him.

So now we know what both Sam and Gollum think about happiness. For them, happiness consists in two different things: For Gollum it is possession of the Ring, and for Sam it is a life of fellowship in the Shire.

The Importance of Friendship

Gollum is not all bad, nor is Sam all good, however. Both are tempted by opposite passions: Gollum by the love of Frodo, and Sam by his jealousy of Gollum. And both are attracted, like almost everyone else, by the power of the Ring.

Even after Gollum had planned to take Frodo and Sam to the giant spider Shelob and in that way revenge himself against Sam, whom he hated, and recover the Ring from Frodo's remains, there is a moment in which his good side could have overcome the bad. The origin of this extraordinary possibility was prompted by affection, the stirrings of love for his "nice master." His expression changes, his eyes become old and tired-looking, he shakes his head as though debating inwardly:

> Then he came back, and slowly putting out a trembling hand, very cautiously he touched Frodo's knee—but almost the touch was a caress. For a fleeting moment, could one of the sleepers have seen him, they would have thought that they beheld an old weary hobbit, shrunken by the years that had carried him far beyond his time, beyond friends and kin, and the fields and streams of youth, an old starved pitiable thing. (TT, p. 366)

The moment is crucial, and Tolkien calls it "the most tragic moment in the Tale" (L, p. 330), but unfortunately Sam destroys the possibility for regeneration it has opened for Gollum. Of course, we do not know whether there was enough fellow-feeling in Gollum to overcome the temptation for treachery in order to recover the Ring. But certainly Sam provides the excuse to make sure that it could not happen. When he wakes up and sees Gollum touching Frodo, his first reaction, prompted by jealousy (L, p. 235), is to challenge him: "Hey you! What are you up to" (TT, p. 366)? Sam is suspicious and he calls Gollum a sneak and villain, something Gollum resents deeply, for his feelings toward Frodo at that moment had been of a finer kind. He responds with bitter irony: "Sneaking, sneaking! Hobbits always so polite, yes. O nice hobbits! Sméagol brings them up secret ways that nobody else could find. Tired he is, thirsty he is, yes thirsty; and he guides them and he searches for paths, and they say *sneak, sneak.* Very nice friends, O yes my precious, very nice." After this he withdraws into himself and the green glint of malice in his eyes reappears. Tolkien notes, in despair: "The fleeting moment had passed, beyond recall" (TT, p. 366). A new venom surfaces, motivated by the bitterness resulting from misunderstanding and rejection. Sam understands it and feels remorse, but he cannot but distrust Gollum.

In his letters, Tolkien speculates that, had Sam not acted as he did, Gollum might still have done all he could to recover the Ring, either by stealing it or taking it by violence, but once he had it, he would have sacrificed himself for Frodo's sake, voluntarily casting himself into the Crack of Doom (L, p. 330). This certainly would have been a dramatic turn of events, but it is doubtful that it could have happened in spite of some indications early on that he wanted to save both his Precious and Frodo. There was not enough time for Gollum's feelings for Frodo to grow strong enough in order for Gollum to overcome his desire to keep the Ring forever. But the issue is unclear in that, from the very beginning, Gandalf does not see Gollum's regeneration as hopeless. He tells Frodo that there is little hope that the evil part of Gollum can be conquered by the good one. "Yet not no hope" (FR, p. 60). And he repeats the point later: "I have not much hope that Gollum can be cured before he dies, but there is a chance of it" (FR, p. 65).

The power of the Ring is a temptation to both Sam and Gollum, to which Gollum gives in completely. After Gollum's moment of hesitation, there is nothing left for him to do but to proceed with the planned treachery. Sam, on the other hand, is tempted by the Ring when Frodo is paralyzed by Shelob, and he takes the Ring from Frodo in order to escape from the orcs that teem in the area. All of a sudden he desires the Ring for reasons similar to the ones we saw in Gollum. He sees himself as "Samwise the Strong, Hero of the Age, striding with a flaming sword across the darkened land, and armies flocking to his call as he marched to the overthrow of Barad-dûr" (RK, p. 186). He sees a transformation in the world brought about by him, Gorgoroth changed into a garden of flowers. He could do it, just put the Ring on and claim it for his own, and this fantasy would become a reality. How could he resist? Gollum could not. They are both hobbits and thus endowed with a plain sense of their limitations, but Sam resists and Gollum gives in. What makes the difference? Sam's love of his master, Tolkien tells us. It is the love that Sam has for Frodo that makes it possible for him to resist temptation.

There is another episode that shows that the great difference between Sam and Gollum lies precisely in their fellow feeling. The reason that the Ring got hold of Gollum in such a way as to have destroyed his will can be traced precisely to how it was acquired: by betrayal, murder, and, most important, the corruption of love. Gollum, as we saw earlier, kills his friend Déagol to get it. By contrast, the reason that Bilbo was never under the complete power of the Ring is precisely that when he acquired it, he was moved by the fellow feeling of pity and spared Gollum's life (H, p. 87).

Gollum cannot resist the desire for the Ring because he has no resources, no friends. One reason, perhaps, why Gollum has no friends is because he has no love for himself. As Aristotle reminds us, "Friendly relations with one's neighbours, and the marks by which friendships are defined, seem [to proceed] from a man's relations to himself."[2] A man who likes himself makes friends easily, and a man who has good friends is more easily prevented from going astray. Gollum lacks this self-love. Even

---

[2] *Nicomachean Ethics*, p. 1081, 1166a1–2

Frodo's friendship is treated with suspicion and scorn because of his own self-doubt. In the face of an enemy with this kind of power, Gollum (like you or I) would have needed a little help from his friends.

Recall that Bilbo nearly did not give the Ring up, and it was only through Gandalf's insistence that he did. Frodo himself became too attached to the Ring and in fact failed to do with it what he meant to do. Instead of throwing the Ring in the fires of Mount Doom, he took possession of it at the last minute: "I have come . . . but I do not choose now do to what I came to do. I will not do this deed. The Ring is mine" (RK, p. 239)! Had not Gollum bitten off Frodo's ring-finger and fallen to his doom with it, it is difficult to envision that Frodo would have come to his senses. But Sam was able to resist the Ring's power, and the reason was his feelings for Frodo. When Sam took the Ring from Frodo in Shelob's cave, he was tempted to keep it, but he did not because his first thought was for his master rather than for himself. Love gave him the strength to resist.

All You Need Is Love

One lesson of Tolkien's saga is clear: For ordinary people like you or me, happiness is achievable only in a social context and its key is love. And love expresses itself in loyalty and sharing, not in possession. Departing from the rule that love prescribes for us leads to misery.

For humans as well as for hobbits, happiness requires fellowship with others, and it is in love for others that we can maintain our course toward it and achieve it. It is by forgetting ourselves that we earn the good life and it is by giving that we receive. This is the old truth illustrated by the lives of Sam and Gollum.[3]

---

[3] I am indebted to Leticia Gracia for an important suggestion concerning the key to happiness in Gollum and Sam.

6

"Farewell to Lórien": The Bounded Joy of Existentialists and Elves

ERIC BRONSON

It could be that country crooner Kenny Rogers got it right. When it really comes down to enjoying this life, "you got to know when to hold 'em, know when to fold 'em." It seems like sound advice (it rhymes, after all), but let's not give the old Gambler too much credit. On that train bound for nowhere, the Gambler left something important out. Exactly how should we play the game, and where can we find the strength to walk away?

Poker players aren't the only ones who have to decide when to call and when to cash in. Over a century ago, existentialist philosophers like Friedrich Nietzsche wrote that lasting happiness requires a delicate balance of holding on to one's past, while knowing when to strike out on one's own. Above all, "knowing when to walk away and knowing when to run" (Grammy award winning Don Schlitz wrote the words) demands spontaneous creativity amidst a changing world of longing and hope. According to many European philosophers, the man or woman of strength must learn to develop and trust that inner voice. Sticking through the bad times and cutting the cords altogether both take great courage, and in such decisions we affirm our identity.

Less than forty years after Nietzsche's death, J.R.R. Tolkien began writing *The Lord of the Rings*. In 1939, as Europe braced for the worst, Tolkien completed the first half of *The Fellowship of the Ring*, emphasizing how terrible riders in black could terrorize even the peaceful oasis of Frodo's beloved Shire. The Ringwraiths of Middle-earth added a touch of evil not present in Tolkien's previous novel, *The Hobbit*. In *The Fellowship*, the Black Riders are messengers of a greater evil brewing in Mordor. When asked about the first eleven chapters, ending with Frodo being stabbed by a Morgul-knife, Tolkien privately confessed, "The darkness of the present days has had some effect on it" (L, p. 41).

However, within the parallel perils of Europe in the twentieth century and Middle-earth at the end of the Third Age, Tolkien elegantly writes of safe havens where even in the darkest times, songs of love are sung under starlit skies. Nestled in the perfumed mountains of Rivendell and the ancients forests of Lórien, many of the elves of old know when to hold 'em and know when to fold 'em. It's a gamble that brings lasting joy to them and everyone they touch. Let's examine Tolkien's elves a little closer. In their fictional world, we too may find an ace that we can keep.

Rivendell and Lórien

It is not unexpected that Frodo should be healed (though never cured) and reunited with Gandalf and Bilbo at the House of Elrond in Rivendell. Readers of *The Hobbit* already are familiar with the charms of The Last Homely House, the westernmost outpost of the elves. "That house was, as Bilbo had long ago reported, 'a perfect house, whether you like food or sleep or story-telling or singing, or just sitting and thinking best, or a pleasant mixture of them all.' Merely to be there was a cure for weariness, fear, and sadness" (FR, p. 252). In Rivendell the Nine Riders of the enemy are turned back, Isildur's sword is re-forged and given to Aragorn, and the Fellowship of men, dwarves, hobbits and elves is formed. Despite, or because of such hard work, there is joyous singing, day and night.

The elves of Rivendell are famous for their singing. Even old Bilbo is tempted to compose a few verses while living there (though he admits he might be somewhat out of line). A good song is addicting, as anyone who has belted a few notes in the shower knows all too well. When the younger Bilbo set out on *his* adventure to slay an evil dragon and steal the gold, the bickering dwarves that made up most of the company met elves headed for Rivendell. Their singing captivated everyone, including the reader. As Tolkien writes, "Elvish singing is not a thing

to miss, in June under the stars, not if you care for such things"
(H, p. 50). And who wouldn't?

In the Christian story of creation, the New Testament tells us
that in the beginning, there was the Word. In Tolkien's spin, we
are told that in the beginning, there was the Song. Before writing even *The Hobbit*, Tolkien laid out the origins of Middle-earth
and how the happy elves found a home there. Though *The
Silmarillion* was first published in 1977, four years after
Tolkien's death, it contains the history behind Middle-earth that
Tolkien had been working on for much of his adult life. As it
begins, the creator of the world, Ilúvatar, made the Ainur, or
Holy Ones, and gave to them the power of song. The voices of
the Ainur, like innumerable choirs and musical instruments,

> began to fashion the theme of Ilúvatar to a great music; and a
> sound arose of endless interchanging melodies woven in harmony
> that passed beyond hearing into the depths and into the heights,
> and the places of the dwelling of Ilúvatar were filled to overflow-
> ing, and the music and the echo of the music went out into the
> Void, and it was not void. (S, p. 15)

Both elves and men (Quendi and Atani) were created as important players of the world's symphony. But though the race of
men will do great things, Ilúvatar proclaims it is the elves who
"shall be the fairest of all earthly creatures, and they shall have
and shall conceive and bring forth more beauty than all my
Children; and they shall have the greater bliss in this world" (S,
p. 41). In the early days, there was a great friendship between
men and the elves along with the occasional mixed marriage
between races. Elrond, master of Rivendell, is born with mixed
blood, courageous in battle with a gift for song; he has the
strength of men with little of their weakness. It was he who
pleaded with Isildur to cast the Ring back into Mount Doom,
and later appoints Frodo to finish the job that men and elves
could not.

Tolkien's Middle-earth, however, is filled with many dangers,
and after the newly-formed Fellowship leaves the comforts of
Rivendell, the participants are beset by snowstorms high atop
Caradhras, and orcs within the Mines of Moria. Before they
escape the Mines, the members of the Fellowship suffer their
greatest loss, as their guardian wizard and mentor Gandalf falls

into darkness at the Bridge of Khazad-dûm. But just when all seems lost for the weary band of travelers, they reach Lórien, a magical forest where elves live and sing in the treetops. Like Rivendell, Lórien is a place for spirits to rise. Even Frodo has difficulty grieving for Gandalf while he rests amidst such beauty. "The others cast themselves down upon the fragrant grass, but Frodo stood awhile still lost in wonder . . . No blemish of sickness or deformity could be seen in anything that grew upon the earth. On the land of Lórien there was no stain" (FR, p. 393).

As Elrond is master of Rivendell, Lórien is ruled by Lord Celeborn and Lady Galadriel. "Very tall they were, and the Lady no less tall than the Lord; and they were grave and beautiful" (FR, p. 398). But Tolkien also informs us that even though Celeborn and Galadriel are the same height, it is clearly the Lady who wields the greater power within the elvish kingdom in the trees. It is Galadriel who wears one of the elvish Rings of Power, and it is she who has seen the evil eye of Sauron long before Frodo first peers into her mirror.

In the New Line Cinema movies, Galadriel is played by Cate Blanchett as a beautiful spirit who walks lightly and speaks as though from another world. Tolkien, though, describes Galadriel as a worldly elf, older and more powerful than Elrond, a woman wiser and sadder than all the others. In Galadriel, we see that there is more to the elves than love songs and happy nights. Unlike Elrond, Galadriel was born in an age when elves were happy and innocent, dwelling in the land of the gods. But *The Silmarillion* tells of trouble brewing between the gods, and it is Galadriel's half-uncle, Fëanor, who takes it upon himself to right the wrongs and fight the growing evil. These Noldor elves rebel against the gods and leave their garden of paradise to take up arms against the forces of darkness. A young Galadriel stands beside Fëanor as he commands his elvish troops: "'Fair shall the end be', he cried, 'though long and hard shall be the road! Say farewell to bondage! But say farewell also to ease!'" (S, p. 83) Though Galadriel does not take the terrible oath of her rebellious kinsmen, she is condemned along with the others as traitors to the gods who protected them. Upon parting, the gods curse their once beloved elves: "The Dispossessed shall they be forever" (S, p. 88).

And so Frodo first meets Galadriel in Lórien, a kingdom named after a more beautiful place where the Noldor once lived among the gods. This concept of lost beauty and dispossession is a major theme in *The Lord of the Rings*. At the end of the Third Age, much that is good of the old world will fall away and nobody is more sure of this inevitability than Galadriel, herself a wanderer in a foreign land, the keeper of all that is beautiful in a world of danger and ugliness. In Rivendell, Elrond is also aware of the coming end, but Tolkien notes how the elves of Lórien suffer more acutely. Frodo observes this change as he walks through the forest. It seems to him as if he has stepped back into the Elder Days:

> In Rivendell there was memory of ancient things; in Lórien the ancient things still lived on in the waking world. Evil had been seen and heard there, sorrow had been known; the Elves feared and distrusted the world outside: wolves were howling on the wood's borders: but on the land of Lórien no shadow lay. (FR, p. 392)

Galadriel presides over Lórien with songs of joy, and that is why the Fellowship takes such comfort in its beauty. But it is a happiness born of sorrow and dispossession, and that is why Tolkien can be placed in a wider tradition of European philosophers who still affirm life, while bearing witness to the passing shadows.

The Sometimes Merry Existentialists

Far away from Middle-earth, in a place disappointingly devoid of elves who whistle while they work, Tolkien's intellectual contemporaries were preparing for their own dark times. Like Elrond and Galadriel, European philosophers at the turn of the twentieth century also contemplated the end of a golden age. European power, which influenced, if it did not control, the far reaches of the globe, was suddenly hanging in the balance. Grandiose words, such as "renaissance" and "enlightenment," that had characterized Europe in its glory were swiftly becoming a distant memory. By the end of World War I, it didn't take a wizard to see that times were changing. In the charred soil of two world wars a school of philosophy called existentialism began to grow and flourish. Without the aid of Galadriel's mirror, existentialist philosophers foresaw the coming of dangerous times, but insisted that one could still sing in the mountains, sleep in the forests, and create real beauty in a chaotic world.

Rightly or wrongly, existentialists are typecast as a rather dour bunch of philosophers who preach only pain and suffering. A glance at some of the more famous book titles supports this stereotype. We have *The Concept of Dread* and *The Sickness unto Death* by Søren Kierkegaard, *Nausea* and *Troubled Sleep* by Jean-Paul Sartre, and *The Plague* by Albert Camus, all depicting the human condition in less than joyful terms. But there are also other strains of existentialism that aren't infected by the sour-puss bug. Philosophers like Friedrich Nietzsche, Karl Jaspers, and Hannah Arendt agree that life carries with it a certain despair, but alongside the suffering stands a spontaneous affirmation of life as it is, though danger lurks behind every tree.

By the late nineteenth century, many European philosophers were predicting the end of the European empire. In Germany, Nietzsche privately worried about the coming cruelty. In his notebook, he writes, "For some time now, our whole European culture has been moving as toward a catastrophe, with a tortured tension that is growing from decade to decade: restlessly, violently . . ."[1] Beside this catastrophe stood the average person, ill equipped to combat it. As Nietzsche again writes, "What is inherited is not the sickness but *sickliness*: the lack of strength to resist the danger of infections, etc., the broken resistance; *morally* speaking, resignation and meekness in face of the enemy."[2]

Even in such dark times, however, Nietzsche promises hope. The artist who is strong, who has *power*, can proclaim joy at just the time when none is evident. Such artists, he argues, "should see nothing as it is, but fuller, simpler, stronger: to that end, their lives must contain a kind of youth and spring, a kind of habitual intoxication."[3] An artist looks at the pain of this world and does more than reproduce our world. She adds to it, enriches it, enlivens it, or in the words of English historian Kenneth Clark, "perfects it." For Nietzsche, the artist can only exist in times of crises. It is the darkness that he lights. First, one must be a

---

[1] *The Will to Power*, translated by Walter Kaufmann and R.J. Hollingdale (New York: Vintage, 1967), Preface.

[2] *Ibid.*, section 47.

[3] *Ibid.*, section 800.

nihilist, finding hypocrisy and futility in life's most sacred projects. All must end in nothingness, after everything is said and done. The true person of power understands this terrible truth and is not crushed; on the contrary, he is empowered. As Nietzsche's Zarathustra affirms, "I carry the blessings of my Yes into all abysses . . . and blessed is he who blesses thus."[4]

Of course, it is not so easy to carry our yeses into all abysses. Even fair Legolas has his quiet moments of self-doubt. Getting through the difficult times takes more than simple yeses. As Nietzsche explains, the man or woman of power needs to learn how to forget experiences that bring pain. Too long do we cling to our past. "But in the smallest and in the greatest happiness, there is always one element which makes it happiness: the power to forget . . ."[5] By carefully forgetting yesterday, one learns to live spontaneously, even happily. Too bad human beings aren't more like computers that can have the past turned on and off, deleting damaged files forever by the casual push of a button. We are born with a history and shaped with experiences. Forgetting the past wholeheartedly is forgetting who we are entirely. Nietzsche doesn't argue for total amnesia, but for a more disciplined remembering of who we are without being slaves to our past. When history reminds us of our own greatness, it is valuable. Such a history "is relevant to the one who preserves and venerates the past, who looks back with love and loyalty to his origins, where he became what he is."[6] Remember that which made you who you are, remember that which makes you unique, and forget everything else that makes you tired, scared, and weak. As Nietzsche argues, none of us are bound to our past, though it's a good place to look for a source of courage and pride.

Through today's news media, we are inundated with the present and the future, often at the expense of the past. We look to

---

[4] *Thus Spoke Zarathustra,* translated by Walter Kaufmann (New York: Penguin, 1985), p. 165. Nietzsche presents us with the image of a light-footed dwarf, who laughs at the bumbling men and women. Nietzsche's dwarf and Tolkien's elves appear to have much in common.

[5] "History in the Service and Disservice of Life," in *Unmodern Observations,* translated by William Arrowsmith (New Haven: Yale University Press, 1990), p. 89.

[6] *Ibid.*, p. 99.

the world of machines to help us escape from the past and lose ourselves in the present. And yet this aspect of industrialization both attracts and repels us. Feel-good movies like *E.T.* and *You've Got Mail* show us how modern technology can bring us closer together, while science-fiction movies like *The Terminator* and *The Matrix* remind us of the growing threat that comes with new machines.

Philosopher Karl Jaspers, a Nietzsche scholar and contemporary of Tolkien, worried that a blind obsession with machines would alienate us from our past; it would prevent us from remembering who we really are. Certainly it is counterproductive to stand in the way of progress, Jaspers admits, "but when the very dwelling-place was machine made, when the environment had become despiritualized . . . then man was, as it were, bereft of his world."[7] Jaspers argues that we are forgetting the wrong things. We are forgetting what makes us human, our critical thinking and our individuality. We are forgetting our love for life. Jaspers asks us, "Have we not long forgotten what it is for man to be himself, to think and live freely, and realize himself in his world?"[8] We should remember our spontaneity and forget the efficient, unthinking orcs who blindly destroy what is most natural, having lost all ability to critically examine their actions.

Jaspers's star student, Hannah Arendt, escaped Nazi Germany and certain death for the crime of being Jewish. Looking back on the Holocaust that had stripped her of all she held dear, Arendt angrily accuses leading Nazi officials like Adolf Eichmann of forgetting his rage, his compassion, and his overall humanity. He loses himself in the technologically advanced German bureaucracy and takes to following orders rather than questioning them. Where was the Nietzschean man of power to see the abyss and affirm life? As Arendt laments in a letter to Jaspers, "Everything does depend on a few. We have all seen in these years how the few constantly became fewer still."[9] But there are that few who still create joy for themselves

---

[7] *Man in the Modern Age*, translated by Eden and Cedar Paul (London: Routledge, 1951), p. 45.

[8] *The Future of Mankind*, translated by E.B. Ashton (Chicago: University of Chicago Press, 1961), p. 234.

[9] *Hannah Arendt–Karl Jaspers Correspondence*, ed. Lotte Kohler and Hans Saner, translated by Robert and Rita Kimber (New York: Harcourt Brace, 1992), #31.

and others, in spite or because of the serious dangers that surround them on all sides. Arendt herself reflects on these few in a book appropriately titled, *Men in Dark Times*. Arendt and Jaspers appear to agree with Nietzsche's guide to happiness. There is much about the past that we would do well to forget, but there is also a history that can give us courage to face even the darkest day. Knowing what to remember and what to forget is the key to living a meaningful and happy life.

The Return of the Sing

Tolkien, like many existentialist philosophers before him, believes that meaningful happiness does not come from ignoring the dangers but from facing the pain and still affirming life. As we read Tolkien's famous essay on the author of "Beowulf," we get the distinct impression that Tolkien might be speaking of himself. He discusses the artistic impulse, "looking back into the pit, by a man learned in old tales who was struggling as it were, to get a general view of them all, perceiving their common tragedy of inevitable ruin, and yet feeling this more *poetically* because he was himself removed from the direct pressure of its despair."[10]

Living through two world wars, Tolkien himself had seen his share of despair and ruin. *The Lord of the Rings* was written during the years 1936–1949, among the darkest years in England's history. We would do well, though, not to overplay the connections between the War of the Ring and Tolkien's own experience. Unlike Nietzsche, Jaspers, and Arendt, Tolkien is not writing of Europe's pain, or of the human condition in the twentieth century. *The Lord of the Rings* is a work of fiction, and should be read as such. Yes, the Shire has obvious similarities to the English countryside and the tea-drinking, pipe-smoking hobbits bear more than a slight resemblance to older English curmudgeons, but Tolkien spends almost his entire Forward to the series pleading that we not mix history and fiction.[11] Though he readily admits, "An author cannot remain wholly unaffected by his experience," neither is he compelled to make an allegory out

---

[10] "*Beowulf*: The Monsters and the Critics," in *The Beowulf Poet* (Englewood Cliffs: Prentice Hall, 1968), p. 28.

of political events. For our purposes, it is enough to observe that Tolkien can be placed in the small group of thinkers who passionately believe in the artist's role to stand resolutely, and create in darkness.

Tolkien's elves share this need to affirm life, especially in dark times. As the sorrowful Fellowship enters Lothlórien, Haldir the elf informs them that even the Golden Wood is no longer safe: "The rivers long defended us, but they are a sure guard no more; for the Shadow has crept northward all about us. Some speak of departing, yet for that it already seems too late. The mountains to the west are growing evil; to the east the lands are waste . . ." (FR, pp. 390–91). The elves are not ignorant of the dangers around them. They face the abyss every day and out of this confrontation their joyous music is born. Beauty is not diminished by dark times. As Tolkien elsewhere comments on the elvish quest for joy, "sorrow and wisdom have enriched it" (S, p. 49).

When Nietzsche cautions us to forget, he does not encourage an obsessive, "technological" attitude with the here and now. Understanding our times means knowing what brought us to the place we are in today. Tolkien's Lady Galadriel remembers who she is and where she came from. As we have seen, the name "Lórien" had been taken from a favored region in her homeland. Her happiness and pride, even her strength, comes from her ability to remember the greatness of her family and people. Sam observes how the elves of Lórien seem more rooted than the singers of Rivendell. "Now these folk aren't wanderers or homeless . . . Whether they've made the land, or the land's made them, it's hard to say, if you take my meaning" (FR, pp. 404–05). In Lórien, the greatness of the past lives on, and that is one explanation for the cheerfulness of the elves.

But Galadriel has a darker side to her as well. Her own personal happiness and her lust for life have been dissipating by the time Frodo and company enter her woods. As Tolkien notes in a posthumously published work, Galadriel had tried to make Lórien "a refuge and an island of peace and beauty, a memorial

---

[11] Not everyone takes Tolkien at his word. Jane Chance, for example, argues that Tolkien wrongly dismisses the influence of WWII on his work. See *Tolkien's Art* (New York: St. Martin's Press, 2001), pp. 31–37.

of ancient days," but she was now "filled with regret and misgiving, knowing that the golden dream was hastening to a grey awakening."[12] What has so filled the strong and seemingly ageless Lady of the Wood so with regret?

Perhaps the cause of Galadriel's growing unhappiness is that she remembers too much. She never really forgets the curse hanging over her from ages long gone. Though Frodo and Sam see only settled bliss, Galadriel feels the burdens of being a stranger in a strange land. She can never be fully happy in Lórien, because she can never entirely let go of the past. Tolkien judges this clinging to the past to be an "error," a futile attempt to "embalm time." Holding on to perfection in an imperfect world is an ultimately tragic attempt by the elves to "have their cake without eating it" (L, p. 151). As long as Galadriel harbors an irrational desire to turn back the clock, her songs are mournful and slow. Bidding farewell to the Fellowship, she sings a poignant, regretful song about the changing of the seasons and the passing of time in Lórien (FR, p. 418).

Because Galadriel cannot forget the past, she is unable to adjust to the changes around her. In Galadriel we see both the blessing and the curse of Tolkien's elves. They are given unnaturally long lives by the gods, and because they can live for thousands of years, it is exceedingly difficult for them to forget anything. Elves only die if they are slain in battle or otherwise mortally injured, or if they develop unbearable "world-weariness" as Miriel does in *The Silmarillion* (S, p. 64).

As Nietzsche warns us, world-weariness is bound to set in when one loses the capacity to forget. It is not surprising then, to see Elrond's daughter Arwen forgo her immortality for a shot at happiness with Aragorn, a mortal man.[13] In Tolkien's fiction, the race of men is blessed with the capacity to forget. Their short lives should make this easy. And yet, throughout *The Lord of the Rings*, we see men remembering when they should be forgetting. Aragorn feels the weakness of his ancestor Isildur,

---

[12] "The History of Galadriel and Celeborn," in *Unfinished Tales of Númenor and Middle-earth* (Boston: Houghton Mifflin, 1980), p. 251.
[13] In *The Two Towers* movie, Peter Jackson creates a particularly haunting vision of Arwen (played by Liv Tyler), standing by Aragorn's tomb, knowing that she is condemned to linger on. For further discussion of mortality in *The Lord of the Rings*, see Chapter 10 in this volume.

Denethor refuses to emerge from his past, and King Théoden has to be thoroughly reprimanded by Gandalf before he can begin to live in the present.

Human beings do have this capacity to forget, as both Nietzsche and Tolkien insist. So why is it so hard to let go? The god-like Valar of *The Silmarillion* are equally puzzled, observing, "Fate may not conquer the Children of Men, but yet are they strangely blind, whereas their joy should be great."[14] If only we could do a better job of remembering some of what we forget, and forgetting some of what we remember, we could share more of the elves' joy and less of their world-weariness.

Country's favorite singing philosopher, Kenny Rogers, recognizes "the secret to surviving is knowing what to throw away and knowing what to keep." But once again, we return to the question: how do we gamblers know when it's time to let go? The twentieth-century existentialists tell us to trust in our own light. If life gives you lemons, the saying goes, make lemonade. But if life gives you rotten lemons, make something else. Use the past when it helps, but trust in yourself when all else fails. Whether it's a bad relationship or a stale job, it is our own freeing light that reminds us we are not slaves to our pasts. This light that each of us carries within us is what Arendt hoped to reawaken in the years following the Holocaust, and it's the same light that can help us leave our unhappy security and strike out for uncharted lands.

Through the wise elf Galadriel, Tolkien teaches us to trust that inner light and be strong enough to leave old problems behind. When Frodo freely offers her the One Ring to rule them all, the very Ring that Galadriel has coveted throughout the ages, she refuses, knowing full well that with the refusal comes her own demise. Though the Lady of the Wood has stayed too long, she can still find happiness by remembering who she is, while walking away from the pronouncements of her past. "'I pass the test,' she exclaims. 'I will diminish, and go into the West, and remain Galadriel'" (FR, p. 411).

More than any other character in the tale, with the possible exception of Tom Bombadil, Lady Galadriel is imbued with the

---

[14] Christopher Tolkien, ed., *The Book of Lost Tales: Part I* (New York: Ballantine, 1983), p. 57.

existentialist's affirmation. As Frodo leaves the friendly borders of Lórien, she presents him with the symbolic light, a crystal phial. "It will shine still brighter when night is about you," she promises. "May it be a light to you in dark places" (FR, p. 423). And perhaps that is all that is meant by Tolkien's imaginary elves. The elves find happiness when they trust in themselves. This self-confidence helps them sing throughout the darkest night, and leave the shores when the music ends. May their world be a light to us in our own dark places.[15]

---

[15] Many thanks to the woodsy elves of Beverly Road, and the mountain elves of Wilkes-Barre for helpful comments on previous drafts.

PART III

Good and Evil in Middle-earth

7

Überhobbits: Tolkien, Nietzsche, and the Will to Power

DOUGLAS K. BLOUNT

> What is good?—All that heightens the feeling of power, the will to power, power itself in man.
> What is bad?—All that proceeds from weakness.
> What is happiness?—The feeling that power *increases*—that a resistance is overcome.
>
> ...The power to control power is self-control
>
> FRIEDRICH NIETZSCHE[1]

The One Ring is, of course, a Ring of Power. Indeed, it is the *ruling* Ring of Power. For, as elven-lore tells us, the One Ring gives its wearer dominion over other powerful Rings. When Sauron, the Dark Lord of Mordor, forged the One Ring, he infused it with his own malevolent power. There were other, lesser rings, but Sauron saw to it that *the* Ring "contained the powers of all the others, and controlled them, so that its wearer could see the thoughts of all those that used the lesser rings, could govern all that they did, and in the end could utterly enslave them" (L, p. 152).

By infusing the Ring with much of his own power, however, Sauron was gambling. For if one with sufficient knowledge and power were to gain possession of it, the Dark Lord could be overthrown. But who in Middle-earth would challenge him?

---

[1] Friedrich Nietzsche, *The Anti-Christ,* in *A Nietzsche Reader,* translated by R.J. Hollingdale (New York: Penguin, 1977) [hereinafter NR], p. 231.

Indeed, who *could* challenge him? Of course, if the Ring were actually destroyed, his power which he had infused in it would be lost. He himself "would be diminished to vanishing point, and . . . reduced to a shadow, a mere memory of malicious will" (L, p. 153). Still, the Ring could be destroyed only in the fires of Mount Doom. More significantly, those who used the Ring came under its sway, eventually becoming dominated by it.[2] And those dominated by it could not bring themselves to destroy it. Its destruction thus seemed highly unlikely. So perhaps Sauron's gamble was not an overly risky one. At any rate, his desire to dominate, enslave, and establish his will over Middle-earth ultimately outweighed the risk.

Ilúvatar, also called Eru, is the one true God, creator of Middle-earth.[3] During the long conflict between light and darkness, the Dark Lord Sauron takes for himself the title "King of Kings and Lord of the World," a title rightfully claimed only by Ilúvatar himself (L, p. 155). Moreover, in seeking to subjugate the whole world, Sauron seeks to supplant Ilúvatar, thus making himself God. Tolkien explains that he sees the fundamental conflict in *The Lord of the Rings* as not about "freedom," though that is certainly involved, but about "God and His sole right to divine honour."

> Sauron desired to be a God-King, and was held to be this by his servants; if he had been victorious he would have demanded divine honour from all rational creatures and absolute temporal power over the whole world. (L, pp. 243–44)

Thus, the conflict in Middle-earth is essentially religious. Sauron seeks to establish his will not only over his fellow creatures in Middle-earth but ultimately over Ilúvatar himself.

---

[2] Tom Bombadil proves to be a notable exception to this rule. As Frodo and his companions discover, the ancient Bombadil remains visible when wearing the Ring, and when Frodo puts it on in his presence, he continues to see the hobbit (FR, pp. 150–51).

[3] Tolkien recounts Middle-earth's ancient pre-history, including its creation, in *The Silmarillion*.

Nietzsche: Philosopher of Power

Sauron's quest to dominate, enslave, and establish his will over all others—even Ilúvatar—makes him the arch-enemy of all that is good in Middle-earth. Still, while it represents a deadly threat to others, the Dark Lord's power play represents to him the hope not merely of life but of abundant life.

German philosopher Friedrich Nietzsche (1844–1900) was an outspoken supporter of the quest for power. For life, according to Nietzsche, is all about suppression of the weak by the strong. "'Exploitation,'" he states, "does not pertain to a corrupt or imperfect or primitive society: it pertains to the *essence* of the living thing as a fundamental organic function, it is a consequence of the intrinsic will to power which is precisely the will of life."[4] Well, if exploitation is indeed the essence of life, no denizen of Middle-earth is more alive than Sauron!

Undoubtedly, this view of life as essentially exploitive will cause many of us to squirm, being uncomfortable as we are with its moral implications. Here, Nietzsche suggests, we might be wise to consider great birds of prey who exploit (eat) little lambs for their own purposes. That the lambs dislike the birds, even see them as evil, certainly does not surprise us. But does this make the birds somehow morally defective? Does it make them evil? Are not the birds simply acting in accordance with their nature? And is it not the nature of strength to control, to dominate, to exploit? "To require of strength," Nietzsche writes, "that it should *not* express itself as strength, that it should *not* be a desire to conquer, a desire to subdue, a desire to become master, a thirst for enemies and resistances and triumphs, is just as absurd as to require of weakness that it should express itself as strength."[5]

The lambs interpret their situation in one way; the birds, finding the lambs especially tasty, interpret it in quite another way. So also Bert, Tom, and William—the trolls who almost roast Bilbo and his dwarvish companions (H, pp. 34–41)—interpret their situation in one way; the hobbit and dwarves interpret it altogether differently. In the end, however, the interpretations

---

[4] Friedrich Nietzsche, *Beyond Good and Evil*, in NR, p. 230.
[5] Friedrich Nietzsche, *On the Genealogy of Morals*, in NR, p. 115.

are merely that—interpretations.[6] None has any binding moral significance—though, of course, the birds and (if not for Gandalf) the trolls have the power to force their interpretations on the lambs and Bilbo and his companions. To see things in this way is to move beyond good and evil.

Now Nietzsche also boldly states that God is dead and life is meaningless—though, he assures us, that ain't all bad. When he announces God's death, he does not mean to be taken literally. For, of course, God has not actually died. Rather, Nietzsche means that humans can no longer harmonize God's existence with other things they know about the world, "that belief in the Christian God has become unbelievable."[7] According to Nietzsche, talk about God's dying does not refer to the deity's demise in fact; instead, it refers to the human realization that God never existed in the first place.[8]

Obviously, the view that God does not exist has important implications. Perhaps the most important conclusion to be drawn from it involves the meaninglessness of life. For if God does not exist, it follows that humans have not been divinely created; and if they have not been divinely created, they have not been designed for any specific purposes. Humans thus exist for no purpose. Their lives have no inherent meaning. "*We* invented the concept of 'purpose,'" Nietzsche tells us, "in reality purpose is *lacking*."[9] Far from being at home in a place where we can pursue our divinely appointed destinies and fulfill divinely intended purposes, we find ourselves in an alien world filled with pointless suffering. This, of course, stands in marked contrast to Middle-earth where each legitimate race (as opposed

---

[6] See Friedrich Nietzsche, *Beyond Good and Evil,* in NR, p. 104: "There are no moral phenomena at all, only a moral interpretation of phenomena . . ."

[7] Friedrich Nietzsche, *The Gay Science,* in NR, pp. 208–09.

[8] See Richard Schacht, *Nietzsche* (New York: Routledge, 1983), p. 121: "That Nietzsche goes well beyond a cautious agnosticism, and shares Schopenhauer's 'unconditional and honest atheism,' is something he makes quite plain time and again." Still, despite the passion with which he espouses his view, Nietzsche does very little by way of actually arguing that there is no God. Thus, his atheistic commitment seems more akin to a fundamental axiom than a well-reasoned conclusion. He nonetheless saw more clearly than most other atheists the implications of that axiom for the rest of one's life and thought.

[9] Friedrich Nietzsche, *Twilight of the Idols,* in NR, p. 211.

to orcs, trolls, and other bastardized races) has a place to call home.

Truth, as Nietzsche sees it, is ugly. If we were faced with the world as it actually is and forced to be honest with ourselves, we could not bear it. *"Honesty,"* we are told, "would bring disgust and suicide in its train."[10] Those who search for a reasonable, good, and beautiful truth by which to live their lives do so in vain. Ultimately, we must deceive ourselves in order to cope with this fact. Otherwise, we would be unable to function.

Fortunately, humans have found in the arts a means of coping. Art keeps our eyes veiled so that we do not despair; art makes our absurd, anguished, meaningless lives bearable by distracting us and obscuring truths which, if faced honestly, would debilitate us. Thus, art serves us as a "kind of cult of the untrue." Notice here the emphasis on beauty over truth, taste over reason.[11] Beauty, *not* truth, will be our salvation. (Indeed, beauty will save us *from* truth.) "There is no pre-established harmony," Nietzsche states, "between the furtherance of truth and the well-being of mankind."[12] In such a case, it seems, taste is far more helpful than reason.

To illustrate the meaninglessness of life, Nietzsche puts forward an unusual view of history, a view according to which everything that will ever happen *has already happened* infinitely many times in the past. Ordinarily, we tend to think of history as progressing forward in a straight line. Such a view fits nicely with the belief that history has some culminating moment toward which it moves. Certainly, the history of Middle-earth—from the earliest events recorded in *The Silmarillion* to those chronicled in *The Return of the King*—seems to be progressing toward some grand climax. Of course, the glimpses which Tolkien allows us of what appears to be the hand of Ilúvatar at work behind the scenes orchestrating events only strengthen the sense that things are moving toward such a climax. On the view put forward by Nietzsche, however, history moves not in a straight line, but rather in a circle. History thus repeats itself over

---

[10] Friedrich Nietzsche, *The Gay Science*, in NR, p. 131.

[11] See Friedrich Nietzsche, *The Gay Science*, translated by Walter Kaufmann (New York: Vintage, 1974), p. 186: "What is now decisive against Christianity is our taste, no longer our reasons."

[12] Friedrich Nietzsche, *Human, All Too Human*, in NR, p. 198.

and over again. Scholars debate whether Nietzsche actually believed in this eternal recurrence.[13] As with his announcement of God's death, he might not have intended his affirmation of it to be taken literally.

Even so, the teaching that history moves in a circle with all events eternally repeating themselves serves a couple of important purposes. First, it undermines the view that life has meaning. For, of course, that view becomes much less plausible if history is not progressing toward some cosmic climax. Second, one who sees eternity not as an otherworldly, pie-in-the-sky experience of heavenly bliss (or, alternatively, as a weeping-wailing-and-gnashing-of-teeth experience of hellish torment) but rather as the infinitely continuous recurrence of the events of this life cannot help but view the here-and-now differently. As Nietzsche writes:

> If this thought [of eternal recurrence] gained power over you it would, as you are now, transform and perhaps crush you; the question in all and everything: 'do you want this again and again, times without number?' would lie as the heaviest burden upon all your actions. Or how well disposed towards yourself and towards life would you have to become to have *no greater desire* than for this ultimate eternal sanction and seal?[14]

So, by his lights, taking eternal recurrence seriously (if not literally) transforms one's life by presenting one with a new standard by which to guide oneself.

Übermensch: **Man of Power**

To summarize the discussion of Nietzsche's thought to this point: God is dead. Or, to put the point differently, we find ourselves unable to believe in God. Moreover, as God has died, so

---

[13] See Schacht, *Nietzsche,* p. 259: "What matters here is not the *truth* of the idea [of eternal recurrence]; it is rather the emergence of human beings capable not only of enduring it (were it to be true), but moreover of embracing it without qualm, and indeed of 'craving nothing more fervently.'"

[14] Friedrich Nietzsche, *The Gay Science,* in NR, p. 250. See Friedrich Nietzsche, *Ecce Homo,* "Why I Am So Clever," in NR, p. 260: "My formula for greatness in a human being is *amor fati* [love of fate]: that one wants nothing other than it is, not in the future, not in the past, not in all eternity."

too have our innocence and naiveté. No divine revelation can distinguish good from evil for us; indeed, "good" and "evil" are interpretations that we assign to things, not actual features of the things themselves. The world, it turns out, is an ugly place filled with much suffering. If that suffering served some greater purpose, we might then be able to bear it. But, alas, it does not! For life is meaningless; we may create beauty to help us cope with this fact, but we cannot change it. History goes monotonously on and on, with the same series of events repeating itself over and over again. Or, at least, so says Nietzsche.

So God is dead, and things go downhill from there. Surprisingly, however, Nietzsche sees the death of God as cause for celebration rather than mourning. "We philosophers and 'free spirits'," he writes, "in fact feel at the news that the 'old God is dead' as if illumined by a new dawn; our heart overflows with gratitude . . ."[15] But, given that God's death makes life meaningless and our suffering (as well as our joy) pointless, why does Nietzsche rejoice in it? What opportunity does he see that others of us do not? Perhaps the following passage gives us a hint.

> God is dead. God remains dead. And we have killed him. How shall we, the murderers of all murderers, console ourselves? That which was holiest and mightiest of all that the world has yet possessed has bled to death under our knives—who will wipe this blood off us? With what water could we purify ourselves? What festivals of atonement, what sacred games shall we need to invent? Is not the greatness of this deed too great for us? *Must we not ourselves become gods simply to seem worthy of it?*[16]

God's demise, Nietzsche tells us, is not debilitating; it is liberating. We have the opportunity to step into the void left by God's death. With God dead and the established moral order undermined, we resemble painters with clean, white canvases. Anything is possible, *if we have the will to make it so!*

Thus, like history on Nietzsche's account, we find ourselves back where we began: *will* and *power*, *will to power*. He calls us to face the meaninglessness of life head-on without blinking. He

---

[15] Friedrich Nietzsche, *The Gay Science,* in NR, p. 209.
[16] *Ibid.*, p. 203 (emphasis added).

calls us not merely to face it, but to embrace it. He gives us clean, white canvasses. But what shall we paint? Whatever we will; whatever pleases us, he says. And what will guide us? Not morality, for it has been overthrown; not reason, for it too has been overthrown. What then? *Taste*; our taste will guide us. "As an aesthetic [or, perhaps, artistic?] phenomenon, existence is still *endurable* to us," Nietzsche writes, "and through art we are given eye and hand, and above all a good conscience, to *enable* us to make of ourselves such a phenomenon."[17] To embrace the meaninglessness of life and make for oneself a life magnificent according to one's own taste—that is the task Nietzsche lays out for us. And he who achieves it is the new man, the overman (sometimes translated as Superman), the *Übermensch* whose coming Nietzsche heralds.

Frodo and Sam, *Über*hobbits

Sauron, whose own will to power initiates the great conflict chronicled in *The Lord of the Rings*, seeks to make for himself a life magnificent according to his own taste. And, while Nietzsche himself argues against both uncultivated taste and technological tedium, his philosophy does not clearly repudiate brute force. Thus, Sauron seems like a candidate for the title *Übermensch* (or overman). But, in *The Lord of the Rings*, the desire to control, to dominate, to establish one's will over others—in short, the unabashed will to power—characterizes not a brave, new kind of person but rather plain, old-fashioned evil. And Tolkien's account of the struggle against Sauron leaves us repulsed by that evil.

The violence of Mordor and its Dark Lord obviously compares quite unfavorably with the beauty of Ilúvatar's children striving together against them. Thus, while Tolkien may not have had this in mind as he wrote *The Lord of the Rings*, he nonetheless gives us a compelling alternative to Nietzsche's vision of reality.[18] Coming by way of artistry rather than argument, this vision challenges the other one on its own terms.

---

[17] *Ibid.*, p. 131.

[18] But, then again, maybe he *did* have it in mind. The Ring, according to Tolkien, symbolizes "*the will to mere power*, seeking to make itself objective by physical force and mechanism, and so also inevitably by lies" (L, p. 160; emphasis added). Given the pivotal role the Ring plays in *The Lord of the*

Nietzsche, so to speak, presents to us a grand, panoramic portrait of reality; Tolkien presents a rival portrait. Which portrait is better? Which vision of reality is more compelling? If we make the decision on the grounds Nietzsche suggests, we will make it on the basis of which vision is more beautiful. What is decisive, after all, is our taste.

Of central importance to Tolkien's vision of reality is community. No hobbit is an island. Dwarves accompany Bilbo on his adventure in *The Hobbit*; in *The Fellowship of the Ring,* Frodo sets out on his trip to Rivendell with Merry, Pippin, and Sam, who refuse to let him go alone. Not surprisingly, given its title, the first book centers around the Fellowship, each of whose members—even the faithless Boromir—contributes to the Ring-bearer's Quest. Sam accompanies Frodo all the way to Mordor and Mount Doom. And it is good that he does; Frodo's Quest surely would have ended in disaster if not for the faithful Sam.

While each member of the Fellowship contributes to the fulfillment of the Ring-bearer's task, that task would have remained undone if not for the help of many others. So, for instance, Fatty Bolger stays at the house at Crickhollow to maintain the appearance that Frodo is still there. Tom Bombadil rescues Merry and Pippin from Old Man Willow; he later rescues Frodo, Merry, Pippin, and Sam from the Barrow-wight. Nob, Barliman Butterbur's employee at *The Prancing Pony* in Bree, rescues Merry from the Nazgûl. Bill, the pony whom Butterbur purchases for the hobbits from Bill Ferny, bears the hobbits' burdens—including Frodo himself after his wounding on Weathertop—from Bree to Rivendell to Moria. Glorfindel's horse carries Frodo to the Ford with the Nazgûl close behind. Gwaihir the Windlord, the Great Eagle, rescues Gandalf from Orthanc; Shadowfax, a horse from the Riddermark, provides the wizard a swift ride when speed is greatly needed.

Bilbo himself gives Frodo the sword Sting and a *mithril* shirt, each of which plays an important role in the Ring-bearer's Quest. Elrond, the Elf-king of Rivendell, heals the wound Frodo received near Weathertop and establishes the Fellowship. The Galadrim protect the Fellowship from marauding orcs, provid-

---

Rings, then, Tolkien seems to intend it in some sense as a response to Nietzsche's "will to power."

ing them sanctuary in Lothlórien. As the Fellowship leaves
Lothlórien, Galadriel presents to its members gifts that later turn
out to be greatly needed. All of these examples come from *The
Fellowship*; discussion of *The Two Towers* and *The Return of the
King* would add significantly to their number, but they suffice to
make the point: The success of Frodo's mission depends ultimately on a very wide community.

Since each member of the Fellowship has a hand in the outcome of the events that shape Middle-earth, a full discussion of
the ways in which its various members contribute to the success
of Frodo's mission would take much more space than I have
here. Still, I want to single out three of their contributions for
comment—Gandalf's sacrifice of himself on the bridge of
Khazad-dûm, Frodo's merciful treatment of the miserable
Gollum, and Sam's refusal to use the Ring himself.

So that the rest of the Fellowship may escape Moria, Gandalf
stands alone on the Bridge of Khazad-dûm to face the Balrog.
Of course, Gandalf is not human. "There are naturally no precise modern terms to say what he was," Tolkien writes. "I
[would] venture to say that he was an *incarnate* 'angel'" (L, p.
202). Of the members of the Fellowship, then, Gandalf is the
most powerful. Yet he allows himself to be killed for the sake
of the others. He subordinates his own good to the good of the
community. Such humility and sacrifice demonstrate not a desire
to control or dominate others, but rather a willingness to serve
others even at great personal loss.

Frodo, following the lead of Bilbo years earlier, has pity for
Gollum and treats him mercifully on several occasions. Twice,
for instance, he asks Faramir to spare Gollum's life. "If you
come on him," Frodo says to Faramir at their first meeting,
"spare him. Bring him or send him to us. He is only a wretched
gangrel creature, but I have him under my care for a while"
(TT, p. 297). Later, at the Forbidden Pool, Frodo pleads for
Gollum's life:

> "The creature is wretched and hungry," said Frodo, "and unaware
> of his danger. And Gandalf, your Mithrandir, he would have bid-
> den you not to slay him for that reason, and for others. He forbade
> the Elves to do so. I do not know clearly why, and of what I guess
> I cannot speak openly out here. But this creature is in some way
> bound up with my errand." (TT, pp. 331–32)

When Faramir insists that Gollum must be "slain or taken," Frodo offers to go quietly to Gollum so that he may be captured, and, he volunteers, Faramir's men may "keep your bows bent, and shoot me at least, if I fail." Here we see not only pity but also a willingness to sacrifice oneself. Whereas Gandalf sacrifices himself for the sake of the Fellowship, Frodo offers himself for the sake of the pitiful, wretched Gollum.

Frodo's pity for Gollum turns out to be deeply important. For, when the Ring finally has him in its grip and he cannot bear to throw it into Mount Doom's fires, Gollum unexpectedly aids the Ring-bearer's Quest. Treacherously attempting to get the Ring from the hobbit, Gollum bites it—and one of Frodo's fingers—off his hand. In his excitement at having reclaimed the Ring, Gollum then stumbles, falling to his death in the fire of Mount Doom. Thus, the Ring is destroyed. In the end, then, the Quest comes to completion despite Frodo's failure to destroy the Ring himself. And Frodo's pity becomes his—and Middle-earth's—salvation.

Sam, according to Tolkien, is the chief hero of *The Lord of the Rings* (L, p. 161). We get perhaps our most interesting glimpse of this apparently unheroic hobbit when the Ring tempts him with a vision of "Samwise the Strong, Hero of the Age, striding with a flaming sword across the darkened land." Two things enable Sam to resist this temptation: his love of Frodo and his unpretentious "hobbit-sense." Sam understands, "in the core of his heart," that he is not big enough to take on any such grandiose role.

> The one small garden of a free gardener was all his need and due, not a garden swollen to a realm; his own hands to use, not the hands of others to command. (RK, p. 186)

His refusal to use the Ring for his own glory stems from the hobbit's deep-seated humility together with his love for Frodo. As with Gandalf and Frodo, who both subordinate themselves for the sake of others, so also Sam subordinates himself for the sake of the Ring-bearer's Quest. He declines to pursue his own glory at his master's expense.

The portrait that Tolkien presents to us, then, is one of community, humility, love, and sacrifice. To be sure, the heroes of Middle-earth have their flaws. Humans long for the immortality of the elves; for their part, the elves long for the mortality of men. Dwarves and elves have deep-seated prejudices against one another that cannot be easily overcome. Frodo himself ultimately gives in to the Ring's temptation. Even so, Middle-earth's heroes overcome their weaknesses—not with power plays aimed at dominating others but rather with humility and self-sacrifice. Strength, according to Tolkien, manifests itself most clearly not in the exercise of power but rather in the willingness to give it up. "The greatest examples of the action of the spirit and of reason," he tells us, "are in *abnegation*" (L, p. 246). Abnegation, the subordination of one's own will for the sake of others—*that,* according to the portrait Tolkien presents, is what characterizes a life lived well; and, given its obvious beauty, such a portrait needs no argument to defend it.

8

Tolkien and the Nature of Evil

SCOTT A. DAVISON

The Lord of the Rings is a story about the struggle between good and evil. We understand it immediately because it is our story, too. In Tolkien's world we recognize the same good and evil qualities that we notice in ourselves and in other people. In fact, the pivotal scene in *The Lord of the Rings* involves Frodo's finally giving in to the temptation to claim the One Ring for himself (RK, p. 239). In a sense, evil prevails for a moment, and only good luck saves Frodo from himself.

 Aristotle said that whereas comedies involve people who are worse than we are, and epics involve people who are better than we are, tragedies are about people who are just like we are[1]. In this sense, *The Lord of the Rings* is a tragedy that turns out well in the end. We understand how Frodo feels when he finally gives in to the temptation to wield the One Ring, since we give in over and over again when faced with temptations in our own lives. But we can still hope that everything will turn out well for us too.

In *The Lord of the Rings*, Tolkien provides us with a vivid picture of the nature of evil. By considering this picture carefully, we can come to understand more fully the evil in ourselves and in our world, and perhaps even begin to fight against it.

---

[1] Aristotle, *Poetics*, Chapter 2.

Is Evil an Independent Force?

Philosophers use the label "Manicheanism" to describe the view that there are two equal and opposite forces in the world, Good and Evil. They use this label because the ancient Persian philosopher Mani (216–276 C.E.) held this view of the world. According to the Manichean view, Good and Evil are locked in a struggle for world domination, and since they are equally balanced in power, it is not clear which, if either, will win in the end. In popular culture, this Manichean view is perhaps reflected most clearly in the *Star Wars* movies, in which there are both good and bad sides to the Force, and neither side is clearly stronger than the other.

The Manicheans thought they could explain many aspects of human experience in terms of the struggle between Good and Evil. They believed that it was possible for things to be perfectly good, perfectly evil, or somewhere in between. Since we find both good and evil things in our world, and the world seems to be better at some times than at others, they concluded that the things we observe are just the visible results of the conflict between Good and Evil that takes place on a cosmic scale.

Does *The Lord of the Rings* contain a Manichean view of evil? Some authors, including leading Tolkien scholar Tom Shippey,[2] have suggested that it does, and some passages appear to confirm this suspicion. Sometimes those who bear the Ring appear to be struggling only with themselves when they are tempted to put it on, but at other times, they seem to be influenced by an external force, something like a principle of Evil. For example, when Gandalf asks Frodo for the Ring in order to check its identity, we are told that "either it or Frodo himself was in some way reluctant for Gandalf to touch it" (FR, p. 54). Is the Ring reluctant or is Frodo reluctant? Does the impulse come from within Frodo, or from an independent Evil principle? Could a Manichean point to the Ring as an example of a completely and utterly evil thing?

We must remember that the One Ring has the powers it possesses only because it was created by Sauron to aid in his quest for world domination. This means that the Ring is not an exam-

---

[2] Tom Shippey, *J.R.R. Tolkien: Author of the Century* (Boston: Houghton Mifflin, 2000), pp. 128–142.

ple of the Manichean idea of an independent evil force in the world, since it is animated by Sauron's will and power. To paraphrase a saying made famous by the National Rifle Association: the Ring doesn't corrupt people; Sauron's power working through the Ring corrupts people.

In addition, the Ring is not an example of a completely evil thing. It is true that Elrond calls it "altogether evil" (FR, p. 300), but his reason for saying this is that nobody can use the Ring for good. The elements that compose the Ring are not themselves evil. There is no "evil metal," not even in Tolkien's world. If those very same particles of precious metal had been forged into a ring by someone else, then it would not have been the One Ring. The power of the Ring is the power of Sauron, which was infused into the Ring through some mysterious process that is unknown to us. As Gandalf says, if the Ruling Ring is destroyed, then Sauron "will lose the best part of the strength that was native to him in his beginning, and all that was made or begun with that power will crumble, and he will be maimed for ever" (RK, p. 160).

But what about Sauron himself? Isn't he an example of a completely evil being?

As Tolkien remarks in a letter, Sauron represents the most corrupt will possible (L, p. 243). But even a totally corrupt person is still a person, an existing creature with powers and capacities that are not evil in themselves. As Elrond says, "nothing is evil in the beginning. Even Sauron was not so" (FR, p. 300). In fact, Sauron is not himself the source of all evil, as Gandalf tells us: "Other evils there are that may come; for Sauron is himself but a servant or emissary" (RK, p. 160).

So *The Lord of the Rings* is not based upon a Manichean view of the nature of evil. This is important because it seems impossible for something to be completely and utterly evil. Everything that exists has some good quality or other. Even things that seem to be evil in themselves are not completely evil. For example, nuclear weapons and land mines are useful only for destroying people and things, but even they have some good qualities. (They are composed of parts that are not in themselves bad things, for instance.)

But if the Manicheans are wrong about the nature of evil, then what is evil? If evil is not an independent force, what is it?

Evil Depends on Goodness

Another way to look at evil is to see it as essentially parasitical on goodness. On this view, goodness is necessary for evil, but evil is not necessary for goodness. Evil is like the darkness of a shadow: light is necessary for shadows to exist, but shadows are not necessary for light to exist. Goodness is primary and independent, whereas evil is secondary and dependent on goodness.

This view of evil is often called "Augustinian," since it was held by St. Augustine (354–430 C.E.), one of the most famous and influential Christian thinkers of all time. St. Augustine writes:

> Wherever you see measure, number, and order, you cannot hesitate to attribute all these to God, their Maker. When you remove measure, number, and order, nothing at all remains . . . Thus, if all good is completely removed, no vestige of reality persists; indeed, nothing remains. Every good is from God.[3]

Tolkien accepts this Augustinian view of evil. In a letter, he writes, "In my story I do not deal with Absolute Evil. I do not think there is such a thing, since that is Zero" (L, p. 243).

To see the Augustinian view of evil at work in *The Lord of the Rings*, remember that it includes the idea that evil is a lack of goodness, as darkness is a lack of light. And since goodness is primary and independent, it follows that the more evil something is, the more nearly it approaches nothingness. There are many illustrations of this in *The Lord of the Rings*.

The Ringwraiths, for example, ride real horses and wear real robes "to give shape to their nothingness when they have dealings with the living" (FR, p. 249). When the Lord of the Nazgûl attempts to enter the Gate of Minas Tirith, Gandalf says to him, "Go back to the abyss prepared for you! Go back! Fall into the nothingness that awaits you and your Master" (RK, p. 100). When Frodo looks into Galadriel's mirror and sees the Eye of Sauron, he sees that "the black slit of its pupil opened on a pit, a window into nothing" (FR, p. 409). And Gandalf remarks that

---

[3] St. Augustine, *On the Free Choice of the Will*, translated by Anna S. Benjamin and L.H. Hackstaff (Indianapolis: Bobbs-Merrill, 1964), p. 83.

Saruman, after the fall of Isengard, has "withered altogether" as a result of his evil life, so that nothing more can be made of him (RK, p. 285).

Tolkien endorses the Augustinian view of evil in the dreary desolation of Mordor when Sam sees a white star twinkling overhead. Its beauty strikes Sam and he starts to regain hope: "For like a shaft, clear and cold, the thought pierced him that in the end the Shadow was only a small and passing thing: there was light and high beauty for ever beyond its reach" (RK, p. 211).

So St. Augustine and Tolkien agree that nothing is completely and utterly evil, because such a thing could not even exist, since existence itself is good. And they both believe that whereas goodness is primary and independent, evil is secondary and dependent on goodness. But if that is true, then where does evil come from? If the world was completely good at one point, then how could evil get started in the first place?

Where Does Evil Come From?

We have seen that nothing is completely and utterly evil. Along the way, we have noted that nothing is evil in itself, not even the One Ring of Power. So where does evil come from? St. Augustine and Tolkien both believe that ultimately all evil comes from the mind of some created person or other.

St. Augustine coined the phrase "inordinate desire" to describe the root of evil, which he identifies as the desire for something that violates the rightful order of things. (So "inordinate" means something like "out of order" or "disordered.") Commenting on St. Paul's statement that "the love of money is the root of all evil" (1 Timothy 6:10), St. Augustine says that "the love of money" must be understood as "any sort of love in which one has immoderate desire and wants more than is enough. This avarice is desire, and desire is a wicked will. Therefore, a wicked will is the cause of all evil."[4]

St. Augustine's idea, then, is that it is possible for evil to arise in a situation that involves only good things. The fall of Satan and the fall of Adam and Eve have a similar pattern, he thinks:

---

[4] *Ibid.*, p. 126.

in both cases, there were good creatures who wanted to have more than their fair share of the good things in the world. This desire is the source of all evil, and when we freely give into it, evil is born. St. Augustine writes:

> Neither the goods desired by sinners, nor the free will itself . . . are evil in any way . . . evil is a turning away from immutable goods and a turning toward changeable goods. This turning away and turning toward result in the just punishment of unhappiness, because they are committed, not under compulsion, but voluntarily.[5]

In other words, evil comes from an exercise of free will.[6] As he says in another place, "Whence comes this turning away, unless man, to whom God is the only Good, replaces God with himself to be his own good, as God is the Good to Himself?"[7]

Tolkien echoes this view in one of his letters. He says that the War of the Ring "is not basically about 'freedom', though that is naturally involved. It is about God, and His sole right to divine honour" (L, p. 243). This view of the origin and source of evil is expressed in many places in *The Lord of the Rings*.

For instance, the pride and greatness of mortal men proves to be their weakness, since Sauron uses it to ensnare them by means of the Nine Rings. Sauron learned the art of ring-making by ensnaring the elven-smiths of Eregion through their "eager-

---

[5] *Ibid.*, p. 83.

[6] It's unclear how well this approach explains so-called "natural evil," evil that results from the forces of nature (floods, tornadoes, earthquakes, and so forth) rather than resulting from the free choices of any created persons. St. Augustine insists that all natural evil is ultimately caused by the free choices of created persons, either human or demonic. On his view, there were no floods, earthquakes, or other natural evils until the Fall of Adam and Eve, and now God permits these evils to occur as just punishments for sin. But today most Christian and Jewish theologians reject this approach and try to explain natural evil as an inevitable by-product of God's desire to create a challenging, predictable world in which free creatures can develop. For good discussions of these issues, see John H. Hick, *Philosophy of Religion*, fourth edition (Englewood Cliffs: Prentice Hall, 1990), pp. 39–48; Daniel Howard-Snyder, "God, Evil, and Suffering," in Michael J. Murray, ed., *Reason for the Hope Within* (Grand Rapids: Eerdmans, 1999), pp. 76–115; and Richard Swinburne, *Is There A God?* (New York: Oxford University Press, 1996), pp. 107–113.

[7] *Ibid.*, p. 145.

ness for knowledge" (FR, p. 272), which apparently blinded them. By contrast, Elrond tells Glóin that the Three Rings of the elves were not made by Sauron, nor did he ever touch them; those who made them desired only "understanding, making, and healing, to preserve all things unstained" (FR, p. 301). The difference between the three Rings of the elves and the One Ring of Power is clear: the Rings of the elves are not aimed at satisfying desires that are out of order, whereas the One Ring points its wearer toward the domination of everyone else. As Galadriel tells Frodo, to use the One Ring, he would need to train his will "to the domination of others" (FR, p. 411).

Tom Bombadil is not tempted at all by the Ring. He is perfectly content with his place in the world, and has no desire at all to get more than his fair share. In fact, he is so immune to the power of the Ring that he can see Frodo when he wears it: "Old Tom Bombadil's not as blind as that yet. Take off your golden ring! Your hand's more fair without it" (FR, p. 151).

Sam is also able to resist the temptation of the Ring because he knows that his humble garden is "all his need and due, not a garden swollen to a realm; his own hands to use, not the hands of others to command" (RK, p. 186). Unlike corporate executives who try to steal from their stockholders and avoid responsibility for the consequences, Sam is content to tend his garden. He resists the desire to occupy a place that is not his own, and thus allows the lure of the One Ring to pass him by. How many of us could resist this same temptation?

Boromir was unable to resist this lure. When Boromir proposes using the Ring in battle against Sauron, Elrond replies that it cannot be used for such a purpose. The Ring was made by Sauron, belongs to him, and is "altogether evil."

> Its strength, Boromir, is too great for anyone to wield at will, save only those who have already a great power of their own. But for them it holds an even deadlier peril. The very desire of it corrupts the heart . . . as long as it is in the world it will be a danger even to the Wise. (FR, p. 300)

This was good advice, but when Boromir was alone with Frodo and the Ring, he was unable to heed it.

Saruman is also unable to resist the lure of the Ring. He tries to persuade Gandalf to join him and Sauron, arguing that Sauron and Gandalf would be able to bide their time, keep their agenda hidden, "deploring maybe evils done by the way, but approving the high and ultimate purpose."

> Knowledge, Rule, Order; all the things that we have so far striven in vain to accomplish, hindered rather than helped by our weak or idle friends. There need not be, there would not be, any real change in our designs, only in our means. (FR, p. 291)

Saruman is willing to justify the means in terms of the ends, hoping to impose his will on the world and everyone in it. Right after saying this, he asks Gandalf if he knows where the Ruling Ring is, and "a lust which he could not conceal shone suddenly in his eyes" (FR, p. 291). After Saruman's fall, Gandalf explains that he would not be turned around because he "will not serve, only command" (TT, p. 209), calling to mind Milton's famous interpretation of the reasoning of Satan: "Better to reign in Hell, than serve in Heav'n."[8]

By contrast, Gandalf has no such designs on world domination. He has no "wish for mastery" (TT, p. 210). To Denethor the Steward of Gondor, Gandalf says that he is given no realm to rule, but rather that he is a steward over "all worthy things that are in peril as the world now stands" (RK, p. 16). There is a big difference between being a steward over something and an owner of it, of course. Gandalf recognizes this difference, and realizes that he is only a steward, not an owner. He refuses to "play God" by marshalling everything at his disposal in order to impose his preferences on the world. Whereas Denethor refers to himself as "Lord of Gondor," Gandalf calls him "Steward of Gondor" instead (RK, p. 129). In the end, Denethor still rules his own end by killing himself, and thus reveals his false conception of the scope of his own authority.

In contrast to these evil desires for what is out of order, we find that the hobbits have something like a natural sense of their proper place. We have already seen this "plain hobbit-sense" (RK, p. 186) in Sam's ability to resist the temptation of the One Ring. Recall also what Thorin Oakenshield says in *The Hobbit* as

---

[8] John Milton, *Paradise Lost*, Book 1, line 263.

he lies on his deathbed and apologizes for speaking so harshly to Bilbo during the attempt to resolve the standoff between the dwarves and men over the treasure hoarded by Smaug the Dragon: "There is more in you of good than you know, child of the kindly West. Some courage and some wisdom, blended in measure. If more of us valued food and cheer and song over hoarded gold, it would be a merrier world" (H, p. 290).

Of course, the hobbits are not immune to temptation. In fact, at the most crucial moment, Frodo gives in to temptation and claims the Ring for himself. As it happens, only the greed of Gollum saves Frodo from becoming another Gollum himself. Frodo was lucky. The destruction of Sauron thus resulted from the apparently coincidental collision of three evil impulses: Frodo's desire to keep the Ring, Gollum's desire to take it from Frodo, and Sauron's single-minded focus on world domination, made possible by his confidence that nobody would ever try to destroy the Ring.

The clearest illustration of the nature of evil comes from Sauron himself. Gandalf says that Sauron calculates everything with reference to his desire for power (FR, p. 302). This focus on domination is so powerful that it even colors his fears about the One Ring, as Gandalf makes clear: "That we should wish to cast him down and have *no* one in his place is not a thought that occurs to his mind" (TT, p. 104). Comparing Sauron to Satan, Tolkien holds that no rational being is totally evil.

> In my story Sauron represents as near an approach to the wholly evil will as is possible . . . Sauron desired to be a God-King, and was held to be this by his servants. (L, p. 243)

Thus, Sauron's evil lies in his desire to usurp God, to assume a place in the world that is not rightly his. As St. Augustine would say, this kind of desire is the root of all the evil in the world.

Overcoming Evil

We have already seen that in order to make something evil, you must start out with something that is good. This is the pattern we see over and over again in Middle-earth. Treebeard the ent notes that trolls are "counterfeits" of ents, just as orcs were made "in mockery" of elves (TT, p. 91). Frodo makes a similar point about orcs (RK, p. 201), and Tolkien describes Isengard as "only a little copy, a child's model or a slave's flattery" of the Dark Tower (TT, p. 175). In all of these cases, evil things turn out to be good things that have been twisted for evil ends.

It is not surprising to find that evil is also connected to the destruction of good things in *The Lord of the Rings*. For example, we are told that orcs invented many clever but horrible devices, especially machines for war (H, p. 62). Treebeard says similar things about Saruman, who "does not care for growing things, except as far as they serve him for the moment," and who created orcs capable of enduring sunlight (TT, p. 76). We are also told that orcs find special delight in going out of their way to destroy living things (TT, p. 11).

The destructive aspect of evil also extends into the realm of relationships. For instance, when they are looking for Denethor, the Steward of Gondor, Gandalf and Pippin find the porter slain along the road to the Closed Door. Gandalf calls this "Work of the Enemy" (RK, p. 127). And Haldir, the elf from Lothlórien, says that the power of the Dark Lord is most clearly seen in "the estrangement that divides all those who still oppose him" (FR, p. 390).

In our world, we see these same evil themes at work. For example, on September 11th, 2001, terrorists used basically good things (box cutters and airplanes) to cause mass destruction, devastation, and death. In doing so, they clearly manifested the essential evil impulse, the desire to impose one's own preferences on the world. By deciding that many innocent people should die, they assumed a position and a prerogative that was not rightly theirs. Their choices reflect the kind of evil will that we would expect to find among Sauron and his minions.

Fortunately, if Tolkien is right about the nature of evil, then there is some good news. This follows from the fact that the Manicheans were wrong about the nature of evil: it is not an independent force in the world, equal to goodness and opposite to it. Instead, as St. Augustine realized, goodness is fundamental and independent, whereas evil is secondary and dependent. Whereas evil cannot exist without goodness, the converse is not true. This means that there always exists some possibility of eliminating evil from the world. Since evil must be produced out of pre-existing goodness, it follows that goodness is, so to speak, the "default mode" for the world. As long as peo-

[handwritten annotation:] Atomic weapons come from the Sun, the Sun made all life, Atomic weapons may end all life

ple have choices, it is possible that they will choose well. So there is always some reason to hope that evil will be overcome.

In conclusion, we have learned that evil is a lack of goodness, that it stems from a desire to have more than one's fair share, and that it is linked to fear and destruction. Knowing this, we are in a position to see more clearly the evil in ourselves and in other people. Do we wish to dominate other people and impose our wills upon the world? What is our proper place? What things do we find satisfying and frustrating? Do we enjoy the simple goods of the world, with a bit of "plain hobbit-sense," or are we bent on achieving some fantastic ideal under the name of "the good life"? Reflecting on these questions, together with Tolkien's illuminating depiction of evil, can bring us closer to understanding and maybe even overcoming the evil in ourselves and in the world around us.[9]

---

[9] I wish to thank those persons whose editorial comments on earlier versions of this chapter resulted in many substantial improvements, especially Greg Bassham and Eric Bronson.

9

Virtue and Vice in
The Lord of the Rings

AEON J. SKOBLE

In an epic tale of good and evil such as *The Lord of the Rings*, it is a virtual necessity that the characters representing good and evil can be identified as such by the reader. One way for them to be identified is through their actions. Another is through the character traits from which those actions proceed. There may be different literary reasons for preferring one approach to the other, but when the characters are given personalities that exhibit virtues or vices, the moral lesson is clearer. The lesson is clearer because right actions may be performed for wrong reasons, or, alternatively, wrongful acts may be performed for the right reasons. So just looking at what people *do* may be less morally instructive than considering who they *are*.

The school of ethical theory that treats character as primary, and as the proper focus of inquiry over actions, is known as "virtue ethics." Its chief intellectual source is the ancient Greek philosopher Aristotle,[1] whose theory stands in stark contrast to those of later figures such as Kant or Mill, who stress other factors such as duty or consequence. By way of analyzing the virtues and vices of several characters in *The Lord of the Rings*, I intend to argue for virtue ethics over its competitors and explore some possible problems with the theory. In particular,

---

[1] Chiefly in *Nicomachean Ethics*, translated by Terence Irwin (Indianapolis: Hackett, 1985).

the process of moral corruption, which of course figures prominently in the novel, will be especially instructive in our account of the virtues and vices and what produces them.

Aristotle's account of virtues and vices is developmental. The primary focus of his account is on what we need to do in order to *become* virtuous. But the concept of "becoming virtuous" seems to imply the corresponding idea of "becoming vicious." That is, just as certain habits of thought and action tend to move our characters in one direction, towards states Aristotle calls virtues, other habits of thought and action may move our characters in the other direction (two other directions, to be precise), towards states he calls vices. Let us begin, then, with an examination of precisely how he thinks this works. I shall illustrate with examples from *The Lord of the Rings*.

Developing Good Character

For Aristotle, moral virtues are states of character one develops which, as they become more integral to one's being, help one to lead a happier, more fulfilled life. This means that we should not make lists of good or bad actions, or try to formulate general principles that allow of no exceptions. The point is that actions proceed from one's character, so it's most useful to develop good character. For example, a simple rule like "don't kill anyone" seems to admit of too many exceptions to be a genuine moral rule. If nothing else, killing in self-defense seems morally permissible. Other possible exceptions might include killing those who would kill or enslave millions. (It would seem morally permissible, if it were possible, to kill Sauron, just as many have argued that it would have been a moral good if the assassination plot against Hitler had succeeded.) Of course, it may be the case that we should generally refrain from killing, or that we should take killing as something that requires strong justification. But how would one tell the difference between these? The point of the virtue-ethics approach is that the person who has cultivated good character is able to figure out when killing would be justifiable and when it would not. What Aristotle calls "practical reason" is a key component of moral wisdom.

Practical reason is not the same thing as experience, but one's ability to learn from experience is part of how practical reason contributes to the development of virtues. In Aristotle's theory, reason operates at two levels. First, reason tells me how to achieve a value or accomplish a goal efficiently, given any goal I might have. But reason can also tell me whether I should have the goals I have in the first place. For example, if I desire to destroy a certain Ring that can't be destroyed by other means, reason can tell me that I ought to toss it into Mount Doom. But reason can also judge whether the desire to destroy the Ring is one that helps me live a better life overall, which seems to be the case for Tolkien's protagonists. Reason can judge the worthiness of a goal only with reference to a predominant goal. In other words, this or that value is good for me to have only if its pursuit is conducive to my overall primary value. On the Aristotelian view, there is such an overall predominant value: life, or more specifically, a flourishing or good life. One *naturally* desires to live a good life, and other desires must be shown to aid, not hinder, that larger goal.

That is why, for instance, there is disagreement at the Council of Elrond. It's a factual matter that the Ring can only be destroyed in the fires of Mount Doom. Simple calculative reasoning thus yields the conclusion, "If we want to destroy it, we must toss it into Mount Doom." The debate is over whether they *ought* to want to destroy it, as opposed to using its power for good. It's true that the Ring would give great power to its user, but as Gandalf and Elrond point out, this power is corrupting, so in a struggle of good versus evil, it's actually counter-productive to use the Ring.

The other use of reason is in deducing the proper course of action in a given situation. Aristotle recommends striving for the mean between extremes. Courage, for example, is said to be not only different from cowardice, but also from a rash *faux*-bravery. In other words, while cowardice is a vice, so is total fearlessness. The person who claims to be unafraid of *anything* is surely mistaken about the way the world works. (Hence Strider's claim, in Peter Jackson's film version, that the hobbits are "not frightened *enough*.") One has ample reason to fear, say, angry grizzly bears, or the Nazgûl. Also, one must temper one's bravery with a prudent consideration of the circumstances—taking a foolish risk may look brave, but if it makes the situation worse, it's hardly virtuous. Aristotle says that one must learn how to be virtuous by performing virtuous acts. Hence virtuous character is something that is developed rather than simply given or chosen.

A crucial factor in this model of self-development is the discovery and emulation of proper role models. The *phronemos*, or person of practical wisdom, is someone to be observed and learned from. Such a person is not the same as a teacher, for one cannot teach virtues the way one teaches the alphabet. To learn swordplay, one must study the fundamentals, observe good swordplay technique, and of course practice. To learn virtue, one must study the fundamentals (for instance, the need for moderation between extremes), observe those who live well, and practice. The difficulty here, of course, is that distinguishing which of the candidates for role models are genuinely good seems to presuppose that one is sophisticated enough to do so. In other words, if I were smart enough to know who is a good role model, I wouldn't need a role model. But this is less a flaw in the theory than it is a reminder about the developmental nature of virtue and the importance of practical reason. Could one come to the conclusion that Saruman would be a good role model? It is said that everyone listens to him in councils. But it turns out that this is due more to tricks of persuasion than to the soundness of his arguments. He certainly *seems* successful, being a powerful wizard (indeed, the chief of wizards, according to Gandalf) with a mighty fortress. But being powerful is not the same thing as living well. As Galadriel, Gandalf, and several others point out, attaining power in certain ways is actually destructive to the soul.[2]

It's possible that only someone already predisposed to vice would identify a vicious character as a role model, because there is a natural affinity of the virtuous for other virtuous people. While there may be such an affinity, that would not explain deception. The fact of the matter is that a vicious person can sometimes deceive others into thinking that he or she is virtuous. An obvious example might be Wormtongue's corruption of Théoden. Théoden did not heed the counsel of Wormtongue out of vice, but because he had been deceived. (Why anyone would listen to the counsel of someone named "Wormtongue" remains a mystery.) But in other cases it seems as though one

---

[2] Complicating matters is the fact that Saruman is not a human but a wizard. The conditions for living a good life may be different for humans and other species. But on the other hand, even other wizards seem to think that Saruman has misjudged the nature of his own good.

must be at least partially complicit in one's own deception, as suggested by clichés such as "I only saw what I wanted to see" or "I was weak." People sometimes say they "let themselves be deceived," thus implying partial responsibility for the error. In any event, the *phronemos* or role model is someone that Aristotle claims is helpful in coming to understand virtue, not a necessary condition. So these sorts of psychological puzzles are not by themselves hindrances to accepting this model. The key thing is the use of practical reason for the purpose of developing good character.

The Characters of Middle-earth

Tolkien seems to think that the hobbits are successful in part because they have good characters.[3] Although there are vicious hobbits, for the most part hobbit culture is portrayed as remarkably healthy and decent. The fundamental good nature of the hobbits is partly why Frodo is able to resist, for the most part, the temptation of corruption offered by the Ring. But can hobbits be described as virtuous? Given the central role of moderation in virtue theory, that's not implausible. They eat more meals than humans do, but relative to their eating habits, they still have a concept of "overdoing it." They seem not to go in for overly ostentatious displays. They recognize the concepts of honesty and laziness, politeness and selfishness, courage and injustice. Thus, they do think in terms of virtues and vices, even if their conception of them may differ from those of humans.

Having the right idea for the wrong reason is only minimally praiseworthy. So if someone is loyal only because he has always been told that loyalty is good, and he never questions it, it's not clear that that person is virtuous, even though we often describe loyalty as a virtue. Indeed, if the object of the person's loyalty is itself evil, we might criticize rather than praise this trait. Wormtongue's loyalty to Saruman is not morally praiseworthy. But if loyalty is only virtuous when the object of one's loyalty is

---

[3] While hobbits are not humans, they are sufficiently like humans that a lot of the same theories of the good life would apply. Elves, by contrast, are strikingly dissimilar to both humans and hobbits. But Aristotle's ethics, like almost everything else in philosophy, is meant for humans, so I will not speculate on what Aristotle might say is the good life for an elf.

itself good, this means that, to be virtuous, one must have the ability to make critical judgments about moral value and steer one's loyalties in the right direction.

Is Sam's deep loyalty to Frodo therefore an example of virtue? I think it is. Some have argued that Sam is a country bumpkin figure, the simple-but-decent sort. But that criticism misses the fundamental nature of their friendship. Sam is a friend to Frodo *because* he recognizes that Frodo is himself good, and thus worthy of Sam's loyalty. So, too, with the friendship and loyalty shown by Merry and Pippin. The hobbits' unshakable loyalty to each other is based on their shared conception of what is good and right.

Sméagol is an interesting case. It turns out that the creature called "Gollum" was once a hobbit, now sadly transformed by the power of the Ring. But the first step in his corruption was the murder of his friend, Déagol (FR, p. 58). Even if we stipulate that the Ring's power was at work, it could not literally compel him to commit murder. The Ring had been in his presence for mere moments, so we cannot account for this in terms of his having been transformed. He must have already been somewhat greedy and malicious for the Ring to have had this effect on him. The Ring has the power to corrupt, but some individuals are harder to corrupt than others. Sméagol is the most obvious case, since he murdered his friend so soon after being exposed to the Ring. We may contrast that with Bilbo's brief flashes of corruption. After possessing the Ring for sixty years, Bilbo has only one or two passing moments of darkness, and can be quickly brought back to his senses. After merely seeing the Ring, Sméagol murders his friend. So the Ring's power seems partly to be contingent upon people's character. Bilbo and Frodo are more virtuous even after coming into contact with the Ring than Sméagol was before finding it. This lends support to the view that as one practices habits of thought and action that produce virtues, one becomes more virtuous; one finds virtuous action easier. That is another sense in which reason is "practical": for the virtuous person, reflection on past experience produces changes in character, but the changed character responds differently to new experiences.

We may also usefully contrast Aragorn and Boromir. Whereas Aragorn recognizes the corrupting power of the Ring, and hopes to defeat Sauron without it, Boromir covets the Ring. Unlike the case of Sméagol, this is not due to a malicious nature. Boromir simply thinks that a powerful tool in the hands of a good man would be used only for good, and would not lead to moral corruption. He realizes too late that this is a misjudgment. This indicates that while Boromir is less practically wise than Aragorn, he may still be fundamentally of a decent nature.[4] But isn't it the case that Boromir has other traits that may have contributed to his downfall? For example, he is resentful of Aragorn's reappearance, angered that the Council of Elrond did not heed his recommendations, and perhaps embittered by the suffering inflicted on Gondor by Sauron. Resentfulness, bitterness, and pride are vices that can make one fall prey to a corrupting force, even if one is basically a good person. By contrast, if anyone has cause to be resentful, it is Aragorn, who ought to be king but has had to live in exile. But he isn't resentful or embittered. He remains temperate and just and magnanimous. Also, importantly, he heeds the counsel of those he recognizes as being wiser, unlike Boromir, who refuses to acknowledge that he could be mistaken. Aristotle specifically singles out for criticism this variety of stubbornness, quoting Hesiod: "He who grasps everything himself is best of all; he is noble also who listens to one who has spoken well; but he who neither grasps it himself nor takes to heart what he hears from another is a useless man."[5] Hence Boromir is a tragic figure, but not an evil one.

If Boromir is flawed but not malicious, then presumably characters in the novel that are clearly presented as evil, chiefly Sauron and Saruman, must bear a greater responsibility for their vices than Boromir does for his. This raises a larger question about how responsible we are for the characters we develop. It's not clear, on this analysis, why we would regard Boromir as a fundamentally good character *despite* his vices, while regarding Saruman or Sméagol as evil characters *because* of their vices. One answer might be that the total lack of virtue exhibited by

---

[4] It doesn't help to note that Boromir is less wise than Gandalf or Galadriel, whose refusals to accept the Ring are informed by magical foresight. Aragorn is capable of discerning this with lesser powers, and is thus a more relevant comparison.

[5] Hesiod, *Works and Days*, 336–340, quoted in Aristotle, *Nicomachean Ethics*, pp. 6–7, 1095b10.

Saruman and Sméagol is evidence of a fundamentally malicious nature, which is not in evidence in the case of Boromir, who is striving for justice even if he fails to see how best to achieve it. Saruman is seeking domination, not justice. Sméagol, on a lesser scale, is sufficiently greedy that he murders his friend to possess the Ring. He is to some extent victimized by the Ring's corrupting influence, but he bears some responsibility for his predicament because it seems he had a vicious character prior to possessing the Ring.

Virtue Ethics in Perspective

The contrast between virtue ethics and other ethical theories is clear here. Simply following a list of rules, such as Kant recommends, cannot account for the role of practical wisdom in developing virtue, in learning how to be good. To the Kantian, morality consists in acting on rules or duties that are said to be universally binding and without exception. Lying, for instance, is forbidden regardless of the consequences. That would mean, first of all, that one would have a moral obligation to speak truthfully to Saruman, or to inquiring Black Riders. But it would also mean that one's ability to use reason would be of no special value—Sam's or to Aragorn's loyalty to Frodo would be no more or less praiseworthy than the Ringwraiths' loyalty to Sauron. Kant says that acts are morally right only if they are performed from a good will.[6] There is little emphasis on developing good character, because on this view, one must already possess good character in order to act morally. That seems like a moral theory suited for the High-elves, who, though corruptible, seem to be *naturally* good, but for hobbits and humans (our ultimate concern), the idea of moral self-development demands that we take seriously our flawed nature. We are capable of becoming better or worse through our dispositions and choices, and while our dispositions color our choices, our choices can alter our dispositions.

Utilitarianism, too, fails to take seriously the role of character in moral choice. Indeed, to elevate "the greatest good for the

---

[6] Immanuel Kant, *Grounding for the Metaphysics of Morals*, third edition, translated by James W. Ellington (Indianapolis: Hackett, 1993), pp. 7–8.

greatest number" to the level of ultimate moral principle is to obviate any discussion of good character, for my motivations would play no role in an assessment of my actions. According to utilitarianism, motivations are unimportant: only consequences have moral weight, and an act is morally right only if it brings about the greatest good for the greatest number.[7] Hence, consideration of a person's character is irrelevant, and we need only determine whether the outcome is desirable in order to discern whether the act was morally good. While there is some intuitive appeal to considering the end results, this can also lead one to conclude that "the ends justify the means," allowing an overall good outcome to stem from even murder or theft. Helping the Fellowship so I can get a cash reward is morally equivalent to helping them because it's the right thing to do. Utilitarianism also suffers from a structural flaw: in order to bring about the greatest good for the greatest number, I must be able to know the future consequences of my actions. This would seem to imply that those with magical foresight, like Galadriel, can behave morally, but Frodo and Aragorn cannot, because their deliberations about good consequences would generally be mere guesses. Since no one in the real world has Galadriel's powers of foresight, this cannot be a useful morality. Aristotle's virtue ethics, on the other hand, can operate in the presence of incomplete knowledge, partly because it focuses moral evaluation on actors, not acts. A person is, or becomes, virtuous *despite* having an incomplete understanding of the future, as a result of moral self-training.

Living a life, then, in which one is actively seeking justice and self-improvement, seems to be a necessary part of the way practical reason is supposed to work, as opposed to living a life devoted to power and domination. On this view, no list of rules will be sufficient. Recognizing that ethics is too complicated to be reduced to any short list of moral rules, virtue ethics offers no simple procedure for making moral choices. Instead, it offers a broad framework for thinking about ethical issues and responsibilities. It urges us to focus, first, on the ultimate goal of human striving: to flourish as happy, fulfilled human beings. It then asks

---

[7] See, for example, Jeremy Bentham, *An Introduction to the Principles of Morals and Legislation* (New York: Hafner, 1948), pp. 1–4; and John Stuart Mill, *Utilitarianism* (Indianapolis: Hackett, 1979), pp. 6–26.

what virtues or admirable traits of character we need to achieve that flourishing or fulfillment. The endeavor to form good character through practical reason is not a certain path to the well-lived life, but it seems to be the most likely strategy. If one can orient oneself towards these virtues, one can seek to act in ways that promote them. As Tolkien reminds us, this is the best insurance against corruption and destruction.[8]

---

[8] I am grateful to Eric Bronson and Gregory Bassham for suggesting several useful clarifications and emendations to this essay.

PART IV

Time and Mortality

10

Choosing to Die:
The Gift of Mortality
in Middle-earth

BILL DAVIS

Aragorn's love for Arwen makes the safety of Frodo and the Ring especially important to him. He very nearly fails to guide Frodo and the Ring from Bree to the safety of Elrond's house. And had he failed, the price would have been very great. In possession of the Ring, Sauron would have been unstoppable. All the good in Middle-earth would have been destroyed. Aragorn would never have been allowed to marry Arwen, Elrond's daughter, and all his hopes would have been dashed.

Arwen's love for Aragorn, however, is even more complicated. The movie *The Lord of the Rings: The Fellowship of the Ring* shows the two of them discussing their future during Aragorn's stay at Rivendell. On a bridge in a lush garden they speak tenderly of their commitment to each other. She asks if he remembers her promise. He does, saying, "You said you'd bind yourself to me, forsaking the immortal life of your people." Her reply is unwavering, "And to that I hold. I would rather share one lifetime with you than face all the ages of this world alone. I choose a mortal life." She clearly loves him, but what does death have to do with her choice?

Aragorn's love will send him on a long and dangerous road to protect Frodo and the Ring. Arwen's love demands even more. If he succeeds, she will marry him and accept his fate as a mortal. How can Aragorn ask this of Arwen? And why would Arwen choose to pay such a high price?

Questions like these can be answered on two levels that ultimately converge. On the first level, we might look for answers
that would make sense to Tolkien's characters inside his story.
Tolkien's world is rich and complex, and explaining his characters' choices is challenging. By the end of this chapter I hope to
show why Arwen doesn't cling to immortality and why Aragorn
accepts death peacefully. Answers on the second level concern
death and immortality in our own lives. The choices made by
Arwen and Aragorn raise important questions about our own
death and what will happen to us afterwards. And thoughtful
answers to these questions are all around us in popular culture
and in religious and philosophical writing. On the way to
explaining Arwen's choice, I will consider some of these
responses. Even though we cannot choose to avoid death, we
can learn to face it more thoughtfully by considering Tolkien's
difficult suggestion that death can be a gift.

Death in Middle-earth

Although they are allies in the struggle against Sauron's efforts
to dominate Middle-earth, elves and men[1] face very different
fates. Like humans in the real world, Tolkien's men and hobbits
are mortal. Whether from old age, sickness or injury, a time
comes when their bodies are no longer able to support life. And
when their bodies die, their souls leave Arda, the earth.[2] Elves,
on the other hand, face a different fate. Elvish bodies can grow
weary or be hurt so that they can't sustain life. But when they
do, elvish souls remain "within the circles of the world." Men
aren't sure what will happen to them after death. Elves know
that no matter what happens to their bodies, their souls will
have an active place in the life of Arda.

Arwen must choose between these two fates because she is
half-elven like her father, Elrond. Half-elves are very rare, but
they must choose whether they will share the fate of men or the

---

[1] Following Tolkien's usage, I will use "men" to refer to the race of humans
in his story, both males and females. For references to non-fictional humans,
I will use gender-inclusive terms.

[2] Arda, in Tolkien's invented world, consists of Middle-earth (the mortal lands
east of the Sundering Sea) and Aman, which consists of Valinor, the home of
the Valar and some elves, and Eressëa, an island inhabited by elves.

fate of elves. Arwen chooses to share Aragorn's fate, making her own death inevitable. The process of dying in Middle-earth is no more pleasant than it is in our world. But even though it involves pain and separation from loved ones, wise men and most elves refer to mortality as a "gift" to men (RK, p. 378; S, p. 265; L, p. 285). Elves have the "gift" of immortality, of lasting as long as the world endures. Curiously, most elves and men wish they had the other race's fate. Most elves envy the ability to die, and most men envy elven deathlessness.

Two groups of mortals, however, do not envy the elves. The first group consists of the Ringwraiths, the shadowy figures who chase Frodo to Rivendell. In the first movie, *The Fellowship of the Ring*, scenes flash of black horses being unleashed, ridden by heavily cloaked shapes also in black. These Nine Riders pursue Frodo and the Ring, nearly catching them in the Inn at Bree. Halfway to Rivendell, five of the Riders attack Frodo among the ruins of Weathertop. Frodo, terror-stricken, reaches for the Ring as they approach him; but when he slips it on he sees them for what they are, emaciated old men wearing crowns. These Black Riders are the Nazgûl, or Ringwraiths, the *undead* human kings that accepted the nine Rings of Power and became Sauron's slaves.

When Frodo puts on the Ring, it is as if he enters another reality. But the reality of the undead Ringwraiths had been there all the time. Putting on the Ring only made it visible to Frodo. The Ringwraiths are horrific because they are undead: they are not dead, and for them *not* dying is a curse. The kings who accepted the rings from Sauron are men. Because their lust for power led the Nine to join with Sauron, their existence continues past the time when they should have received the gift of death. They are thus the "undead," specters who *should* be dead, but who are held in existence by the cruel will of their master, Sauron, and an undying lust for the Ring. They pursue Frodo because he possesses the Ring; and their existence is consumed completely by the desire to get it. At the Ford of Bruinen a watery torrent of horses washes away the horses they are riding, but the Nine are not drowned. The horses are lost, but the undead *cannot* die, and that is part of their punishment for their greed.

In his treatment of the Ringwraiths, Tolkien assumes that existence isn't always better than non-existence. While we are tempted to think that living is always better than dying, Tolkien follows the philosopher Aristotle in thinking that only *natural* existence is a good thing. Continuing to exist in any other way—any *unnatural* way—is worse than death. Like every natural thing, Ringwraiths have a *nature*, a way that they are supposed to be. Even though the Ring dominates them, they are still by nature men. The way a thing is supposed to be—its nature—determines not only the limits of what it can do, but also how it finds fulfillment.[3] A flower finds its fulfillment in blossoming and providing the seeds for reproducing itself. A beaver dams a river, builds a lodge, and mates. Men by nature develop civilizations and reproduce; and they die when their time is spent.

When any natural thing is prevented from fulfilling its natural purpose, it is frustrated. If it is conscious, it feels this failure and knows it is incomplete. A beaver prevented from building and mating would languish, aware that something was missing. Similarly, for the Ringwraiths, unending existence is a fate worse than death; it involves the perpetual pain of having their natures frustrated.

A second group of mortals who do not envy elven deathlessness includes noble men like Aragorn and faithful hobbits like Frodo. They are somehow able to embrace death without despair. As a reward for his heroism and suffering, Frodo is permitted to cross the Sea to the Undying Lands. In this land of peace and deathlessness Frodo recovers from his wounds and sadness. But he doesn't remain in Aman forever. Eventually he chooses to give up his life and pass beyond the circles of this world (L, p. 328). After defeating Sauron and reigning as King, Aragorn also accepts death freely (RK, p. 378). So, eventually, does Arwen. Aragorn, Frodo and Arwen all reap the "gift" of being able to leave Arda when their years are full.

It isn't hard to see why the Ringwraiths would welcome death as a release from endless torment. But it is harder to understand why both the men and elves of Middle-earth would call death a "gift." Most elves expect that when men die their souls will be annihilated, ceasing to exist altogether.[4]

---

[3] Aristotle, *Physics* II.1–2, 192b10–194b16.

[4] J.R.R. Tolkien, *Morgoth's Ring: The Later Silmarillion*, edited by Christopher Tolkien (Boston: Ticknor and Fields, 1993), pp. 330–360.

Why then would elves envy the ability to die? Elves admit that men have the "gift" of not being bound to the circles of this world, but they don't distinguish between two very different ways this might be true. An example might help to illustrate the difference.

Suppose an ingenious police officer has put you and a friend under house arrest in two different houses. Both of the houses are full of things to do, but if your friend ever attempts to leave, the doors will either be locked or will lead back into some other part of the same house. Your friend has the fate of the elves: lots to do, but no way to leave. If instead you had the fate of men, before long you would be required to leave the house/prison. Some of the doors would open and lead somewhere other than another part of your house. In this situation, your friend might well say that you have the "gift" or "privilege" of being able to leave.

But is this gift a blessing? If at least one of the doors leads away from the house to somewhere else with things worth doing, then it is a blessing to be able to leave. In this case being able to leave the confines of the house—or the circle of the world—is good. But what if every open door leads to unending pitch-black nothingness, or off the edge of an enormous cliff onto jagged rocks? In that case is it a *blessing* to be able to leave? Feeling trapped in a world with no escape,[5] elves envy even the possibility of annihilation. In uncertainty and despair, most men in Middle-earth fear that their fate is the enormous cliff (annihilation). Concerning our own uncertainty about death, philosophers have had a lot to say.

Death on Planet Earth

Because we share with Tolkien's men and hobbits the "gift" of death, we don't find it difficult to understand their fears about death and what comes after it. Hamlet's famous "To be or not to be" speech deals with the problem directly: death is "the undiscovered country."[6] It may be sleep; it may bring fantastic

---

[5] Jean-Paul Sartre presents us with a similar scenario in *No Exit and Three Other Plays* (New York: Random House: 1989). In the title play, three strangers are stuck in a room with each other for all eternity.

[6] Shakespeare, *Hamlet*, Act III, Scene 1.

dreams; or it may bring hellish torment. For Hamlet, not knowing what comes next is a good reason to avoid death. Classical
literature like Dante's *Inferno*, cartoons like *The Far Side*, and
even television commercials depict hell as a fiery land of per-
sonalized torment. Similar sources depict heaven as a happy
place—angels lounging on clouds, winged saints with harps and
no cares—but one that might be a bit boring. The standard story
is that after death souls continue to live, but that their quality of
life depends upon whether they were good or evil while on
earth. We are fascinated by the afterlife because of the great difference between torment and bliss. Uncertainty about what we'll
find can make the subject frightening. It also makes the topic
attractive to philosophers.

The most common conclusion among philosophers is that
we shouldn't be afraid of death. Their reasons differ, but the earliest Western argument against fearing death is probably the
most famous. In 399 B.C., Plato's mentor, Socrates, was convicted
of a variety of crimes. The jury that had convicted him then had
to decide whether to have him executed (as the prosecution
wanted) or to impose whatever Socrates offered as a suitable
punishment. The jury expected Socrates to propose exile instead
of death, but he surprised them. At first he asked to be treated
as a town hero with the right to free meals for life, but finally
he proposed a small fine. In his *Apology*, Plato records Socrates's
reasons for taking such a bold step. Refusing to be ruled by fear
of what he didn't know, he was confident that after death he
would be better off. He may sleep forever. Or he may end up
talking to heroes who have already died. Neither prospect
scared him enough to make him beg the jury for a lesser punishment than execution. He reasoned his way to accepting death
calmly.

Socrates is famous for accepting death "philosophically,"
meaning that he based his actions on a reasoned argument
rather than on his emotions. For over two thousand years intellectuals have pointed to Socrates as a shining example of a
philosophical approach to death. But part of Socrates's reason for
accepting death was his confidence that his soul would continue
to exist afterwards. He believed that his soul was immortal.

Not everyone expects death to be followed by a conscious
afterlife. Some philosophers have warned that it is possible that
after death we will simply cease to exist altogether. Like many

elves in Tolkien's world, these philosophers insist that human death won't be a transition; it will be the very end. But many of the same philosophers who expect annihilation refuse to fear death. In his book, *On the Nature of Things*, the Epicurean philosopher Lucretius argued that only the superstitious fear death. He was convinced that we are only our bodies and that we cease to exist completely when our bodies die. While this might seem to be a depressing conclusion, he insisted that we should find it liberating. The process of dying may be unpleasant, but being dead isn't scary, because once we're dead we won't experience anything at all. For Lucretius this is good news. It means that we can stop wasting time trying to please priests or saying useless prayers.

Lucretius is not alone in thinking that impending annihilation can be liberating. Existentialists such as Jean-Paul Sartre and Albert Camus want us to see that the inevitability of death can be helpful. Because we know that we are going to die soon, we are not tempted to take this life for granted. Our impending death keeps us from forgetting that this life is all there is, and that we have only a short time to live as richly and meaningfully as we can. It takes great courage to live with full knowledge that this is all there is, but death keeps us from thinking that we have forever to get it right. For Sartre and Camus, dying itself isn't a blessing, but unflinching awareness that we will die is a great advantage.[7]

Immortality in Middle-earth

While many philosophers wrestle with the possibility of their own annihilation, the elves of Middle-earth face the prospect of unending consciousness. Unlike the Ringwraiths who persist without bodies of their own, elves always have bodies. Even if their bodies die, their souls do not long remain disembodied; they get new bodies, and even recover all their past memories (L, p. 286). The most common afterlife fate depicted in Tolkien's story is reincarnation (L, p. 189). The clearest and

---

[7] Jean-Paul Sartre, "Existentialism," in *Existentialism and Human Emotions* (New York: Philosophical Library, 1957); and Albert Camus, "Absurd Reasoning," in *The Myth of Sisyphus and Other Essays* (Harmondsworth: Penguin, 1991).

most spectacular example of reincarnation in *The Lord of the Rings* is Gandalf's return. Passing through the Mines of Moria, Gandalf enables the other eight members of the Fellowship to escape by standing alone against the Balrog. He prevents the black menace from passing the bridge, but Gandalf is dragged into the abyss by a last desperate stroke from the Balrog's whip. As far as anyone can tell at the time, the wizard plummets to his death (FR, p. 371).

It is a crushing blow to the company, and their hopes steadily fade until a changed Gandalf reveals himself to Aragorn, Legolas, and Gimli as they search for Pippin and Merry. The story that Gandalf tells of his long fall into the pit, his struggle with the Balrog and eventual return is vague, hinting at both death and victory. But as Tolkien makes clear in his letters, Gandalf the Grey *did* die, was given a new body, and was returned by Ilúvatar to Middle-earth as Gandalf the White (L, pp. 201–03).

In Tolkien's Middle-earth, reincarnation always involves getting a body of the same kind as the one lost. Elves that die in battle or from mishap in Middle-earth are reincarnated as elves in the Blessed Realm. Gandalf returns as a wizard. He is wiser and more powerful, but that is the result of the growth of his soul. Gandalf the White doesn't have the same body as Gandalf the Grey. If he had, his return would have been a case of resurrection rather than reincarnation.

But if elves can be sure that death will lead to getting another body, why would the elves envy the ability men have to die? Even the elves in the Blessed Realm are jealous of the human ability to die and leave altogether. Why? What could be missing? One possible explanation is that these elves find unending delight *boring*. Even a good thing over and over without end can become dull. The idea that such a paradise might be undesirable has contributed to philosophical discussions about the possibility of human immortality.

Immortality on Planet Earth

Only a minority of philosophers today believes in personal immortality. Before the last century, however, many philosophers expected that their souls would continue after their bodies died. Usually this expectation arises from a religious conviction. Socrates's belief that his soul would live after his body had died probably rested on a version of a Pythagorean mystery religion. A number of Eastern philosophical traditions are based on either Hindu or Buddhist religious commitments. These philosophers expect that we will be reincarnated, a fate very similar to that of Tolkien's elves. Human souls, they say, are clothed in bodies made of flesh. When the body dies, the soul is given a new body as its house or covering. Some hold that every living thing is a soul, and at the death of any particular body the soul transmigrates (moves) into another body. In these traditions it is usual to think that the kind of body the soul gets next depends upon the actions of the soul in its previous life. Souls of humans may be reincarnated as lesser beasts if they live wicked lives as humans.

Religious and philosophical schools that believe in reincarnation are most common in Eastern cultures. Christian and some Jewish philosophical systems also hold that humans are immortal. But instead of expecting reincarnation, these traditions look forward to resurrection in the afterlife. Unlike reincarnated souls, a resurrected soul gets the very same body back,[8] but with all its diseases and weaknesses removed. Just how this works is ultimately mysterious, involving a miracle that God performs to reunite soul and body. For Christians, the mysteriousness of how resurrection *could* happen is usually overwhelmed by the wonder of knowing that it *has* happened. Jesus Christ was executed on a cross, his body was sealed in a tomb, and on the third day he rose from the dead. His body was the same body— the holes left from having nails driven through his hands were still there—but it was a glorified body, beyond pain, disease, and death.[9] As a Roman Catholic, Tolkien himself believed this about Jesus, but none of his characters in Middle-earth experience resurrection.

Philosophical attention to the afterlife reached its high point in the Middle Ages. Christian philosophers such as Augustine,

---

[8] At least this is the traditional view. See for instance St. Thomas Aquinas, *Summa Theologica*, Supp., Q. 79, art. 1; John Calvin, *Institutes of the Christian Religion*, Volume 2, translated by Ford Lewis Battles (Philadelphia: Westminster, 1960), p. 998. Many contemporary theologians reject this view of the resurrection.

[9] Matthew 24, John 20-21, and I Corinthians 15.

Bonaventure, and Thomas Aquinas wrote extensively about the nature of the soul, its connection to the body, and reasons for thinking that the soul is immortal. Many of these arguments continue lines of reasoning found in the ancient Greek philosophers Plato and Aristotle. Similarly detailed discussions of the soul's immortality and resurrection can be found in the works of Jewish and Muslim philosophers, such as Maimonides and Al-Ghazali. And philosophical defenses of resurrection are not limited to the Middle Ages. Peter van Inwagen and Trenton Merricks are two leading philosophers today who argue that humans will be resurrected after they die.[10] In all of these discussions immortality is depicted as one of eventual and unending bliss. Some believe that purgatory lies between death and the heavenly paradise. But just as with Tolkien's character Niggle (in "Leaf by Niggle"), perfect happiness is the final condition.[11]

Philosophical confidence about human immortality, though, has been under attack in recent years. And religious pictures of heaven have been subjected to special scrutiny. Many philosophers still argue that annihilation is all we can expect after death. Others insist that stories about heaven are just fantasies used by powerful priests to trick gullible people into obedience. Still other philosophers contend that even if there were a heaven of endless delight, it wouldn't be a blessing to go there.[12] Tolkien's elves in the Blessed Realm grow weary of unending life. Why not think that the same would be true in the heaven expected by many Muslims, Jews, and Christians?

Philosophers who doubt the existence of heaven have drawn attention to this difficulty. In Greek mythology Sisyphus is cursed in the Underworld with the task of endlessly rolling a rock to the top of a hill, only to see it immediately roll back to the bottom. Albert Camus focuses on the hideousness of this

---

[10] Peter van Inwagen, *The Possibility of Resurrection and Other Essays in Christian Apologetics* (Boulder: Westview, 1997); Trenton Merricks, "The Resurrection of the Body and the Life Everlasting," in Michael J. Murray, ed., *Reason for the Hope Within* (Grand Rapids: Eerdmans, 1998).

[11] "Leaf by Niggle," in *The Tolkien Reader* (New York: Ballantine, 1966).

[12] Bernard Williams, "The Makropulos Case: Reflections on the Tedium of Immortality," in *Problems of the Self* (Cambridge: Cambridge University Press, 1973), p. 82; Garth L. Hallet, "The Tedium of Immortality," *Faith and Philosophy* 18:3 (July 2001), pp. 279–291.

fate in his essay "The Myth of Sisyphus." Not only must Sisyphus struggle to raise the rock each time, but his punishment is made infinitely worse by his awareness that it is all pointless. Every time he walks down the hill to start again, Sisyphus has time to think about the futility of his existence. Heaven isn't supposed to have the painful labor of pushing a rock, but why not think that it would be nearly as undesirable as Sisyphus's fate: endless, pointless, and boring?

The awful tediousness of unending existence has also been a significant theme in recent popular works. Wowbagger the Infinitely Prolonged of Douglas Adams's *Hitchhiker's Guide to the Galaxy* series finds himself sorry that he is deathless precisely because it is boring. With nothing meaningful to do and absolutely forever to do it in, he decides to insult everyone in the universe one at a time, in alphabetical order.[13] Here again, deathlessness looks a lot more like a curse than it does a blessing. Similar stories of boring immortality can be found in the *Star Trek* series[14] and in the LucasArts video game *The Dig*.

Not everyone, though, is convinced that endless existence must be painfully dull. Heaven has its philosophical defenders, going back at least to Boethius (c. 480–525 A.D.). Facing his own execution, Boethius confidently looks ahead to life after the death of his body. He expects that his heavenly afterlife won't be boring because heaven is beyond time. His afterlife won't be an endless series of dull or pointless moments. Rather, it will be a completely full existence where time has no meaning. More recent defenses of heaven have compared it to the embrace of lovers—where time seems to stand still—or to the delight children take in doing the same thing over and over.[15]

Boethius's solution wouldn't apply to the elves of the Blessed Realm. Their existence is certainly time-bound. But while a heaven beyond time avoids the boredom problem, it doesn't

---

[13] Douglas Adams, *Life, the Universe and Everything*, in *The Ultimate Hitchhiker's Guide* (New York: Random House, 1996), pp. 317ff.

[14] *Star Trek: The Next Generation*, Season 1, Episode 22, "Skin of Evil." *Star Trek Voyager*, Season 2, Episode 18, "Death Wish."

[15] Lauren A. King, "Life in Heaven: Sometimes It Sounds Boring," *Christianity Today* 27 (April 8th, 1983), p. 66; G. K. Chesterton, "Orthodoxy," in *The Collected Works of G.K. Chesterton*, Vol. 1 (San Francisco: Ignatius Press, 1986), p. 263.

make heaven all that attractive. We have no way of picturing ourselves as existing outside of time, so we have no way of imagining life in a heaven of this kind. The time-stands-still embrace solution and the child-like delight solution could apply to Tolkien's elves and might apply to us. But both of these approaches look more like short-term evasions than solutions. Eventually the embrace must end; and even children who are easy to please get tired of the most interesting toys.[16]

Why Arwen Chooses Death

At this point it is tempting to conclude that Tolkien calls death a "gift" simply because it releases men from the wearying tedium of endless existence. But it is unlikely that Tolkien intends for us to draw this conclusion about death. Apart from his insistence that the story wasn't written as an allegory of any kind, *The Lord of the Rings* is part of a larger history that is purposely written from an elvish point of view (L, p. 147). What elves would value dominates the way the story is told. Release from the burden of endless existence is a source of eager interest because it is something the elves cannot have. The fact that they cannot leave the circles of the world makes them emphasize that life can be wearying, futile and boring. The best existence elves can hope for (the Blessed Realm) is one where work is rewarded and pain is rare, but it is still a finite world. Because it is finite, it is possible for them to know all there is to know about it. For the elves, immortality is simply living as long as this finite world of limited goods endures.

Unlike the elvish "immortality" of deathlessness in a finite world, the Christian heaven that Tolkien looked forward to is an endless afterlife of fellowship with a limitless good. The most blessed of the elves would at some point run out of things to learn about the circles of this world. For theists, on the other hand, heaven involves getting to know God—an infinite good—better and better. The blessed in this kind of afterlife cannot exhaust all that can be known about God. Elvish immortality has to be repetitive eventually, but the immortality Tolkien expected can't be. It will always be possible to learn

---

[16] Hallet, "The Tedium of Immortality," pp. 285–87.

more about God. And since Tolkien believed that what might be learned about God is always amazingly good, it will never be boring.

But even if heaven won't be boring, Arwen's choice still needs explaining. Although they call death the "gift" of men, elves do not expect that dead men will enjoy an afterlife where delight increases forever. And while wise elves simply admit that no one is sure what happens when men die, most elves believe that dead men cease to exist. Wise men do not know any more than the wise elves. And most men fear that the common expectation of annihilation is true. Arwen and Aragorn, however, are not common. They are uncommonly wise, and they love uncommonly deeply. Arwen's choice of Aragorn, and their willing acceptance of death, can both be explained by focusing on their wisdom and their love.

In her choice of Aragorn and his fate, Arwen prefers a finite life of deep love to an unending life without that love. In order to marry Aragorn and enjoy that relationship, she would have to take on his mortal nature. It wasn't possible to have the great joy of his love and be deathless. Had she chosen elvish immortality instead, endless life without love would not give as much joy as sharing a brief life with Aragorn. Arwen does not choose death for its own sake. She chooses life with Aragorn for its own sake and accepts eventual death as a price she is willing to pay to get it.

But that was not her only choice. In the end, like Aragorn and Frodo, she also chooses to accept death before it is forced upon her. Although Arwen, Aragorn, and Frodo know very little about what comes after death, they know two crucial things. First, they know that those with the "gift" do not remain within the circles of this world. Second, they know that death is a gift from Ilúvatar, the creator-God of Tolkien's world. They are Ilúvatar's children, special objects of a love more profound than the love between Aragorn and Arwen. In the end they accept death both because it releases them and because they expect that what comes next will also be a blessing.

What kind of blessing it will be hasn't been revealed. The oldest among the elves look forward to a "last battle" and the destruction of this world. But their stories don't end there. They go on to tell of this world being "remade" without the presence of evil. The souls of the elves (and in some stories the souls of men) return to this world and enjoy unending bliss.[17] The origin of these stories is unclear, but they are consistent with what they know about their creator's love for them. Aragorn's last words to Arwen before he gives up his life speak of this hope: "In sorrow we must go, but not in despair. Behold! We are not bound for ever to the circles of the world, and beyond them is more than memory. Farewell!" (RK, p. 378) Death delivers them from the pains and frustrations of life in this world. And as beloved children of their creator, Arwen, Aragorn, and Frodo look forward to an even better life in a world remade. We should be so blessed.[18]

[17] Tolkien, *Morgoth's Ring*, pp. 319ff.

[18] I'm indebted to my son, Jonathan Davis, and my students Ryan Davidson, Matt Fray, Matthew Krueger, and Ryan Wright for research assistance and insightful comments on earlier drafts of this chapter.

11

Tolkien, Modernism, and the Importance of Tradition

JOE KRAUS

It's all a very close call, isn't it? The Ring and its evil almost win at the end of *The Lord of the Rings*, and it's not hard to think about all of the ways that things could have turned out catastrophically. If Gandalf hadn't realized that Bilbo's ring was the One Ring before Sauron could mobilize the Black Riders, that would have been the end before it started. If Frodo hadn't focused on everything he had learned from Bilbo, Gandalf, and Elrond, then he and Sam would have been lost once the Fellowship disintegrated and they found themselves alone. If Aragorn hadn't outsmarted Sauron—if he hadn't revealed himself at the perfect moment or if he had failed to lead a convincing counter-attack on Mordor and drawn Sauron's attention away from Frodo—then the whole War of the Ring would have been hopeless. If the forces of the good, Gandalf, Elrond, Galadriel, Aragorn, and Frodo, hadn't realized that using the Ring would ultimately corrupt them, then Sauron's evil would have won no matter how the battles had ended.

Too many close calls in a story can get boring or comical—think of how many machine-gun bullets never hit Rambo as he runs across one open field after another—but there's a pattern to the way Tolkien allows his characters to make many of their escapes. That is, the heroes of *The Lord of the Rings* often rescue themselves because they remember something important that their enemies have forgotten. Gandalf, for instance, discovers the Ring because he, and he alone of the powers in Middle-earth, remembers to look after the Shire. He, Aragorn, and Faramir are brave, but they are also prepared. They venture into places where they know they will face danger, but they never rush in. They have studied history, lore, tactics, languages, and geography, and they know as much as they can about whatever it is they are attempting. They have their trusty swords and their quick wits with them all of the time, but they have also done their homework. Thus, Tolkien seems to tell us, knowledge, is a crucial part of what it takes to be a hero.

In this essay, I argue that one element of Tolkien's vision in writing *The Lord of the Ring* was to imagine a world where scholarship and respect for tradition provide real and tangible power. Remember that Tolkien was a professor who studied and taught the languages of Northern Europe, so he was committed to the values of the humanities. In addition, however, he also served as a soldier in World War I and watched his son Christopher serve in World War II. As a consequence, he knew all too well that engineers and industrial leaders were the sort who determined victory in modern warfare. He knew as well that there were entire schools of thought with little regard for the religion, history, philosophy, and ancient cultures that he prized. Part of what he does in *The Lord of the Rings* is offer the fantasy that, in a time of tanks and machine guns, ancient languages and arcane history still matter, that without them there is no hope for the final victory of the good. In other words, he creates a fantasy that many of us English and philosophy teachers probably share: if you listen carefully to everything that we tell you in class, then maybe you will be able to go out and help save the world.

Shooting Arrows at Modernism

Tolkien is saying more than simply "pay attention in class," though. He values a particular kind of study, a study that leads to an understanding of the philosophy of the past and so offers a moral arsenal in the struggle against technology and the temptations of power. He calls for his characters—and presumably his students—to recognize their personal link to the moral and philosophical traditions of Europe because the alternative is disaster. He asks them to regard their connection to Western history and culture as an almost religious one. As he describes his own affinity for that tradition in a letter to his son, Michael, "I was never obliged to teach anything except what I loved (and do) with an inextinguishable enthusiasm . . . The devotion to 'learning', as such and without reference to one's own repute, is a high and even in a sense spiritual vocation" (L, p. 337). That is, Tolkien wants to communicate a sense that the most important thing an educated person can do is to understand what the great thinkers of the past have to teach us about the moral structure of the universe. If we cling to tradition, we will find the wisdom to survive today. While such an idea may sound conventional—and in many ways it is as conventional as the English countryside ways that the hobbits of the Shire follow— it was distinctive for the time in which he wrote. A generation earlier, thinkers as different as Ezra Pound, Pablo Picasso, and Sigmund Freud had proposed radical new ways of thinking about art and humanity that threatened to tear down established ideas of conduct and beauty. While most of Tolkien's own contemporaries in the humanities embraced and extended such ideas of the "modern," he called for a return to tradition. During the half-century in which technology went from the Wright Brothers to the atomic bomb, Tolkien insisted that older values could still make a difference in the real world.

Philosophers and students of culture debate the best way to define "modernism" but most agree that it refers to a wide range of ideas and perspectives that come together as a kind of mood, a sense that everything is impermanent. As Marshall Berman puts it, modernity "is a paradoxical unity, a unity of disunity: it pours us all into a maelstrom of perpetual disintegration and renewal, of struggle and contradiction, of ambiguity and anguish. To be modern is to be part of a universe in which, as Marx said, 'all that is solid melts into air.'"[1] That is, we experience modernism as the loss of the institutions and philosophies that have guided us. It means that there are new and exciting possibilities before us, but the old certainties are gone. Some scholars see the modern period emerging full-born with the end of World War I, when so much of Europe was destroyed and so many of the shocked survivors questioned why the world's leading civilizations had fought at all. Others see the seeds of it as early as the

---

[1] *All that Is Solid Melts into Air: The Experience of Modernity* (New York: Simon and Schuster, 1982), p. 15.

Renaissance, when, with Europe's rediscovery of Greek and Roman philosophy, the Catholic church lost its monopoly as an intellectual framework. In either case, by the time Tolkien set out to write *The Lord of the Rings*, that modern mood was coloring most contemporary Western academic thought.

Berman's definition shows how difficult it is to characterize something that is simultaneously so broad and so nearly universal. Above all it shows that many observers understand modernism as the extreme rejection of traditional values. No matter how dramatically the major modern thinkers disagreed with one another, they shared the sense that previous generations had gotten most of the major questions wrong. One manifestation of modernism was Karl Marx declaring that class conflict was the only significant engine driving history; another was Sigmund Freud insisting that everything turned on the human drive for sex. Both ways of seeing the world insisted that traditional explanations of human activity, ones that came out of religion or Classical philosophy, were not merely wrong but extinct. Philosopher Friedrich Nietszche put it most succinctly when he famously declared "God is dead." In the modern world, the new—the "modern" in all of its senses—was almost always better than the old and traditional. There simply wasn't room for ideas that had no direct basis in science, and traditional philosophy and religion struck many leading thinkers as little more than superstitions.

Tolkien understood that he was in a minority when it came to rejecting modernism. As he put it in a letter to Joanna de Bortadano, "If there is any contemporary reference in my story at all it is to what seems to me the most widespread assumption of our time: that if a thing can be done, it must be done" (L, p. 246). In other words, he wrote *The Lord of the Rings*, in part, as a protest against the sense that the past no longer had any relevance, that humans could act, in the absence of God, however they wished. Tolkien knew that many of his fellow academics embraced such sentiments, yet he deliberately went in the opposite direction. He went looking for the past, and he tried to find ways to make his discoveries useful to the modern world. He knew that the world was changing—both the real world and the world of ideas—and he reacted to that change by studying forgotten works and reintroducing them to his students and the public at large. In response to the chaos that many others celebrated and even worshipped, he reasserted the importance and value of tradition.

Above all, Tolkien saw modernism as a self-destructive reaction to the dizzying present that called for eliminating the remnants of the past. As someone who loved nature, it troubled him to see the reckless and unplanned development of much of the countryside that he knew. (In that light, it is easy to see the ents as the fantasy that our forests will fight back if we abuse them too much.) As someone who took his own religious identity very seriously, he seemed to feel a sad sympathy for modern thinkers who dismissed religion, Catholicism in particular, without investigating what they were dismissing. Tolkien saw modernism as, at least in part, a knee-jerk rejection of many of the things he valued. He did recognize that it took intellectual and emotional work to believe in the wisdom of tradition in a generation that had seen World War I, but he also knew that it had been difficult in every age to sort out central, guiding ideas. He saw too many of his contemporaries taking an easy road, abandoning the Western tradition that made possible their own skepticism. He mistrusted the modern mood in most of its manifestations, understanding it as a kind of despair, and he resisted it, in part, by writing a fantasy that showed it as such.

The Modern Despair of Saruman and Denethor

The most modern character in the entire trilogy is Saruman, even though he was once, ironically, the most learned in ancient lore. For many of the centuries before the events of *The Lord of the Rings* take place, he was the leader of the White Council, the most powerful force in Middle-earth resisting Sauron. Even though he becomes a villain in the story, he never stops fighting against Sauron. He wants the Ring so that he can use it to destroy Sauron and take over the world himself. The trouble is that Saruman has forgotten his own wisdom. He has withdrawn into his private study, allowed himself to be distracted by what he learns from the *palantír*, and has lost faith in the tradition of which he was a noble part. He thinks he knows the world, even though he is a virtual hermit in his tower at Orthanc. As he sneers to Gandalf about the Ring, "Have I not earnestly studied this matter? Into Anduin the Great it fell; and long ago, while

Sauron slept, it was rolled down the River to the Sea" (FR, p. 281). He is wrong, of course. The hobbits have the Ring, and we readers have the distinct pleasure of knowing that he is making a fool of himself.

Saruman's real mistake is more than just factual, though. It is that he comes to conceive of the world only in the same terms that Sauron does. He cannot imagine victory without the Ring and he can no longer see the virtues of elvish wisdom and natural power. He tells himself that he does not want to see a world ruled by Sauron, but he simultaneously throws away his faith in the traditional powers of Middle-earth. As he says to Gandalf, "The Elder Days are gone. The Middle Days are passing. The Younger Days are beginning. The time of the Elves is over, but our time is at hand: the world of Men, which We must rule" (FR, pp. 290–91). So saying, he sounds a bit like Nietzsche. He sees the old world as spent and withered, and he proposes conquering what's left. To that end, he makes himself into a parody of Sauron, breeding his own race of orcs and inventing great fiery machines that belch black smoke. He continues to study, but he does even that under the influence of Sauron; he searches through overlooked details of the past for personal power rather than as a means of reconnecting with the gods and powers who have sent him as their emissary from the remote West. In his twisted effort to save Middle-earth, he makes the literal error of seeing the trees without recognizing the forest. Because he makes a strip mine of Treebeard's forest, the ents rise up and overwhelm him.

Denethor, the Steward of Gondor, has an almost identical experience, falling from his position as the most powerful man in Middle-earth into paranoia and despair. Like Saruman, he has foolishly made use of a *palantír* to learn what he can of the world without having actually to venture into it. He should have known from his studies that only the true king could master one, but he tries all the same. He compounds that foolishness by imagining that he really can control what he sees. He is strong enough to resist the eye of Sauron that stares back at him, but he does not realize the degree to which Sauron nevertheless directs his vision so that he sees only dark tidings that demoralize him. As he declares to Gandalf, "I have seen more than thou knowest, Grey Fool. For thy hope is but ignorance" (RK, p. 130). He has turned away from the traditional and valuable course of the stewards who came before him. Rather than acting in the stead of the departed king, he acts as if he were the king. His speculations have shown him that there is no hope, and he never tests them. Instead, he retreats to his rooms and tries to kill his son Faramir so that he can make a glorious end to the great history that he feels certain is about to come to a close. Like Saruman, he finds himself caught in Tolkien's critique of modernism: if you do not embrace the wisdom of the past in a time of crisis, the only choice you have is to try to destroy the present. Although there is still hope, a tiny hope resting on the fading strength of Minas Tirith and the advice that Gandalf has to offer, he decides it is easier to despair than to depend on the traditions and teachings that are the source of his own strength.

Samwise or Wise-guy Pippin?

An interesting dynamic of wisdom and the failure to appreciate wisdom plays out between Sam and Pippin. For much of *The Lord of the Rings*, Pippin is notoriously reckless, forgetting what Gandalf and the others have told him and taking foolish chances. He should know that he has to be as quiet and unobtrusive as possible, but he still drops the stone down the well in Moria (FR, p. 351). Doing so alerts the Balrog that they are there, and that leads to the confrontation where Gandalf falls to his doom. Later, he cannot resist stealing the *palantír* and looking into it. In doing so, he narrowly avoids revealing Frodo's Quest, and he flouts what he knows is the wise course of staying far away from the stone. As Merry tells him, "Don't forget Gildor's saying—the one Sam used to quote: *Do not meddle in the affairs of Wizards, for they are subtle and quick to anger*" (TT, p. 216). He knows what the elves would tell him, and he knows that he is flying in the face of the very authority that has helped him survive that far, but he cannot help himself. He is acting on an impulse that Sauron has strengthened—touching the Orthanc-stone when Wormtongue hurls it at him puts him in reach of its spell—but he could have resisted it if he were more conscious of clinging to what he knows is right and good.

Pippin is too child-like to be afflicted with anything like the modern despair of Saruman and Denethor, but his carelessness has some of the same roots. When he refuses to respect what he learns from Gandalf and the elves, he shows a disinterest in the values that underlie Tolkien's most successful heroes. His failing is that he cannot be serious enough. At one level he knows he is part of a Quest that will determine whether the world will survive. At another, he remains so light-hearted that he overlooks the context of that Quest. He loses his concentration at the worst possible moments, acting, in effect, as if he has no restraints other than his physical weakness. He does what he wants, when he wants, and comes across as if he is choosing to reject the wisdom that has come to him. In that way, he is a classic example of the class clown. He isn't trying to be malicious with his mischief; he is simply not mature enough to stay focused throughout the course of a serious adventure. If he had concentrated on where he was and what he was doing, he might have avoided some of the serious harm he causes.

In contrast, Sam, whose lower-class manners sometimes make him seem like a clod, studies and concentrates all of the time. He is the only member of the Fellowship who correctly guesses Frodo's plan to venture off alone, and he routinely insinuates himself into serious meetings, such as the Council of Elrond, where he has not been invited. The Gaffer boasts of him that when he was still a child he had learned everything that he could from Bilbo. As he says, "Crazy about stories of the old days he is, and he listens to all Mr. Bilbo's tales. Mr. Bilbo has learned him his letters—meaning no harm, mark you, and I hope no harm will come of it" (FR, p. 24). That is, Sam turns out to be an extraordinary scholar for someone born into an illiterate family. By studying with Bilbo, he learns about elves and the history of the First Age, and, with that knowledge, he manages to survive the Tower of Cirith Ungol. He knows that he should rely on Galadriel's phial and not the Ring to overcome the Watchers, and he knows to use the elvish word "Elbereth" as his secret password with Frodo. Using his limited book knowledge to its fullest, he overcomes one of Sauron's great barriers, saving himself, Frodo, and the Ring at the darkest hour of the Quest. He is even a Ring-bearer for a brief while, and he and Bilbo are the only ones who are clear enough in their thinking to give it away of their own accord.

Pippin does eventually reform, maturing to the point that he embraces some of Frodo's and Sam's strengths. As a member of the Guard in Gondor, he takes his duties very seriously and so has a role in saving Faramir's life, and later he is a key leader in rescuing the Shire from Saruman's vengeful depredations. Even more strikingly, Tolkien tells us in the Prologue to the story that Pippin becomes one of the great librarians of Middle-earth after the War of the Ring (FR, pp. 16–17). Under his guidance, the Took family mansion gathers many of the most important manuscripts of the age, and Pippin himself brings a complete copy of Bilbo and Frodo's history of the War of the Ring to Gondor where it enters into the main history of Middle-earth. It's an extreme transformation—in essence he goes from Bart Simpson to Ben Stein—but it underscores the degree to which Tolkien insists that being heroic ties into being scholarly. With the coming of the Fourth Age, the golden era that Aragorn ushers in with his return as the King, many of the characters find that they can put away their weapons and begin to study simply for the sake of study. Pippin, returned from his adventures and mature at last, finds his eventual calling as an important hobbit leader and as a thoughtful scholar himself.

Escape to Middle-earth

If remembering the great tradition of the elves and Númenor makes it possible for Tolkien's heroes to escape one crisis or another, remembering—or discovering—that tradition offers his readers a different kind of escape. Twenty-first-century readers may not find themselves confronting Shelob or orc-hosts, but we do wrestle with a variation of the despair that claims Saruman and Denethor. It may be easier today than at any time in history for us to get distracted. At a trivial level, ask yourself how often you've watched television or surfed the net instead of doing something more substantial. More seriously, think about the ways in which you find your motivation sapped by the barrage of images and ideas that come at you from media of every sort. It is hard to stay focused, and the result for many people is a sense of emptiness, a sense of unfulfillment that takes a step toward full-blown despair. As Bruce Springsteen sings, "There's 57 channels and nothin' on." For readers of *The Lord of the Rings*, though, that isn't so. It offers the fantasy that there are real truths and real things to believe in. We may be doing little more than sitting around reading a stack of paperbacks with cheesy covers, but it *feels* as if we are discovering a greater purpose for our life.

As Marshall Berman understands modernism, there is no way to escape from it. In his view, even if we reject the negative sense that the world we have known is melting, we find ourselves overwhelmed by the opportunities of the contemporary world. That is, he sees modernism as offering the perpetual sense that we can create endlessly new things. As Berman puts it, "To be modern is to find ourselves in an environment that promises us adventure, power, joy, growth, transformation of ourselves and the world—and, at the same time, that threatens to destroy everything we have, everything we know, everything we are."[2] In other words, the modern world promises great power, but it offers no framework within which to exercise it. It holds out the inspiring hope that we can build new things, but it also offers the evidence that nothing lasts, that nothing is intrinsically good. Modernism is beguiling; it attracts us with promises of every variety and shape, but it also betrays us. In the modern world, whatever success we have is ultimately a prelude to disappointment and perhaps even despair.

In the face of that notion, Tolkien offers his Middle-earth as a fantasy of anti-modernism. Unlike Berman, he imagines a way in which it is possible to create change for the good without relying on power that we cannot control. In that light, the Ring itself is a kind of modernism. The characters who most clearly despair are the very ones who cannot imagine escaping its power. They succumb to evil because they dream of using evil's power to accomplish the good. In contrast, the ones who "pass the test" of the Ring, the ones who are able to go without using it, manage to escape from what Tolkien presents as a false dilemma. Frodo, Aragorn, and Gandalf defeat Sauron by making him irrelevant, by finding a way of making him impotent rather than confronting him directly. As a metaphor, that suggests Tolkien's fantasy toward modernism. The Ring holds out the false hope of power that people can use to remake the world. Readers can escape the dilemma of modernism, as Berman characterizes it, in the same way that Tolkien's heroes can: by turning to a mythical past and finding themselves in a history that keeps unfolding.

Some critics fault Tolkien for rejecting much of the substantial philosophy of his own era. They see *him* as the one who

---

[2] *All that is Solid Melts into Air*, p. 15.

takes the easy way out, and they accuse him of rejecting ideas that he has not fully considered. One of the most dramatic of those critics is Catharine R. Stimpson, who declared in her 1969 study, "Tolkien is bogus: bogus, prolix, and sentimental. His popularization of the past is a comic strip for grown-ups . . . to those who have studied over the ambiguous texts of twentieth-century literature in the classroom, he offers a digest of modern despair: *The Waste Land*, with notes, without tears."[3] In her view, Tolkien rejects the modern, both as it exists in the real world and as an artistic approach, without first wrestling with it. She sees him ignoring the challenge that modernism throws before us all, the challenge of finding our own truth in a world where there is no capital 'T' truth available. She perceives him as offering an impossibly simple answer. She proposes that he glamorizes many of the elements that our contemporary world has appropriately discarded: hereditary kingship, a stubborn faith that supernatural powers will resolve human crises, and a sense that the darker and shorter peoples of the South are generally pagan evil-doers. Stimpson regards *The Lord of the Rings* as a fad—although it is now more popular than ever, more than a generation after she made her claim—and she cannot imagine that future audiences will turn to Tolkien for any kind of inspiration.

To be fair, though, Tolkien wanted his stories to serve as an imaginary history for the modern world. As the appendices to *The Return of the King* make clear, he understood his Middle-earth as our earth at a much earlier time. With the end of the War of the Rings, Aragorn ushers in a new golden age, but it is only a temporary one. His descendents gradually lose the nobility that they inherit from him and, as ages pass and people forget the glory that was the kingdom of Aragorn, lesser humans come to power and forget the "Truth" that was the secret weapon for the heroes of the War of the Rings. In other words, *The Lord of the Rings* is, in part, a history of how modern discontent came to be. As Tolkien puts it in a letter about why he abandoned the only story he sets in the Fourth Age, adventure is very different when it begins and ends with decisions that humans make. He started the story but stopped, explaining, "I

---

[3] *J.R.R. Tolkien* (New York: Columbia University Press, 1969), p. 43.

could have written a 'thriller' about the plot and its discovery and overthrow—but it would be just that. Not worth doing" (L, p. 344). Story functions differently for him when there are no superhuman evils remaining. What evil there is, apparently an "orc-cult" of young boys who try to revive interest in the now extinct orcs, comes from humans, and it falls to humans to wipe it out. There are great truths and great powers over the Sea, but they no longer act in visible and defined ways. The world is different, sometimes thrilling still, but it is somehow diminished, changed so that we can see that it really is our own world.

In the end, Tolkien seems to explore a middle ground in his flight from contemporary crises back to his imagined origins for them. He does not address the twentieth-century conditions that caused modern ideas to have such widespread acceptance. Instead, he invents a crisis for Middle-earth that forces his characters to confront some of the same intellectual challenges as his readers. His characters have to make some of the same difficult decisions that we do about what to believe, but they have the good fortune to live in a world where there is a right answer. Their crises seem familiar, but their triumphs and successes can never be anything more than fantasies to the rest of us. One reason *The Lord of the Rings* works for so many contemporary readers is that it provides a world in which we can glimpse an authentic and powerful truth, one that we know is correct even though great powers of evil and error threaten to overwhelm it. His heroes seem like authentic heroes because doubt and despair—the great threats of the modern world—are legitimate enough threats that they claim would-be heroes such as Saruman and Denethor.

Tolkien may have little to tell us about what modernism is, but he does provide one key insight into how it works. He knows that, in a world of ambiguity, his readers crave certainty. He himself is saddened to find that the intellectual and cultural traditions he prizes seem as if they are fading away or under attack. In the world that he invents, such traditions are better than our own because they are the Platonic originals of the ones we know in our own lives. His gods send out angels, such as Gandalf, whom we can touch and with whom we can talk. His messiahs really do return to establish their kingdoms on earth. Tolkien acknowledges that he is creating a fiction, something that he hopes will entertain his readers, but something that he hopes as well will give them a place of temporary retreat from the modern world. The same wisdom that his heroes use to escape from the evils of Middle-earth serves as a story that lets his contemporary readers escape, briefly, from the challenge of the modern. Middle-earth has enough landmarks to tell us that it will one day develop into our own, but it remains more magical. In it, Tolkien imagines what it would be like if we could know what was good and right without having any doubts, and yet he still presents the good as threatened by evils that seem dimly familiar to our own. Through his works, he offers us the fantasy of a world heading toward modernism but not quite there yet, a place where we still have the power to reject what threatens to overwhelm us.

12

Tolkien's Green Time: Environmental Themes in *The Lord of the Rings*

ANDREW LIGHT

I'm talking to my friend Julia who asks what I'm working on at the moment. Somewhat sheepishly I tell her that it's an essay on *The Lord of the Rings* for a book in a series that has included collections on *Seinfeld, The Simpsons, The Matrix*, and other bits of popular culture. I'm somewhat embarrassed because she's a serious art historian and I worry that she'll mistakenly think I'm dabbling in cultural studies.

Her response, however, surprises me: "Tolkien is wonderful!" she says. "Seriously, I read *The Lord of the Rings* twice as a kid and his writing made a huge impression on me. For years I forbade my brother from reading it because I wanted to have this world all for myself." For many people like Julia, Middle-earth is a world of importance to them, not simply a fictional realm; it's a safe haven of sorts that they visit over and over again to find re-enchantment and renewal.

But Julia and I both agree that my assigned task, to write a chapter on the environmental elements in *The Lord of the Rings*, is a daunting one. Isn't the entire series about the environment, or nature, and aren't all the characters in the novel representations of some part of nature? Scholars such as Patrick Curry have argued that Tolkien's works are thoroughly infused with a strong environmentalist message.[1] Curry goes so far as to claim that

---

[1] Patrick Curry, *Defending Middle-earth* (London: HarperCollins, 1998).

The Lord of the Rings served as a kind of clandestine environmental manifesto that was later most appreciated during the rise of the radical environmental movement in the late 1960s and early 1970s. Tolkien himself, who disliked allegory, would have demurred if offered such a characterization of his own work. When faced with comparisons between the plot of *The Lord of the Rings* and the events of World War II, he insisted that there was no intended connection to any contemporary events.

Yet it is impossible to ignore the strong environmental themes in the book, especially in the devastations wrought by Sauron and Saruman, keepers of the fictional two towers. For example, at the end of the cycle when the hobbits return to the Shire to find that Saruman has transformed their pastoral Eden into a nineteenth-century industrial wasteland (a kind of Middle-earth version of turn-of-the-century Manchester or Pittsburgh), don't we get a clear critique of the ravages of industrialism pulling apart the traditional connections between people and the land? Couldn't this be used as a launching pad for a discussion of sustainable development or globalization today and the struggle to prevent what happened in the industrialized North from happening in the rural South?

Probably. But it is a virtue when appreciating any text to try to respect the unique integrity of a work and what it does differently from other texts. Discussing this issue with Julia I hear myself saying that if I wanted to write something about the representation of struggles for sustainable development in novels or films I wouldn't choose Tolkien as my focus. The reason is not because we can't distill such a message from *The Lord of the Rings* but because such a claim seems more peripheral to the power of these texts to create a world where other more unique things are happening. This is not to pander to Tolkien's wishes on how he should be read, but to try to do justice to the very real magic that these works have played in people's lives.

This chapter, then, will not go so far as a reading like Curry's but will still highlight one important aspect of the environmental associations to be found in these works: the representation of a kind of geologic or naturally scaled time in *The Lord of the Rings*. Though not literally a representation of geological time as we know it (which measures the billions of years of existence of the earth from its primordial birth to the present through the geologic record), *The Lord of the Rings* nevertheless embodies a time scale attuned more to the natural world and upon which the main drama of the cycle of the story is played out. Especially through the characters of Tom Bombadil and the ents, *The Lord of the Rings* makes comprehensible a sense of the past through which "nature" sets the context for events in the present. From this long perspective, which I will call "green time," Tolkien helps us understand the importance of nature as the foreground and background of all events of any significance to us, while at the same time encouraging our responsibility for it. Once we recognize this part of the text we may be in a better position to appreciate how it can help us to overcome our current environmental problems, whether those solutions were intended by Tolkien or not.

Who Stands for What?

On a first pass it is tempting to take the various peoples of Middle-earth, especially the nonhuman ones, as stand-ins for various parts of nature. According to such a view, appreciation of those peoples should in turn help us to appreciate different parts of the natural world. We might see elves as embodying the forest, dwarves the mountains, and hobbits the domesticated countryside. After all, each of these peoples almost exclusively occupies these places. While they will venture between these locations in the course of the story, they appear to feel truly at home only in their own environment.

Gimli the dwarf, for example, is the only one in the Fellowship who seems to relish the idea of taking a route through the Mines of Moria underneath the Misty Mountains. While this is partly because he hopes to find his relative Balin still holding the dwarf fortress there, he also seems the only one truly unbothered about being underground. Later, in *The Return of the King*, we are given a description of the passing of Aragorn, Legolas, Gimli, and others underground through the Paths of the Dead from the perspective of Gimli. This is done to impart to us how unusual it was for him to be so disturbed by a place under a mountain and so magnify how terrifying it must have been for the rest of the party.

Humans, in contrast, are interlopers in Middle-earth, as too many environmentalists see them today in our world, living in all of these environments as well but not intimately connected with them in the same way as the elves, dwarves, or hobbits seem to be. We know, too, that after the end of the Third Age, which concludes with the War of the Ring, the Fourth Age will see humans as the dominant people in Middle-earth, much as they are now the dominant species on our own planet. With the passing into memory of the other peoples of Middle-earth we have a possible allusion to the evolution of humans from only one among equals of other species in our prehistoric past to our current state as undisputed master of all.

But a view connecting Tolkien's peoples to their environments confronts a significant hurdle: the existence throughout the narrative of other characters and peoples who are more direct extensions of parts of the natural world itself. Take the example of the forests. Throughout *The Lord of the Rings*, as well as in *The Hobbit*, the elves are strongly associated with the forests of Middle-earth, especially Mirkwood, home of Legolas's kin, and Lórien, where Galadriel and Celeborn dwell. There is a constant fascination with forests, evinced for example by Legolas's desire to see Fangorn, the mysterious wood near Isengard. Just as with Gimli and Moria, Legolas is the only one of the Fellowship who seems genuinely interested in visiting Fangorn, another place with a bad reputation. While it is true that elves live in other places as well, there is nonetheless a temptation to see them as more closely connected with this environment than the others they inhabit.

A bigger problem with such an association however is that Fangorn, at least, is home to another people entirely. In *The Two Towers* we are introduced to the ents, another of the "free peoples" of Middle-earth by their own reckoning. They are first encountered by Merry and Pippin after their escape from the Uruk-hai, the powerful subspecies of orcs bred by Saruman. Merry and Pippin have escaped by hiding in Fangorn and there meet Treebeard, leader of the ents, who goes on to play a critical role in the overthrow of Saruman.

Upon meeting Merry and Pippin, Treebeard is confused. He cannot figure out what sort of thing they are since he has never encountered one of their kind. When they tell him they are hobbits, Treebeard realizes that he must amend the "old lists" which each ent commits to memory. The lists include descriptions of other peoples of Middle-earth such as the elves, described as the "eldest of all" peoples. Indeed, it is the elves, we are told, who awakened the ents and trees in the early days of Middle-earth. "The Elves cured us of dumbness," according to Treebeard, and even though we know that the ents were not literally created by the elves, in some sense they helped to animate them (TT, p. 75). What does Treebeard mean by this? Apparently that the elves helped to nurture in the ents a capacity for reason and eventually for speech. But the ents were not bred by the elves in the same way that "the Dark Power of the North" originally bred the orcs (RK, p. 457). The elves enlightened, if you will, part of the raw material of the earth that was there before them. Though the ents are not trees themselves, we know from Treebeard they are very close to them. Treebeard says that many of his kinsmen were barely moving at all now, essentially becoming trees, and perhaps in some sense returning to their primordial state. The ents are represented as thinking much as one would imagine trees would think—slowly and methodically and unhurriedly—and they act essentially as anthropomorphized trees.

If we were to argue that the elves personify the forests of Middle-earth, for something along the lines of the reasons offered earlier, we would be confronted with a hurdle in explaining the ents. Do they also stand for the forests along with the elves? And if so, who stands for the forests more? Treebeard certainly has an opinion, telling Merry and Pippin that "nobody cares for the woods as I care for them, not even Elves nowadays" (TT, p. 75). But what he and the other ents do is not simply care for the forest as much as they serve as a narrative device that allows part of nature to speak for itself. In the end it is the ents, not the elves, who best represent the forests. The same could be said for the relationship between the mountains and the dwarves even though the latter do not have as clear a competitor as the ents for representation of one of their preferred environments. Though at home in underground places, the dwarves share these places with other races as well and do not personify them as such. In this sense no one stands for anything in Middle-earth, but the place itself is fully animated so that it stands for itself, and even speaks for itself at times.

Green Time

But if parts of Middle-earth stand and speak for themselves, what makes such representations of natural entities and places different from other anthropomorphic representations in other forms of literature? One significant difference is that the ents, Tom Bombadil, and other primordial inhabitants of Middle-earth either implicitly or explicitly acknowledge a different time scale than the other peoples and characters in the story. If what they offer is not literally a different time scale (for remember that the elves are immortal and certainly exist in a different temporal perspective than humans), then at least it is a time scale more attuned to the rhythms of the natural world.[2] Most striking, in terms of the main events of the story, we can see this point in how this set of characters appears largely indifferent to the outcome of the War of the Ring. Though drawn into one side or another at times, most often their participation in the War is more a matter of circumstance than anything else.[3] Though they can be harmed by the other peoples of Middle-earth, they are largely indifferent to the events of the story, just as the earth is to us.

In *The Fellowship of the Ring* we find this perspective expressed most clearly in the character of Tom Bombadil. Tom is first encountered by the four hobbits on their journey from the Shire to Rivendell. Along the way, the party travels through the mysterious Old Forest. As we learn later, this is just a small frac-

---

[2] Some may see the immortality of the elves as a counterexample to the long-temporal perspective that I am attributing to green time. If the elves are immortal, why are they not green and hence indifferent to the affairs of humans? But a clear difference is that the elves are the historical enemies of Sauron (and the earlier manifestations of evil that preceded him) and so do take an interest in the affairs of men, rather than only of nature or something else, at least for the reason of overthrowing their enemy. The relationship between elves and humans is actually unique and quite intimate. As Tolkien tells us, the elves stand for the perfected capacities of humans to one degree or another. According to Tolkien, "The Elves represent . . . the artistic, aesthetic, and purely scientific aspects of the Humane Nature raised to a higher level than is actually seen in Men" (L, p. 236).

[3] Peter Jackson gives the elves a more direct role in determining the outcome of the War by having them come to Rohan's rescue at Helm's Deep in the movie version of *The Two Towers*.

tion of a once tremendous forest described by Elrond as a place where "a squirrel could go from tree to tree from what is now the Shire to Dunland west of Isengard" (FR, p. 297). There they fall under the spell of Old Man Willow, an ancient, conscious tree that tries to devour Merry and Pippin by trapping them in its trunk. Just in the nick of time Tom happens by and sings a song that compels the tree to free the hobbits. Tom invites the four to his nearby house on the edge of the forest and the Barrow-downs where he lives with his lady, Goldberry, the "river daughter." The hobbits experience the stay with Tom and Goldberry in mystical and magical terms, reveling in a kind of trance of natural purity, wanting for nothing and for a time fearing nothing. When the hobbits ask Goldberry who Tom is, she answers first simply that "He is," and then adds, "He is the Master of wood, water, and hill" (FR, p. 140). This is not to say that he is master over the things themselves ("the trees and the grasses and all things growing or living in the land belong each to them"), but that he thoroughly understands them. Part of the reason is that, as he explains, he is "eldest . . . here before the river and the trees; Tom remembers the first raindrop and the first acorn" (FR, p. 148).

Unfortunately, Tom remains wrapped in mystery, and among Tolkien scholars and die-hard fans, a matter of some debate. The most common interpretation of this character is that Tom is some kind of anomalous nature spirit, different from everything else in the book, but accounting for his understanding and power over the natural world. Some however claim that he is a Maia (a kind of powerful immortal spirit, such as Gandalf or Sauron), or even one of the Valar, the archangelic guardians of the world.[4] In a letter, Tolkien explains that Tom represents "a particular embodying of pure (real) natural science: the spirit that desires knowledge of other things, their history and nature, because they are 'other' and . . . entirely unconcerned with 'doing' . . ." (L, p. 192; italics omitted). Tom could certainly be lots of things and still embody this ethos of investigation, either as an independent nature spirit or as a god.

---

[4] See Eugene Hargrove, "Who is Tom Bombadil?" at http://www.cas.unt.edu/ ~hargrove/bombadil.html. Hargrove makes a strong case that Tom is the Valar Aule and that Goldberry is Yavanna.

Regardless of what or who Tom is, what is important to us here is that he is represented as essentially unconcerned with the events of the War of the Ring. At the Council of Elrond, when it is debated what to do with the Ring, a suggestion is made that it be given to Tom. Frodo had told the Council that when he gave the Ring to Tom he was able to control it (making it temporarily disappear) and that moreover he could see Frodo when the latter put on the Ring and was invisible to everyone else. Perhaps Tom could keep the Ring safe from Sauron. Gandalf however argues against the idea, saying that it is not so much that Tom has power over the Ring but that "the Ring has no power over him." Even if Tom were persuaded to keep the Ring, "he would not understand the need. And if he were given the Ring, he would soon forget it, or most likely throw it away. Such things have no hold on his mind. He would be a most unsafe guardian; and that alone is answer enough" (FR, p. 298).

Whether angel, god, or spirit, Tom is attuned to the natural world above all things. This is his chief concern, and no matter the explanation, he has been in Middle-earth since its creation watching all things slowly evolve, take root, and grow. In part this may be why Tom would be unconcerned with the Ring, since the struggle over it happens at only one snap-shot in time and is important mainly to the self-conscious peoples of Middle-earth rather than to the earth itself. Though one of the elves at the Council of Elrond does point out that both Tom and the earth will suffer if Sauron wins, since he can "torture and destroy the very hills" (FR, p. 298), still, we are told that Tom would fall last of all, and then "Night will come."

But if this were true wouldn't Tom be concerned with the victory of Sauron and so want to help the Council? Such an outcome for Middle-earth sounds like the hypothetical future of our own world where the planet is made uninhabitable for any life forms by a nuclear holocaust. But just as we should be skeptical of any claim that the earth itself would be concerned in any coherent sense with such a turn of events, Tom as the embodiment of the natural world in some form is also believed to be indifferent. Part of the explanation for Tom's indifference may be temporal. Time for him is green; it is bound with the long-rhythms of nature as they come and go, and not with the relatively brief experiences of the self-conscious beings (and especially mortals) of the planet. In addition, this perspective is not only temporally different but green also in terms of its different perspective. It is more "collective" than "individual." From Tom's perspective, attuned to natural cycles, the welfare of individuals does not matter as much as the sustainability of the continuing and evolving processes of nature. Tolkien saw something of this in his reflections on Tom's relationship to the Ring. From Tom's perspective we see that "The power of the Ring over all concerned . . . is not the whole picture, even of the then state and content of that part of the Universe" (L, p. 192). As I will point out below, however, this does not imply that we should be unconcerned with the fate of our own planet because it is unconcerned with us, just as it is not the case that the free peoples of Middle-earth should be indifferent to the destruction of their own world.

We see a similar kind of indifference to short-term affairs, as well as a kind of collective perspective on the world with the ents. For example, shortly after the battle of Helm's Deep, as Gandalf leads the victorious men of Rohan through the mysterious wood that had appeared at the end of the battle, a group of ents are seen walking swiftly towards them. Surprised, "The riders cried aloud in wonder, and some set their hands upon their sword-hilts" (TT, p. 168). Gandalf calms the company, saying, "You need no weapons. These are but herdsmen. They are not enemy, indeed they are not concerned with us at all." What does Gandalf mean by this? Arguably that the ents are unconcerned with the riders in part because to them the men of the company are only fleeting figures who will come and go on the larger timeline of the world, eventually passing into oblivion, no matter what they do.

The perspective of the ents is again quite different from the other characters, and it is not just their long individual lives that seems to differentiate them. The ents, as the forest given the power of speech and human-like locomotion, see the affairs of men in much the same way as we might imagine how our own forests might view our affairs if they were made conscious. But even more peculiar is that their perspective appears to be more collective than individual. While there is not much direct evidence for this suggestion in the text, it is a reasonable inference given how closely connected the ents are to the forest. While they must be individuated in order to be characters that we can more effectively empathize with, their orientation is driven by their intimate collective identity with the forest. We can learn the personality of a particular ent, such as Treebeard, but they do not appear to exist as independent from each other or independent from the forests that they protect. The ents in the scene just mentioned do not notice the riders of Rohan but they do take care to notice what each individual tree is doing.

This perspective makes sense given the kind of things they are supposed to be. Particular trees live and die, just as individual humans live and die, but a forest goes on as a collective ecosystem and does not exist as a single tree. So too, it seems, with the ents. The temporal perspective they have is thus most likely not one confined to their particular life-span, but is more akin to what we would imagine to be the perspective of a whole forest as it continues from a past into a future with different individual entities coming into being and passing away as part of a larger life cycle. When a tree dies in a healthy forest it does not simply pass away but becomes nourishment for both flora and fauna in a forest that regenerates into yet more forest continuing on into the future. And the same, we can assume, may be true of the ents, or, at the very least, we can imagine that this is how they see themselves in relationship to the larger ecosystem of which they are a part. As Treebeard puts it, "We are made of the bones of the earth" (TT, p. 91). In contrast we humans (either here or in Middle-earth) can more easily abstract ourselves away from the ecosystems which nourish us and reshape our environment to suit our particular needs. The ents however are so intimately connected to their environment that they cannot live outside of it. Indeed, the population of ents is said to have diminished as the forest has dwindled.

There is however another reason why the ents are diminishing which may also help make the case for their collective identity as tied to the forests. Treebeard tells us that the ents are also in decline because they have lost their mates, the "entwives." The entwives are represented as beings that both nurture and personify domesticated agricultural environments in a similar way to the relationship between the ents and the forests. As Treebeard tells the story to Merry and Pippin, the entwives evidently became so caught up in their agricultural environments that they abandoned the forests entirely and the ents eventually lost touch with them. While this may be evidence that the entwives did not care for the future of their overall species, it instead points to the very different perspective taken by these characters in their intimate relationship with their environments. The ents and the entwives grow distant from each other because they are drawn toward more involvement with the environments that they personify, or perhaps grew out of. In this sense they do not really act as one species at all—with a species interest in procreation and reproduction—but rather two different species concerned with the flourishing of two different environments. It is a strange tale, and one of the mysteries of the book as Tolkien saw it, himself admitting that he did not know for certain what had become of the entwives (L, pp. 179, 419). The situation that is represented, however, is one of a kind of mutual loss. The ents must have been as preoccupied with the rhythms and time scale of the forests as the entwives were with their environments in order to have let them stray so far and disappear. But it is evidence of a close collective identity between the ents and the forests, one that is even closer than that to beings of their own kind.

This perspective of the ents again points to a kind of representation of the indifference of nature. While the temporal view of the ents again is not that of billions of years of geologic time, it is at the very least a green time from the perspective of the long history of nature that pre-exists humanity in Middle-earth and which, it is assumed, will continue after humans are gone. Though the ents are brought into the War of the Ring, this occurs mainly because Saruman and the orcs have destroyed part of Treebeard's forest. Without Saruman's sins against the forest it is not clear the ents would have become involved in the War at all.

Just as the philosopher Ludwig Wittgenstein said, "If a lion could talk we could not understand it," no doubt if a forest or ecosystem could talk we wouldn't understand it either. Its perspective would be too foreign to us. But when we anthropomorphize a natural entity it is not simply to imagine what a thing would say if given a voice, but also to say something about how we can look at the world differently from our own limited perspective. In part, Tolkien's representation of a green time in the experience of ents and Tom Bombadil does just this: it encourages us to take a longer view of our own history and our relationship to the other living things with which we share the earth.

Into the Future

With the benefit of the sciences of geology and cosmology we know that our earth was in existence for billions of years prior to the appearance of humans on the planet. The evocative metaphors invented by geologists and evolutionary biologists to represent this deeper sense of time are familiar to most of us: we humans are relative newcomers on the scene, here in only the last few seconds of the earth's history as represented by a twenty-four-hour clock. Assuming that the extinction of all life on earth does not happen at the same time as the end of our own species, then life will go on without us for billions of years after we are gone. Many like myself are certain that the universe itself will go on for billions of years after the earth is destroyed by the inevitable death of the Sun.

It's extremely difficult to imagine ourselves in relation to this deeper time and history, even if we consider only the history of life on earth. Failure to consider the consequences of our own actions in relation to this longer time span is therefore quite understandable. But if we could take on even a little of that perspective, it would help us to acquire the humility to recognize that we are part of a story much longer and grander than ourselves.

I said above that part of the power of Tolkien's representation of green time was that it showed the basic indifference of nature to even the most momentous events in the book, and by extension of our own brief existence. This indifference results partly from the long time spans of the green-time characters and partly from their ecosystemic or collective perspectives. Still, the representation of this form of green time in *The Lord of the Rings* does not ultimately encourage the principal characters to become indifferent to what happens to the natural world. When nature becomes personified it does fight back in the story, and the forces allied with the Fellowship mourn the loss of parts of the natural world spoiled by Sauron and Saruman and want to defend it too. The different perspective of the green-time characters in *The Lord of the Rings* is something that the others must engage with and which they come to respect. They can then count among their ultimate victories not only protecting their respective peoples and places but also the personified earth itself. If we were to take a lesson from these themes then I think it would be that we should also try to similarly empathize with the nature of our own planet whenever possible and to defend it when it needs defending. The indifference of the green-time characters in these works should not be taken as a reason to be indifferent to nature. Rather, it should help us to feel all the more awe-struck by the more ancient and in some ways more complex forms of life with which we share our world.

Can such a view help us? It could. Daily we are confronted with global environmental problems that challenge our ability to understand their long-term implications and our part in either causing or mitigating them. Daily we are given reasons not to worry about these problems or, more commonly, confronted with trade-offs that require us to set them aside. Global warming is a good example. Fifteen years ago there was clear disagreement in the scientific community about global warming. Today there is near-unanimity that the planet is heating up and that the consequences could be dire, especially for poorer countries in the Southern hemisphere.

The worst consequences of global warming however are far off in time and space, most likely only harming those places that cannot retool their economies in the future to respond adequately to such a change. How do we encourage people to become concerned about such remote harms they are causing? What will motivate people now to set aside short-term economic gains through continued use of technologies that aggravate global warming in favor of long-term environmental sustainability? In part, it will involve taking a longer view of human welfare than we are accustomed to, one where we take responsibility for our actions that create consequences in the future for people and places we will never know. Such a perspective begins to approximate Tolkien's green time. Though it would be too much to suggest that we think like a forest (though many environmentalists have said things very similar to this), *The Lord of the Rings* at least helps us to imagine what it is to care for things as a process and into a future that may or may not include our species. It is a challenge for us to live our lives without only considering the moments of our own lifetime as always the most important.

Reading Tolkien is surely no panacea for our environmental ills. Still, there is a recognizable call here for us to appreciate the longer perspective of other things in the world and to take responsibility for our actions given our dominant position on our planet. This is something Tolkien understood and represents in the book by means of the diminishment of the non-human peoples of Middle-earth. As the War of the Ring comes to an end and the Fourth Age begins, the future of humanity is uncertain. At one point, Legolas and Gimli become philosophical about this issue:

"It is ever so with the things that Men begin: there is a frost in Spring, or a blight in Summer, and they fail of their promise."

"Yet seldom do they fail of their seed," said Legolas. "And that will lie in the dust and rot to spring up again in times and places unlooked-for. The deeds of Men will outlast us, Gimli."

"And yet come to naught in the end but might-have-beens, I guess," said the Dwarf.

"To that the Elves know not the answer," said Legolas. (RK, p. 153)

Our future is uncertain. But Tolkien is an entertaining and engaging guide for us to think about that future. When those like my friend Julia go back to Middle-earth, they enter into a landscape populated by very different kinds of relationships than are possible in our own world, though not ones that we cannot imagine ourselves taking part in. In Middle-earth we can be put in relationships with the natural world where we come to take responsibility for it because it is so wonderfully different from ourselves. This seems a lesson we can take back to our own world and put to good use.[5]

---

[5] My thanks to Eric Katz, Meg Kilvington, and especially Julia Voss for helpful advice on this chapter.

PART V

Ends and Endings

13

Providence and the Dramatic Unity of *The Lord of the Rings*

THOMAS HIBBS

At the very end of the Quest in *The Lord of the Rings*, Frodo and Sam reflect on the completion of their task. The Ring has been destroyed in the Cracks of Doom and Frodo, after his battle with Gollum, is now safe, except for the finger Gollum bit off in his ferocious desire to seize the Ring. A joyful and grateful Sam remains angry with Gollum, until Frodo recalls Gandalf's premonition that "even Gollum may have something yet to do." He then explains to Sam, "But for him . . . I could not have destroyed the Ring. The Quest would have been in vain, even at the bitter end" (RK, p. 241). Frodo is referring to his own unwillingness at the crucial moment to part with the Ring; only Gollum's theft of the Ring and his accidental fall into the Cracks of Doom with the Ring accomplished the task with which Frodo, the Ring-bearer, had been entrusted.

It seems then that good triumphs in Tolkien's fictional world not only over the power and will of the evil characters but even against the momentary wishes of those most trusted to defend the good. In this and other ways, Tolkien manages to suggest the working of a higher, benevolent power, a providential orchestration of events. Unlike Sauron, whose attempt to see and control all is obvious to those involved in the cosmic war between good and evil, the hand of providence is neither clear nor compelling. Indeed, Tolkien repeatedly suggests that the fate, destiny, or providential design of things is not available to human beings in advance of events. How then can we detect its presence?

We must be careful here about what sort of account of providence to expect from *The Lord of the Rings*. This is a novel or epic, not a philosophical treatise or even a philosophical dialogue. Even in terms of drama, we will find very little direct evidence of the providential power at work in Middle-earth. What we find are suggestions, clues, and hints that enliven and deepen our appreciation of the mysterious way in which all things seem to work together for the good.

From the vantage point of the characters in *The Lord of the Rings* and the readers of the books, providence first appears under the guise of chance, of seemingly fortuitous events that turn the tide for good and against evil. These events, which often bring good out of intended evil, occur contrary to the will or at least outside of the intention of those who cause them. But providence is more than simply one or more fortuitous events; it involves the orchestration of an entire sequence of events; whatever glimmer we have of the workings of providence can generally be seen only in hindsight, the discernment of an order or intelligibility in what initially appeared to be merely a sequence of chance events.

Since Gollum's role in the drama of the Ring illustrates all of these, we shall begin with a brief summary of Tolkien's depiction of him as an instrument of providence. Then we will turn to two difficulties or problems traditionally associated with providence: (a) the role of freedom and finite agency, and (b) the existence of evil. In each case, we will attend not so much to abstract philosophical arguments as to the way Tolkien offers a dramatic demonstration of the reality of human freedom and action and of the way patience and compassion is used to overcome evil.

Gollum As an Instrument of Providence

Early in the story, when Gandalf is explaining the history of the Ring to Frodo, he mentions that Gollum both hated and loved the Ring as he hated and loved himself. Frodo wonders why, if he hated the Ring, he did not simply get rid of it. Gandalf responds that Gollum "could not get rid of it. He had no will left in the matter. A Ring of Power looks after itself, Frodo. *It* may slip off treacherously, but its keeper never abandons it . . . It was not Gollum, Frodo, but the Ring itself that decided things.

The Ring left *him*" (FR, pp. 60–61). "What, just in time to meet Bilbo?" said Frodo. Gandalf comments that Bilbo's appearance at that precise moment, inadvertently putting his hand on the Ring in the dark "was the strangest event in the whole history of the Ring so far."

> "There was more than one power at work, Frodo. The Ring was trying to get back to its master . . . it abandoned Gollum. Only to be picked up by the most unlikely person imaginable: Bilbo from the Shire! . . . I can put it no plainer than by saying that Bilbo was *meant* to find the Ring, and *not* by its maker. In which case you also were *meant* to have it. And that may be an encouraging thought."

"It is not," said Frodo, "Though I am not sure that I understand you" (FR, p. 61).

In this early exchange, we find the elements of Tolkien's dramatic depiction of providence. First, the role of chance; Bilbo did not enter the cave looking for the Ring, yet he ends up leaving with it. Second, at least according to Gandalf, the Ring itself left Gollum in an attempt to return to its master, but its will was thwarted by the chance arrival of Bilbo. This implies for Gandalf the workings of some other, perhaps higher, power, "beyond any design of the Ring-maker" (FR, p. 61). Third, what appears to be chance allows for the possibility that good may now be brought out of evil. Gandalf predicts that the malicious and deceptive Gollum may yet have an important role to play in the events unfolding. He observes that not even the wise know all ends. Thus, fourth, whether and precisely how things will turn out remains unclear until the end of the entire drama.

Later, in a chapter entitled, "The Taming of Sméagol," Gollum engages in a bloody battle with Sam, who is saved only by the timely and forceful intervention of Frodo. When Sam urges slaying Gollum, Frodo hears voices "out of the past." The voices remind him, "Many that live deserve death. And some that die deserve life. Can you give that to them? Then be not too eager to deal out death in the name of justice, fearing for your own safety. Even the wise cannot see all ends" (TT, p. 246). At this point, Gollum becomes their guide on an arduous trek that will enable them to fulfill their Quest in ways they could never have imagined.

Finally, in the dramatic ending of the Quest at Mount Doom, Gollum seems to pass beyond the bounds of hope. Yet, even here we should pause. We cannot be certain what Gollum would have done had he lived and remained in control of the Ring, especially once he became aware that Sauron was bearing down upon him with all his concentrated might. At this crucial point in the drama, Sam is separated in the darkness from Frodo and from Gollum. Suddenly he sees Frodo standing at the very Crack of Doom, speaking with a "voice clearer and more powerful" than he had ever heard before: "I have come," he said, "but I do not choose now to do what I came to do. I will not do this deed. The Ring is mine!" (RK, p. 239) As Frodo puts the Ring on and disappears, he becomes visible to the Dark Lord, who realizes how precarious is his power and turns his attention away from his armies to concentrate exclusively on Frodo. Sam is knocked down and briefly loses consciousness; when he awakes, he sees Gollum "fighting like a mad thing with an unseen foe" (RK, p. 240). Gollum eventually locates the Ring on Frodo's finger and bites it off, chanting wildly, "Precious." In his exultation, he loses his balance and falls into the Crack of Doom, effectively fulfilling the quest of the Ring-bearer. Gollum is, as Gandalf had predicted, an unwitting instrument of divine providence, but he manages to serve this role only because Frodo had earlier recalled Gandalf's words and taken to heart his plea for mercy and patience.

Freedom and Duty in a Providential Cosmos

The mysterious, incomprehensible designs of providence underscore the importance of human effort, a sense that, in spite of the apparent odds, one must press on to do one's duty in the fight against evil. Why? Finite creatures must take their bearings by what they can discern, by fulfilling the limited role assigned to them—a theme that pervades *The Lord of the Rings*. This requires a virtuous and prudential sense of what is within one's power, what falls under one's jurisdiction, and what does not. Concepts like duty and providence are often seen as limits to our freedom to make our own unique ethical choices. In Tolkien's world, however, doing one's duty is a free choice made by good beings in the fight against evil. The working of providence may initially be perceived as an external or miraculous intervention, say, for example, in the return of Gandalf. Ultimately, however, providence involves an ordering of the entire narrative; this is evident in and through the dramatic structure of *The Lord of the Rings*. Rather than undermining freedom, providence presupposes that finite creatures are real agents, responsible in various measures for their actions. Without this, there could be no drama.

These points are driven home after the death of Boromir and the splitting of the Fellowship. Aragorn tells his few remaining comrades, "my choices have all gone amiss . . . With [Frodo] lies the True Quest. Ours is but a small matter in the great deeds of this time" (TT, p. 19). This is a remarkable expression of humility on the part of Aragorn, an expression that is rendered all the more striking by its contrast to the hubris of Boromir. Humility here is not a matter of groveling subservience; instead, it has to do with acknowledging one's part within a larger whole, with discovering and filling one's role in a cosmic battle between good and evil. Of course, Boromir manages in his repentance to die well, an alteration that underscores the contingency of human choice, the mysterious presence of freedom even in those whose characters seem to have been formed in a certain determinate way.

The notion of submission to one's proper part within the whole means that one's ultimate destiny is not in one's own hands. It means that the assertion of human autonomy or the celebration of raw will is a dangerous illusion. In Gandalf's confrontation with the despairing Denethor, the latter asserts that against the Power that now rises there can be no victory. Gandalf does not dispute the claim (indeed, he will soon quote Denethor's claim to others), but he urges Denethor not to imitate the "heathen Kings," who slew themselves in "pride and despair" (RK, p. 129). Boasting of his own autonomous control over himself, Denethor asserts that his will is to rule his "own end" (RK, p. 131). The use of "end" here by Denethor calls to mind Gandalf's earlier assertion that not even the wise can see all "ends" (FR, p. 65). After Denethor's death, the Captains of the West hold a counsel to decide what path to take. Gandalf reiterates Denethor's claim that the Power they oppose cannot be defeated directly. It is "not our part," he adds, "to master all the tides of the world, but to do what is in us for the succour of those years wherein we are set, uprooting the evil in the fields that we know, so that those who live after may have clean earth to till. What weather they shall have is not ours to rule" (RK, p. 160).

Gandalf explains that while we can't always control life's storms, we can control how we react to the inclement weather. Though we cannot always choose our duties, we can freely decide whether we are willing to accept those duties. Denethor freely chooses not to carry out his duty to Gondor. In the eighteenth century, German philosopher Immanuel Kant argued that freedom and duty are not opposites and that duty must be obeyed even when doing so fails to bring happiness. A rational being freely compels himself to obey universal laws. For Kant, conformity to duty is the very expression of one's freedom, "and such a power can be found only in rational beings."[1]

Tolkien first shows us this interplay between freedom and duty in Frodo's decision to be the one who takes the Ring to Mordor. At the Council of Elrond when Bilbo asks who will take the Ring (in the movie version Bilbo is not present and it is Elrond who asks), Frodo feels the weight of his duty. "A great dread fell on him, as if he was awaiting the pronouncement of some doom that he had long foreseen and vainly hoped might after all never be spoken" (FR, p. 303). Frodo grudgingly accepts his duty to be the Ring-bearer. Although Elrond admits that he believes the task was "appointed" to Frodo, he allows the hobbit the freedom to choose this path for himself.

Still, there are important and instructive differences between Tolkien and Kant. Kant argues that the source of the moral law could not reside in nature or God or anything external to human reason itself. Any external source of the moral law would create heteronomy, the opposite of autonomy. Kant is an advocate of this opposition in part because he believes that the natural world is not a moral world; instead, the natural world is governed by the mechanistic laws of science and hence precludes freedom. Kant thus accepts what has come to be called the disenchantment of the natural world. For Tolkien, by contrast, the entirety of nature is not just enchanted but is permeated with

---

[1] *Groundwork of the Metaphysic of Morals*, translated by H.J. Paton (New York: Harper and Row, 1964), p. 95.

reason and a moral sense. For all his stress on freedom and duty, Tolkien does not operate with a Kantian dichotomy between autonomy and heteronomy; indeed, certain forms of autonomy signal the vice of pride. In place of Kant's isolated individual will, which in order to be free must turn from God, nature, and society, Tolkien gives us characters who can only understand themselves and their duties by seeing themselves as parts of larger wholes, as members of nations and races, as participants in alliances and friendships for the good, and ultimately as part of a natural cosmos.

When we freely accept our duties, we rarely know how the story will end. Providence may help us see our path, but it can never promise ease or peace. The finite intellect's limited apprehension of ends should teach us patience and determination in the endurance of suffering and deprivation.

A good example of this occurs in the scene in which Sam finds Frodo apparently killed by Shelob. "'What shall I do, what shall I do?'" he said. 'Did I come all this way with him for nothing?' And then he remembered his own voice speaking words that at the time he did not understand himself, at the beginning of their journey: *I have something to do before the end. I must see it through, sir, if you understand*" (TT, p. 385).

Still, he is caught in a conflict of duties, to stay with Frodo, or at least to bury him, to take his sword and the Ring and continue the Quest in Frodo's place, or to resist that out of cowardice or a temptation to supplant the rightful Ring-bearer. Sam comes close to despair, believing that even if he and Frodo accomplish their goal, they will perish near Mount Doom, "alone, houseless, foodless in the midst of a terrible desert. There could be no return" (RK, p. 225). Yet, in the face of despair, resolve grows in Sam.

> Sam's plain hobbit-face grew stern, almost grim, as the will hardened in him, and he felt through all his limbs a thrill, as if he was turning into some creature of stone and steel that neither despair nor weariness nor endless barren miles could subdue. (RK, p. 225)

A grim determination to press on in the performance of one's allotted role marks a peak of virtue or heroism, which is motivated no longer by the expectation of reward or even "return."

Kant believed that while doing one's moral duty did not always bring pleasure, it gave the rational being a certain level of dignity. As Denethor counsels at one point, "after hope" there remains only the "hardihood to die free" (RK, p. 82). Of course, so long as they are able to fulfill their duty and continue the fight, they continue in some sense to hope, to cling to the good that their virtue renders them incapable of denying.

Providence, Patience, and Endurance

The survival of hope in the face of the seemingly imminent victory of the enemy marks the endurance of good in the face of evil. Indeed, the language of a "cosmic battle between good and evil," which I have been using in this essay, can be terribly misleading. It invites a Manichean vision of two forces, roughly equal to one another, and suggests that one can neatly divide the adherents of darkness from the warriors of virtue.[2] The metaphysical underpinnings of such a view render divine providence questionable. As Augustine pointed out long ago, if evil is actually something, some independent power operating in the universe, then divine providence would be in doubt.[3] For, if that were the case, then some things would seem to elude providence.

The doctrine of providence seems to entail a classical metaphysics of good and evil, wherein evil is parasitic on the good and, contrary to appearances, has no independent existence. It is a privation, the absence of a good that ought to be present. Of course, writers like Augustine and Tolkien try to reconcile this teaching with the psychological experience of the seeming existence of evil. Augustine shows that in the sinner's departure from God, the fullness of being, he makes himself "a land of want."[4]

For Tolkien, Gollum is once again the central dramatic character. When Frodo first hears the story of Bilbo's taking the Ring from Gollum, he states that he wished Bilbo had killed Gollum

---

[2] For more on the Manichean view of evil, see Chapter 8 in this volume.

[3] Augustine, *Confessions*, Books V and VII, translated by F.J. Sheed (Indianapolis: Hackett, 1993).

[4] *Ibid.*, Book II, Chapter 10.

and never found the cursed Ring. Gandalf replies that "Gollum was not wholly ruined. . . . There was a little corner of his mind that was still his own, and light came through it, as through a chink in the dark: light out of the past . . . Alas! there is little hope . . . for him. Yet not no hope" (FR, p. 60). Still, Gollum's devotion to the evil Ring divides him against himself. Moreover, the pursuit of the Ring severely diminishes his entire life, even his enjoyment of pleasure. As Gandalf explains, there remains nothing more for him "to find out, nothing worth doing." He retains "only a nasty furtive eating and resentful remembering" (FR, p. 60).

Tolkien underscores the role of providence in bringing about the fulfillment of the Quest not only through Gollum's role but also through Frodo's succumbing to the power of the Ring at the last moment. Concerning Frodo's "failure" at the Crack of Doom, Tolkien writes,

> Frodo had done what he could and spent himself completely (as an instrument of divine Providence) and had produced a situation in which the object of his quest could be achieved. His humility (with which he began) and his sufferings were justly rewarded by the highest honour; and his exercise of patience and mercy towards Gollum gained him Mercy: his failure was redressed. (L, p. 326)

Through patience, tolerance, and compassion, the designs of Providence are brought to fruition.

Even Saruman, who embodies a kind of anti-providence, seeking to bring evil out of good, is treated as not being utterly beyond hope. When Saruman is discovered wreaking havoc in the Shire, Frodo decides to banish him rather than kill him. In his pettiness, Saruman laughs scornfully, "I have already done much that you will find it hard to mend or undo in your lives. And it will be pleasant to think of that and set it against my injuries." When the hobbits chant, "Kill him!" Frodo says, "I will not have him slain. It is useless to meet revenge with revenge: it will heal nothing" (RK, p. 325). Even after Saruman pulls a knife and attempts to kill him, Frodo still spares his life. Saruman responds bitterly, "You have robbed my revenge of sweetness, and now I must go hence in bitterness, in debt to your mercy. I hate it and you!" (RK, p. 325) But as he is leaving, his lackey Wormtongue, turns on Saruman, pulls a knife and cuts his throat.

Saruman's insidious activities in the Shire and his manner of dying depict in brief the logic of evil in a providential world. Evil is parasitic on the good and can never supplant it; evil is able only to eat away at the good, to cause disorder in the midst of a larger order. His murder by one of his own servants illustrates the way evil deeds return to plague their doer. "Oft evil will shall evil mar" (TT, p. 221).

Sometimes evil mars itself by acting in accord with its own distorted vision of things, by assuming that its enemies will act in the way it would act. After Gandalf's reunion with Aragorn, Legolas, and Gimli, the wizard explains that Sauron "is in great fear, not knowing what mighty one may suddenly appear, wielding the Ring . . ." (TT, p. 104). This, coupled with Sauron's knowledge that two hobbits were captured at Parth Galen by orcs from Isengard, deflects the Dark Lord's attention from true threats to imaginary ones and allows the now scattered members of the Fellowship to continue to pursue their plan. What seemed at first to be mistakes, now seem to work in the favor of the Fellowship. Thus does providence bring good out of evil.

Providence and Joy

If the appropriate response to evil is courageous endurance and hopeful patience, the fitting response to unanticipated good fortune is wonder, joy, and gratitude. In one of greatest events of "chance" in the story, Aragorn arrives at the Pelennor Fields to support the forces of Gondor just at the moment when their fortunes look most bleak. As Aragorn's side is filled with "wonder" and "great joy," the hosts of Mordor grow despondent, realizing that the "tides of fate [have] turned against them" (RK, p. 122). The passage illustrates the way providence works to fortify the good just at the moment when they are most in need. It also shows that the natural response to such astonishing and unanticipated good fortune is not to calculate the odds of the event or demand a proof that what happened was more than chance. Instead, the appropriate response is wonder, joy, and thankfulness. If the reader feels these emotions during and especially at the end of *The Lord of the Rings*, then the dramatist has done his job.

Certainly the most dramatic and most unanticipated providential event is the return of Gandalf after his battle with the Balrog in Moria. Gandalf recounts how he was "delivered," how he and the Balrog fell into an abyss, and how he finally threw down his enemy. Then, he states, "darkness took me, and I strayed out of thought and time, and I wandered far on roads that I will not tell. Naked I was sent back—for a brief time, until my task is done" (TT, p. 111). Although what happened to Gandalf is never clearly stated, we can detect a kind of death (in his straying beyond thought and time) and a return (in his being sent back among the living). Indeed, the hand of providence is explicitly announced here. Gandalf is "sent back" to perform a "task." Of course, his friends are shocked, and at first are not even able to recognize the transformed Gandalf:

> His hair was white as snow in the sunshine; and gleaming white was his robe; the eyes under his deep brows were bright, piercing as the rays of the sun; power was in his hand . . .
> At last Aragorn stirred. "Gandalf," he said. "Beyond all hope you return to us in our need!" (TT, p. 102)

No matter how much we may feel wonder and joy at the orchestration of the events depicted in *The Lord of the Rings*, Tolkien makes clear that the providential restoration of order does not return all things to their previous condition. Some, like Sam, can go home again, but for others, like Bilbo and Frodo, there is, as Frodo puts it, "no real going back." Frodo suffers intermittently from his wound, which, he says, "will never really heal" (RK, p. 333). As Sam and Rosie celebrate the birth of their first child, Frodo comes to the realization that he cannot stay in the Shire. "I tried to save the Shire, and it has been saved, but not for me. It must often be so, Sam, when things are in danger: some one has to give them up, lose them, so that others may keep them" (RK, p. 338). So long as finite minds have to reckon with life in a temporal, imperfect world, there will still be uncertainly as to the ultimate fate of individuals. We end in this sense where we began. Just as Gandalf had to pass on the memories of the past to prepare Frodo for his tasks in the present, so now Frodo urges Sam to "keep alive the memory of the age that is gone, so that people will remember the Great Danger and so love their beloved land all the more" (RK, p. 338).

The fascination with stories and histories, with finding one's bearing in the cosmic history, is perfectly compatible with, indeed seems necessitated by, belief in a providentially structured universe. In such a universe individuals can have confidence that there is an order for them to discern and tasks for them to fulfill, since a providential world is one in which human history has the structure of a plot, an intelligible dramatic unity. Just before announcing his departure, Frodo gives Sam the Red Book of Westmarch, the one Bilbo began and Frodo nearly finished, relating the tale up to the return of the King. Frodo tells Sam that the last few pages are for him to fill in. Here we have a final accentuation of the indeterminacy and uncertainty of the future. Even when Sam finishes the book, there will be others to write, detailing adventures not inferior to the ones contained in *The Lord of the Rings*.

14

Talking Trees and Walking Mountains: Buddhist and Taoist Themes in *The Lord of the Rings*

JENNIFER L. McMAHON and B. STEVE CSAKI

Readers of Tolkien's *The Lord of the Rings* may recognize similarities between it and classic epics like Homer's *Odyssey,* Virgil's *Aeneid,* and Dante's *Divine Comedy.* Frodo's journey certainly parallels that of Odysseus, with its perils, adventures, and final reclamation of the Shire. Similarly, Frodo's trek through the darkness and fumes of Mordor is reminiscent of Dante's expedition through hell in *The Divine Comedy.* Drawing from such classic epics as well as from familiar myths and fairy stories, Tolkien weaves a tale that is replete with archetypes that resonate with Western readers.

Nevertheless, *The Lord of the Rings* also begs comparison with works and ideas issuing from Eastern traditions. This chapter will offer such a comparison. In particular, it will examine themes evident in *The Lord of the Rings* that are also prominent in Zen Buddhism and Taoism. Specifically, this chapter will address the themes of sentience in non-human entities, man's relationship with nature, the importance of the master and student relationship, and the balance between good and evil. In addition to exploring the parallels between Tolkien's work and the Zen Buddhist and Taoist traditions, special care will be taken to discuss the salient differences between them. This latter enterprise is essential to the objective of this chapter, namely to encourage an understanding of both the thematic commonalities and real differences that exist between the Eastern and Western viewpoints.

Sentience and Sensibility

Perhaps the most obvious point of comparison between Tolkien's *The Lord of the Rings* and Buddhist and Taoist texts lies in their treatment of nature. In Tolkien's work, nature figures not only as the principal setting for the plot, but also as a vital force. Thus, far from being simply an unassuming backdrop for the action, nature is presented as a nurturing ground for the primary characters, an imposing obstacle to their endeavors, and an integral aspect of their values. In particular, there are two features of Tolkien's treatment of nature that invite comparison with elements of the Buddhist tradition: his recognition of consciousness in natural entities and his emphasis on kinship with nature.

Tolkien's acknowledgement of consciousness in nature[1] is most apparent in his talking trees. Tolkien introduces these entities in Chapter VI of *The Fellowship of the Ring*. Here, as Frodo and his friends proceed through the Old Forest, they have the uncomfortable feeling that they are being watched by the trees (FR, p. 125). Later, both Tom Bombadil and the ent, Treebeard, confirm this suspicion when they tell various members of the group about the "voices" (TT, p. 16) and "thoughts" (FR, p. 147) of trees. While Treebeard has them under his care, he tells Pippin and Merry that while "most of the trees are just trees of course . . . many are half awake" (TT, p. 69). Indeed, earlier Pippin and Merry discovered just how wide awake some trees are when Old Man Willow took them captive and it required the magic of Tom Bombadil to set them free.

For most Western readers, Tolkien's talking trees contribute to the fanciful quality of Tolkien's *The Lord of the Rings*. They do this because most Westerners do not believe that trees are conscious. In fact, consciousness is one of the main qualities Westerners have used to distinguish humans from other living things. Thus, while we may be willing to grant animals some degree of awareness, we typically elevate ourselves above animals by virtue of the consciousness we possess, and we deny plants and most other natural entities consciousness altogether.

---

[1] At least in his works of fantasy. We don't mean to suggest that Tolkien personally believed that trees are conscious or sentient, or that animals such as eagles or horses can talk or understand speech.

While the belief that natural entities like trees possess aware-ness is not commonly accepted in the West, it is central to the Buddhist tradition. From the Buddhist perspective, sentience is not found only in humans, and enlightenment is not a uniquely human possibility. Rather, Buddhists believe that the myriad things of the world are sentient and have the capacity to reach enlightenment. Repeatedly, the authors of the canonical texts of Buddhism speak of "all sentient beings" and make it clear that this class includes, but also extends beyond, humans. This is particularly true of Japanese Buddhist sects, which have incor-porated some of the animistic elements of Shintoism.

It is important to note, however, that the consciousness Tolkien attributes to trees is not truly analogous to the sentience of which Buddhists speak. For example, although Zen master Dogen describes mountains as "walking,"[2] his language is poetic and metaphorical, not literal. In contrast, Tolkien's trees literally talk and act in ways similar to humans—as do hobbits, dwarves, elves, and wizards. For instance, Tolkien suggests that trees in the Old Forest "do not like strangers" (FR, p. 124). Passages like these make clear that Tolkien tends, in his fiction, to anthropo-morphize natural entities. Instead of having their own type of sentience, nonhuman entities are represented as having thoughts and emotions that are essentially analogous to those of humans. Ultimately, Tolkien attributes human consciousness to nonhuman entities to various degrees. Humans are more con-scious than trees, but the consciousness that trees exhibit mim-ics human awareness. Hobbits, dwarves, and elves manifest awareness that is essentially identical to that of humans, whereas wizards—and the Dark Lord, Sauron—exhibit a kind of super-human consciousness that is nonetheless derived from a human model.

An obvious difference between Tolkien's treatment of non-human entities and that offered by Buddhism is that Buddhists do not anthropormorphize nature. Instead of projecting the model of human consciousness onto other forms of life, Buddhists assume that sentience manifests itself in different ways in different beings. In particular, that the awareness some

---

[2] Dogen, *Mountains and Waters Sutra,* in *Moon in a Dewdrop* (San Francisco: North Point, 1985), p. 97.

beings have may be primarily affective, not reflective. While some modes of sentience may be qualitatively similar to human consciousness, human consciousness is not necessarily the only or the best type. For Buddhists, the reflective form of consciousness that humans exhibit is a type of sentience, but consciousness is not the only form of sentience. Indeed, in many Buddhist texts, ordinary human consciousness is portrayed as an impediment to enlightenment.[3]

Back to Nature

Another point of comparison between Tolkien and Buddhism is their emphasis on the relationship that individuals have with nature. For example, throughout *The Lord of the Rings,* Tolkien stresses the relationship that Frodo and Sam have to the Shire. Clearly, Frodo and Sam are creatures whose characters are shaped by their pastoral surroundings, even as they act to shape those very settings. Indeed, their hobbit holes symbolize the depth of their connection to nature. Importantly, Tolkien suggests that the relationship that the hobbits have to their environment is not atypical. Rather, he indicates that other beings also have a profound connection to nature. For example, he suggests that orcs are formed—and fouled—by their relationship to the sordid land of Mordor. Regarding elves, he says, "whether they've made the land, or the land's made them, it's hard to say" (FR, p. 405). Finally, not only do the ents embody their relationship to nature with their bark-like hide and limb-like appendages, their connection to particular natural environments is so powerful that it has engendered a split between the males, who prefer forests, and the females, or entwives, who prefer tilled terrain. As Treebeard explains to Pippin and Merry, the force of this connection is so strong that the male ents have in

---

[3] See T.P. Kasulis, *Zen Action, Zen Person* (Honolulu: University of Hawaii Press, 1981) for further discussion of this point. There, Kasulis distinguishes between thinking, not-thinking, and without-thinking. While humans tend to identify with thinking (reflective thought), Kasulis explains that reflective thought tends to promote the mistaken impression that things have autonomous essences and are therefore not fundamentally connected to one another. Thus, reflective thought creates an obstacle to understanding and enlightenment because it obscures the true nature of things.

fact lost the entwives and the species has become threatened as a result.

Like Tolkien, Buddhists believe that individuals have a deep relationship to nature. This belief finds expression in the Buddhist doctrine of dependent origination. According to this doctrine, things obtain their being by virtue of their connection to other things. Buddhists believe both that we are shaped by the context in which we find ourselves, and that we shape the environment in which we live and the beings that we encounter in it. Put simply, Buddhists deny that individuals exist in isolation. Instead, they believe that all beings exist and are defined in relation to one another. Rather than perceiving nature as a collection of independent beings that have only incidental relations to one another, Buddhists see nature as a matrix of connection, a dynamic totality in which each individual component is affected by and affects the whole.

While the emphasis on the relation that individuals have to nature is something that Tolkien and the Buddhists share, they differ in how they envision that relationship. Tolkien emphasizes stewardship over, and even domestication of, the natural environment. Thus, while Tolkien acknowledges that individuals are shaped by their environment, he also suggests that they have a certain authority over nature. This point is conveyed through the text's implicit critique of models of improper stewardship of nature as well as in its suggestion that certain beings either have, or are destined to have, dominion over all or part of the earth.

Tolkien's critique of improper stewardship of nature is most apparent in his treatment of the environmental destruction wrought by Saruman and Sauron as well as the industrialization that threatens the Shire. Tolkien's portrayal of the ecological harm caused by such improper stewardship is likely expressive of the Judeo-Christian belief that individuals have a special obligation to act as stewards of their natural surroundings.

Though Buddhists would not oppose the notion of stewardship and would likely commend Tolkien for his critique of individuals who do "not care for growing things, except as far as they serve" them (TT, p. 76), Buddhists do not see individuals as having some special authority *over* nature. Rather, they hold that individuals are members *of* nature. While Buddhists recognize that humans exert a more significant influence on the environment than other species, they do not privilege humans over other natural entities or nature generally. Instead, they seek to correct the egoistic assumption that humans are superior and thus have special rights when it comes to the control and use of nature. Buddhists stress the fact that humans are like other beings with respect to their dependency on nature. They do this in part to remind us that we risk ourselves by denying or damaging this relationship. In essence, Buddhists suggest that humans should seek the harmony or equilibrium with nature apparent in other species. While this desire for greater harmony with nature certainly seems to motivate Tolkien's critique of the destruction wrought by improper stewardship, a subtle privileging of human types still colors *The Lord of the Rings*.

A more significant difference between Tolkien and the Buddhist tradition concerns their representation of nature. In *The Lord of the Rings*, there are two main types of environment: quaint pastoral fields or downs and treacherous wilderness areas. Essentially, Tolkien divides nature into two categories, domesticated nature and wild nature. While Buddhists would certainly admit a difference between cultivated terrain and untamed forests, a difference in perspective becomes apparent when one notes Tolkien's preference for domesticated nature. Throughout *The Lord of the Rings,* Tolkien characterizes the Shire and other cultivated areas positively. In contrast, Tolkien represents the forests and other wilderness areas as "sinister" (FR, p. 111), "unfriendly" (FR, p. 108), and "full of peril" (FR, p. 339). One could argue that Tolkien is merely trying to convey the threat that wild environments pose to his protagonists. However, this mode of portrayal effectively aligns wilderness areas with the forces of evil and the Shire and other domesticated areas with the forces of good, a maneuver that is certainly common in Western literature.

Of course, it would be a mistake to think that Buddhists are uninterested in the control and cultivation of nature. Indeed, what is more contrived than a Zen garden? However, in Buddhism one does not encounter the elevation of domesticated nature and denigration of wild nature that is found in Tolkien's work. Rather, there seems a more balanced appreciation of diverse natural environments. This appreciation may be inspired by the Buddhist goal of appreciating things in their "suchness" rather than with respect to how they affect humans.

Consistent with the Buddhist notion that the ego distorts our understanding of things and impedes harmonious engagement with both nature and others, Buddhist texts and art forms influenced by them try to avoid foregrounding humans. As D.T. Suzuki reminds us, the objective in creating a Zen garden or tea room is to reproduce the appearance of unadulterated nature by avoiding the introduction of elements that are indicative of humans, such as regularity and symmetry.[4]

Ultimately, while *The Lord of the Rings* displays an emphasis on nature that is similar to that in the Buddhist tradition, important differences do exist between their accounts of nature. Though it is beyond the scope of this essay to offer a detailed examination of what motivates these differences, it appears that some of these differences can be attributed to differing background beliefs. Just as the religious doctrines of Buddhism influence its view of nature, Tolkien's treatment of nature is clearly affected by Judeo-Christian notions, specifically the tendency to give humans special status in nature, and the tendency to be suspicious of wild nature. These tendencies likely contribute to the differences between Tolkien's account of nature and those in Buddhism.

Sensei Samwise

Another parallel that exists between Tolkien and the Buddhist tradition is their similar emphasis on mentoring. *The Lord of the Rings* is replete with examples of relationships that are best described as master-student relationships. This view of the importance of a mentor, and perhaps more importantly the notion of developing precisely as a result of mentoring, seems to be very closely paralleled in the master-student relationship that is central to many forms of Buddhism, particularly Zen Buddhism. In this tradition, it is generally accepted that mentoring is not merely helpful, but essential to the achievement of enlightenment.

In *The Lord of the Rings*, the master-student theme is most apparent in the character of Frodo. Frodo has several mentors

---

[4] Daisetz T. Suzuki, *Zen and Japanese Culture* (Princeton: Princeton University Press, 1970), pp. 269–314.

throughout the novel. First, there is Bilbo, who acts as a surrogate father to Frodo. Then there are Gandalf and Aragorn, on whom Frodo constantly leans for guidance. Finally, there is the most unlikely of all masters, "Master Samwise." Throughout *The Lord of the Rings*, there is no sense that Frodo's various mentors are discarded. Instead, as one mentor becomes unavailable, another takes his place. As Frodo adopts different mentors, the roles of the mentors change to a certain extent as well. Finally, due in no small part to Sam's guidance, Frodo completes his development and, at the end of the book, embodies the role of the master and reclaims the Shire. While we shall focus primarily on Frodo's mentoring and how it conveys ideas about the master-student relationship that may be similar to those in Zen Buddhism, we will also look at Sam and his simultaneous role as teacher and student.

While Tolkien presents different kinds of master-student relationships, the differences are due to the differing roles and expectations of each character. By providing Frodo with a series of mentors, Tolkien offers a view of the master-student relationship that is similar to that of Buddhism. Specifically, he demonstrates that a student needs a master who is suitable to both the student's potential and ultimately to the student's goal or task. As Frodo matures and his needs change, so do his mentors.

In keeping with the belief that individuals need multiple mentors who are suited to their changing aptitudes and goals, Buddhists believe that individuals can learn from a host of sources. Tolkien conveys this belief through Frodo's various mentors. Bilbo, who is Frodo's first mentor, is also his cousin. However, Bilbo takes on the role of a parent to Frodo. He guides Frodo through his protracted hobbit adolescence and departs when Frodo is mature enough to begin living on his own. Bilbo's presence demonstrates that family members, particularly parents, are essential sources of instruction.

Frodo's second master or teacher is Gandalf. He takes the role of a wise elder and is more self-conscious with respect to his role as a teacher. After Bilbo's departure, Gandalf takes Frodo under his wing—or more appropriately his wand. Gandalf begins Frodo's education by informing him of the history of the Ring and the dangers that accompany it. Gandalf also imparts more general life lessons. For example, when Frodo bemoans the fact that Bilbo did not kill Gollum, Gandalf states,

"Do not be too eager to deal out death in the name of judgement. For even the very wise cannot see all ends" (FR, p. 65). With this comment, Gandalf not only reminds Frodo that he is not yet wise, he informs him that humility is characteristic of wisdom because the world is too wide for even the wise to comprehend it completely. This sentiment runs throughout Buddhist literature as it is expressive of the Buddhist belief that the ego is one of the greatest obstacles to understanding. Ultimately, Gandalf guides Frodo in a manner that encourages Frodo's independence. He provides Frodo with instruction but then lets him confront challenges on his own. For example, in the film version of *The Fellowship of the Ring*, Gandalf asks the "Ring-bearer" to decide if they should leave Caradhras and go on to the Mines of Moria.

Through Gandalf, Tolkien not only shows that we can learn from the wise, he illustrates what it means to be a good master. Rather than dominate those under his tutelage, he shows that a good master fosters independence and personal development. Clearly, this distinguishes Gandalf, the good master, from Sauron, the evil master, whose goal is to permanently enslave his underlings, not to aid them in the attainment of wisdom and autonomy.

Frodo's third master is Aragorn. Unlike Gandalf who gives Frodo lessons, Aragorn teaches Frodo largely through example. Even when they first meet, Frodo realizes that there is something special about Aragorn. Frodo watches Strider intently and clearly learns much from him. Aragorn is a role model of courage, independence, and commitment. As a master, Aragorn illustrates not only important traits, he also demonstrates that a mentor can teach by example as well as by means of a conventional lesson.

Frodo's fourth and final master is Sam. Sam is Frodo's friend, but he is also Frodo's servant and companion on the journey to Mordor. Though it is Sam who refers to Frodo as "Master" throughout *The Lord of the Rings,* it is clear that Frodo learns as much—or more—from Sam as Sam does from him. Sam instructs Frodo through both discussion and example. Through his selfless commitment to Frodo and his perseverance in the face of adversity, he teaches Frodo about loyalty, humility, and character. One obvious example of this is when Sam (who cannot swim) risks drowning rather than abandon

Frodo as Frodo attempts to leave the Fellowship at Parth Galen (FR, p. 456).

Sam is a particularly interesting "master" to Frodo because he seems to be such an unlikely candidate for the role. He seems more simple than scholarly, and he lacks the prestige of the Ring-bearer, the power of a wizard, and the renowned ancestry of Aragorn. However, Tolkien makes Sam's role explicit by titling Chapter X of *The Two Towers,* "The Choices of Master Samwise". By drawing our attention to "Master Samwise," Tolkien reminds his readers that guidance often comes from unexpected sources and that we can learn from even the humblest of teachers.

In Zen Buddhist literature, there are many accounts of masters attaining enlightenment from the teaching or example of simple people. For example, Dogen's search for the right master took him from Japan to China where he met a most unlikely mentor. As the story goes, there was a load of shiitake mushrooms on the boat that brought Dogen to China. A cook from a Ch'an (Zen) monastery came to the boat to purchase some of the mushrooms. This cook was able to answer some of Dogen's difficult questions and thus served as a master for Dogen. There are many stories like this, and they typically involve questions and answers between a master and a student. In virtually all cases, the student cannot find the path to enlightenment on her own. Rather, the guidance of a master, a master suited to the particular student and her stage of development, is essential. Here, Tolkien and Buddhism agree not only about the importance of a master, but perhaps more importantly, the necessity of the right master at the right time.

Beyond Good and Evil: Tolkien and Taoism

Arguably, the battle of good versus evil is the most prominent theme in *The Lord of the Rings.* Indeed, as one of the preceding sections indicates, this theme is conveyed in part through Tolkien's polarized characterization of nature. For anyone familiar with Eastern thought, Tolkien's emphasis on opposing forces calls to mind the symbol of the Tao with its intertwining yin and yang. The question, however, is whether Tolkien's view of opposing forces is truly analogous to Taoism's.

According to Taoism, all things are comprised of the cosmic principles of yin and yang or some combination of the two. Yin and yang are opposites. Yin is associated with darkness, passivity, and femininity, whereas yang is associated with light, activity, and masculinity. Taoists maintain that harmony or goodness exists when the forces of yin and yang achieve the state of dynamic equilibrium illustrated in the symbol of the Tao. In the symbol, yin is portrayed as an internal element of yang and vice-versa, illustrating that the relationship is a complex one. Taoists maintain that evil occurs as a result of an imbalance between yin and yang.

In some ways, Tolkien appears to present a view of opposites that is similar to that found in Taoism. Specifically, throughout most of *The Lord of the Rings*, Tolkien depicts a world where two opposing forces exist in balance. Like Taoists, he associates one force with light and the other with darkness. Moreover, we see a sort of equilibrium emerge between representatives of each force insofar as Tolkien actually balances his nine Walkers with the nine Black Riders. Finally, an equilibrium of forces is suggested when, in a conversation about the future, Haldir the elf suggests that the balance between opposing forces may persist in the form of a "truce" (FR, p. 391).

Though Tolkien suggests that there is a balance between the opposing forces of light and darkness, crucial differences exist between Tolkien's view and that of Taoism. Indeed, while Tolkien's text may call to mind the symbol of the Tao, there are more differences than similarities between Tolkien's and Taoism's account of opposites.

The first major difference between Tolkien's account of opposites and that found in Taoism is that while Tolkien depicts a time when opposing forces exist in balance, he also makes it abundantly clear that this balance has not always existed and that it should be overcome. Insofar as Tolkien likens the force of darkness to a "shadow" (FR, p. 391) that descends upon the earth and endangers all good things, he makes it clear that a "truce" between opposing forces is not a goal to be sought. Rather, Tolkien envisions the relation between opposing forces as a "war" (TT, p. 489) that needs to be won. In *The Lord of the Rings*, the goal is the defeat of the forces of darkness, not reconciliation with them. The position that one of the oppositional forces of nature should be overcome is not in keeping with the basic principles of Taoism.

Tolkien's negative characterization of the Dark Power also makes it evident that he privileges one of his two forces over the other. Clearly, Tolkien associates the Dark Power with evil and the forces of light with goodness. While the association of light with goodness and darkness with evil is commonplace in the West, Taoists do not characterize the cosmic forces of yin and yang in this manner. Though Taoists associate yin with darkness and yang with light, yin is not bad and yang good. Taoists do not maintain that one of their cosmic principles is the origin of evil while the other is the epitome of goodness. Given the emphasis that Taoists place on achieving a balance between yin and yang, the association of one force with evil would imply that evil is necessary, which Taoists do not believe to be the case.

Rather, Taoists maintain that evil results from disharmony or imbalance in the Tao. Taoists believe that both yin and yang are necessary for the optimal functioning of nature. They assert that goodness is only achieved when these principles are balanced. Indeed, this is another important difference that Tolkien's war metaphor makes apparent. Because Tolkien identifies goodness with light and evil with darkness, he is compelled to assert that harmony in nature can only be achieved through the defeat of its enemy, the Dark Power. However, Taoists believe that harmony emerges when opposing forces are balanced. Thus, while Tolkien suggests that goodness and harmony can emerge fully only in the wake of the Dark Power's defeat, for Taoists the destruction of either one of the two cosmic forces would destroy natural harmony and generate evil.

Another difference between Tolkien's account of opposites and that of Taoism is that Tolkien personifies his forces and Taoists do not. In *The Lord of the Rings*, one particular individual embodies the force of darkness. While he has various underlings, Sauron is described as the "Dark Lord," and the darkness sweeping over the earth is said to find its origin primarily in him. Likewise, though he is not its sole representative, "Gandalf the White" personifies the force of light and goodness. While Taoists hold that the yin and yang are found in individuals, they do not personify the forces of yin and yang. Rather, Taoists see yin and yang as "completely impersonal natural forces."[5]

The final difference between Tolkien's view of opposites and that of Taoism concerns the relation between their respective forces of opposition. As the symbol of the Tao illustrates, Taoists believe that the cosmic forces of yin and yang are interdependent. The symbol of the Tao conveys this belief insofar as the yin and yang intertwine with one another and because a seed of yin is found at the heart of the yang component and a seed of yang at the center of the yin. Taoists believe that yin and yang depend upon, even originate in, one another. This is not the case with Tolkien.

As we hope to have shown, while aspects of *The Lord of the Rings* call to mind ideas and themes evident in the Buddho-Taoist tradition, close examination reveals that many of these similarities are merely apparent. In fact, many of the similarities that exist between Tolkien and Taoism are, while quite striking, somewhat superficial. However, several parallels with Buddhist and Taoist thought do survive scrutiny, particularly the general emphasis on nature and the significance attached to the master-student relationship. In the final analysis, it is in the themes of nature and humanity that we find the bridge that connects Buddhism and Taoism to *The Lord of the Rings*.

---

[5] Fung Yu-Lan, *A Short History of Chinese Philosophy* (New York: Macmillan, 1948), p. 142.

15

Sam and Frodo's Excellent Adventure: Tolkien's Journey Motif

J. LENORE WRIGHT

> I view life as a journey. It's not so much having some goal
> and getting to it. It's taking the journey itself that matters
> . . . I don't think life is about arriving somewhere and then
> just hanging out. It's expanding and expanding and trying
> and trying to get somewhere new and never stopping. It's
> getting out your colors and showing them.
>
> GEENA DAVIS[1]

J.R.R. Tolkien never expected to become famous. Like his reluctant pilgrim, Frodo, character was more important to him than
mere reputation. But famous he is, for as Hamfast Gamgee "the
Gaffer" might say, "famous is as famous does." In addition to
Peter Jackson's film version of *The Lord of the Rings*, Tolkien's
work has inspired everything from Internet chats to fashion
designs. *The Lord of the Rings* discussion boards continue to
erupt on the World Wide Web. The August 8th, 2002, edition of
The New York Times, advertises an English-designed child's tent
as "Just the Burrow for Your Little Hobbit." Even the world-
renowned fashion designer, Vivienne Westwood, appears to
have embraced the Tolkien spirit. On CNN's "Fashion Report,"

---

[1] Quoted in Tom Morris, *Philosophy for Dummies* (Forest City: IDG Books
Worldwide, 1999), p. 320.

she described her fall 2002 collection as "woodsy" and "pilgrim-like." Cloaks and folded fabrics define that particular line, along with its gray, brown, and green color scheme.

Like Frodo's quest, Tolkien's fame is imbued with irony: he did not seek it; it sought him. By his own account, he never intended to write an allegory for contemporary culture when he began *The Lord of the Rings*:

> As for any inner meaning or 'message', it has in the intention of the author none. It is neither allegorical nor topical . . . I cordially dislike allegory in all its manifestations . . . I much prefer history, with its varied applicability to the thought and experience of readers. I think that many confuse 'applicability' with 'allegory'; but the one resides in the freedom of the reader, and the other in the purposed domination of the author. (FR, p. x)

We hear Tolkien's plea imbedded within these words—please don't mistake me for a prophet!—and yet we cannot help but see our world in his. The greedy corporate leaders who helped to bankrupt Enron and WorldCom look a lot like orcs fighting over pillaged goods. In reports of the insider-trading scandal implicating Martha Stewart, she resembles poor-old Sméagol, chasing after "good things" even when they do not belong to her. And the bulldozing and burning of tropical rain forests in South America bears a frightening resemblance to the environmental devastation wrought by Saruman's goblin-men. Tolkien's story plays upon the themes that have shaped and continue to shape the narrative history of contemporary culture. His story is our story. But what does his story have to do with philosophy?

In *Love's Knowledge*, Martha Nussbaum offers a partial answer. Nussbaum argues that literature humanizes philosophy by giving philosophy a corpus, a body, in which to live. Outside of this humanizing process, philosophy remains abstracted and disconnected from life experience. Moreover, in portraying characters whose actions mimic the lived experiences of human beings, literature offers us a lens into the philosophical dimensions of human action—ethical, aesthetic, and ontological. If this is true, then Tolkien's characters can be said to humanize and clarify aspects of Western philosophy.

The Journey Out of the Cave

The narrative of Western philosophy is a journey-narrative. Considered together, the narratives that form the history of Western thought reflect journey motifs of two general types: a journey directed *outwardly* into the world, and a journey directed *inwardly* into the self. The former—the journey without—is typified by a series of conflicts often initiated by the introduction of evil in the journey narrative.[2] The latter—the journey within—is typified by a series of dramatic encounters either within oneself (an inner psychological battle) or with another character. This encounter is often initiated by a strong emotion or force, such as love, and culminates in a union with the force against which a character struggles.

One of the most famous journeys in Western thought (long before the movie, *Thelma and Louise*) is St. Augustine's. In his autobiography, *Confessions*, Augustine depicts his early childhood in North Africa, his adulthood spent teaching rhetoric in Carthage, Rome, and Milan, and finally his conversion to Christianity and his subsequent rise to the position of Bishop of Hippo. In reading his life story, we also bear witness to his philosophical journey toward a vision of Truth found in the tri-une image of the Christian God. Augustine's description of his conversion draws heavily upon Plato's Allegory of the Cave, which appears in Book VII of the *Republic*. The Allegory of the Cave tells the story of a slave who breaks free from his shackles inside a dark dwelling and makes his way out into an unknown world filled with sunlight and "real" objects. As the slave comes to recognize the world beyond the cave, he denounces his allegiance to shadowy images and affirms eternal Forms, the source and constituents of all that is true and knowable. Plato offers an epistemological account of this experience in the *Phaedrus*, where he claims that every human soul once lived in communion with the Forms, contemplating the Beautiful and the Good, aware of true being in its supreme and uncorrupted state.

---

[2] See John S. Dunne, "Myth and Culture in Theology and Literature: A Conversation with John S. Dunne, C.S.C.," *Religion and Literature* 25.2 (Summer 1993), p. 83.

Following in Plato's footsteps, Augustine searches to understand goodness and beauty in the world. He begins his journey out of the cave of Pagan Rome by embracing Manichean philosophy, a materialist philosophy of good and evil. After meeting the spiritual guide of the Manichean sect, Faustus, Augustine flirts with astrology and then Academic skepticism, until he finally encounters an allegorized rendering of Christian thought in the preaching of St. Ambrose. Once Ambrose teaches Augustine how to allegorize scripture, Augustine sees himself in the image of God and begins his pilgrimage of faith.

As we have seen, a journey is a movement from one place to another. But not all journeys are movements in space or through time. Many are spiritual, like St. Augustine's passage from Manicheanism to Christianity. Others are intellectual, such as the journey of the townspeople in the movie, *Pleasantville*, who see the beauty of reality once the stifling veil of repressive rules is removed from their lives. Although a journey involves movement—physical, spiritual, intellectual, or philosophical—there is more to a journey than reaching one's destination. As Bilbo points out, "Not all those who wander are lost" (FR, p. 278). Indeed, movement requires freedom of varying kinds, but the movement away from both one's physical space and one's perspective on reality requires one to accept and act upon at least two kinds of freedom: freedom from material belongings (a freedom to uproot and wander), and freedom from conflicting duties.

In *The Lord of the Rings*, Frodo's journey out of the cave is a journey out of the Shire. He frets over his journey and delays the decision longer than he should. Though he has longed to travel for some time, he confesses that leaving home under these conditions is an "exile" (FR, p. 69). Frodo becomes increasingly burdened by his outward journey as he recalls Bilbo's admonition that leaving one's home is dangerous business. The first step Frodo takes outside of his cave occurs when Gandalf recites the history of the Ring and Frodo infers the role he might play in its destruction. A second step occurs when Frodo sells Bilbo's home and belongings to the Sackville-Bagginses, the relatives he despises (FR, pp. 64–69). A third step occurs when Elrond offers Frodo freedom from the burden of the Ring. "Frodo glanced at all the faces, but they were not turned to him. All the Council sat with downcast eyes, as if in deep thought."

> At last with an effort he spoke, and wondered to hear his own
> words, as if some other will was using his small voice. "I will
> take the Ring," he said, "though I do not know the way." (FR,
> p. 303)

As Frodo and his hobbit companions journey further and
further from the comfortable Shire, they forge new self-identi-
ties. Though typical hobbits are passive and fearful, Sam,
Merry, and Pippin face their fears and confront the horrors of
war, engaging in varied forms of battle themselves. They suffer physical and psychological wounds, wounds that with
each stage of healing, make them stronger, braver, and more
confident. As a result of the wounding and healing process
they undergo, they unchain themselves from their natural
instincts and hobbit-like desires. Only then does their physical journey become existential. Once this transformation
occurs, their self-conceptions become harmonized with their
duties, and they fulfill the Nietzschean charge to "become
who you are."

Though Frodo makes his decision to carry the Ring to
Mordor without obvious compulsion, his choice illustrates the
limits of human freedom. Not only is freedom tethered to
responsibility, it is contingent upon a willingness to choose
between two viable options—a choice that is shaped by many
historical situations. Frodo is the Ring-bearer in part because his
uncle, Bilbo, surreptitiously acquired the Ring from Sméagol
(a.k.a. Gollum) and then passed it down to him. He is also the
Ring-bearer because the Ring remains in his possession—"the
ring chooses the bearer." Clearly, Frodo's choice is not a choice
for himself; his lack of knowledge regarding the location of the
Cracks of Doom compels others to bear his burden along with
him. His decision to carry the Ring, however, means that he is
not only responsible for destroying the Ring, but he is also
responsible for the individuals who help him achieve his Quest.
His decision offers freedom *for* the Ring, not from the Ring. And
Frodo's decision to destroy the Ring *creates* the Fellowship; it is
productive. It simultaneously binds the fellows to Frodo, and it
frees them to travel with Frodo on his journey to Mordor.
Hence, Frodo's commitment to carry the Ring is a commitment
to create freedom in fellowship.

The Journey into the Self

Like philosophical inquiry, Tolkien's journey motif moves in two directions: it is a movement outside the dark cave of illusion and into the light of knowable reality, and it is a turning away from the facade of the self into the innermost psyche. The journey inward into the psyche presupposes an existential freedom that is itself part of the structure of authentic human existence. The characters' inward investigations of their own psyches is a journey toward radical freedom—a recognition that life is defined by events without purpose or meaning. Following in Heidegger's footsteps, philosopher Charles Taylor argues, "My sense of myself is of a being who is growing and becoming . . . It is also of a being who grows and becomes. I can only know myself through the history of my maturations and regressions, overcomings and defeats."[3]

During the seventeenth century, the journey motif received further elaboration at the hands of the French philosopher, Réne Descartes. For Descartes, the journey toward Truth—the journey that Plato tethered to the Good, the journey that Augustine believed culminated in a reunion with God—is turned inward toward the contemplation of innate ideas. As a young soldier, Descartes traveled widely, "visiting courts and armies, mixing with people of diverse temperaments and ranks, gathering various experiences,"[4] and witnessing the carnage of the Thirty Years' War. In the end, however, he decided that conquering himself was an easier and worthier goal than conquering the world, and he resolved "to undertake studies within myself too and to use all the powers of my mind in choosing the paths I should follow."[5] As we follow Descartes into the depths of the self, we come to know the *cogito*, the thinking thing, the symbolic essence of the human mind.

---

[3] *Sources of the Self* (Cambridge, Massachusetts: Harvard University Press, 1989), p. 50.

[4] *Discourse on the Method*, in *Selected Philosophical Writings*, translated by John Cottingham, Robert Stoothoff, and Dugald Murdoch (Cambridge: Cambridge University Press, 1988), pp. 24–25.

[5] *Ibid.*

Descartes creates and uses a system of methodological doubt to tear down the weak foundation of belief. By doubting all that he formerly believed, Descartes shows that the senses may systematically deceive us. He then draws the further conclusion that because our senses deceive us, knowledge cannot be based upon sensory experience, but rather has to be based on mental processes—processes that lead to the contemplation of ideas. Only when we base our beliefs on immediate experience and innate ideas can we know reality absolutely and with certainty. Like Descartes, the Ring-bearer and his fellows must break free from their assumptions and false beliefs if they wish to be transformed by the journey inward.

Like so many thinkers who recognize the need to free themselves from existential doubt but lack the willpower to embrace radical freedom, Boromir attains his philosophical transformation and self-knowledge only at death's door, when he confesses to Aragorn, "'I tried to take the Ring from Frodo . . . I am sorry. I have paid . . . Go to Minas Tirith and save my people! I have failed'" (TT, p. 4). Aragorn replies, "No! . . . You have conquered. Few have gained such a victory. Be at peace!" Burdened by his wish to save his people, Boromir succumbs to his deep desire to use the Ring to destroy enemies of his land. His enslavement to this desire brings about his own demise.

A key step in the transition from enslavement to freedom is personal transformation. Once we break free from our inner chains, we are free to grow as individuals. For example, Gandalf's transformation from "Gandalf the Grey" to "Gandalf the White" begins in the bowels of Moria while battling a Balrog. When he reappears in *The Two Towers*, he represents a new beginning, the dawning of a new day. And as Aragorn assures Gamling, "dawn is ever the hope of men" (TT, p. 152). Other characters that achieve personal transformation include Aragorn, who began the journey as "Strider" and in the end is crowned "King Elessar," and Sam Gamgee who becomes "Master Samwise."[6] But other characters never accomplish this existential

---

[6] The endowment of new titles and the changing of names is a sign of pilgrims making progress in journey tales. In the Eastern tale, *Monkey*, the main character acquires a new name along each stage of his journey toward Buddhahood. He begins as "Handsome Monkey King," then he is named by the Patriarch Subodhi, "Aware of Vacuity." And finally he becomes "Buddha Victorious in Strife."

feat. For instance, though he pretends to be a devoted disciple of Frodo, Sméagol secretly plans to take the Ring from him, with the help of the hideous spider-like creature, Shelob.

Tolkien suggests that Sam and Frodo's physical journey may have been mapped out for them by the circumstances of time and history. But he also suggests that their existential journey—their choices to either affirm or deny each element of the journey—is a matter of their own choosing. By choosing to affirm the journey—choosing to become a Nietzschean Yea-sayer—they choose to affirm even life's "strangest and sternest problems, the will to life rejoicing in its own inexhaustibility . . ."[7] Like the Yea-sayer, Sam and Frodo overcome their history and what they take to be their nature. Then and only then do they fulfill their quest and achieve existential freedom.

Unlike the hobbits, Sméagol and Saruman are Nay-sayers, lamenting their own failures, licking their wounds, and wallowing in self-pity. Sméagol remains enslaved by the Ring even when it is out of his possession, pitying himself for his lack of food, lack of rest, and lack of trustworthiness. Saruman refuses to accept the mercy of Gandalf and company, stating, "Pray, do not smile at me! I prefer your frowns" (RK, p. 283), to which Gandalf replies, "alas for Saruman! I fear nothing more can be made of him. He has withered altogether" (RK, p. 285). Both Sméagol and Saruman live inauthentic lives, lives committed only to the past and present, refusing to acknowledge future possibilities, or to recognize what Heidegger calls one's "potentiality-for-Being." Inauthentic characters define themselves only in terms of their pasts, refusing to be free from "the idols we all have and to which we are wont to go cringing."[8] Despite being burdened by the struggle against nature and history, Tolkien's little hobbits, Sam and Frodo, set their own course as they journey toward self-knowledge and authentic living.

Though most journey narratives adopt either the outward or inward model of journey narratives, *The Lord of the Rings* utilizes

---

[7] Friedrich Nietzsche, *Twilight of the Idols*, translated by R.J. Hollingdale (New York: Penguin, 1968), p. 121.

[8] Heidegger, "The Quest for Being," reprinted in Walter Kaufmann, ed., *Existentialism from Dostoevsky to Sartre* (New York: Penguin, 1989), p. 257.

both. As John Dunne remarks, Tolkien's saga is "a great journey, but it's a conflict, a war, between good and evil; it's both of those at the same time."[9] By drawing out the philosophical implications of the outward and inward journeys within *The Lord of the Rings*, we not only connect the past to the present historically, we confront and affirm the past existentially—we find ourselves in Tolkien's story. By confronting both the historical and existential facets of human experience, we begin to understand something new about our tasks as contemporary philosophers—the task to gaze into the fragmented abyss of postmodern culture and find meaning and value therein.[10]

Pilgrims and Guides

Throughout *The Lord of the Rings*, Tolkien describes the journey of Frodo and his fellows not as a heroic escapade, but as a "Quest." Like most quests with great or exalted purposes, the hobbits' journey is unexpected and undesired. It begins in the familiar Shire and moves quickly to lands unknown to them. Like Monkey's journey to India in search of sacred Buddhist scrolls in the Chinese epic, *Journey to the West*, Sam and Frodo's journey occurs primarily on foot, takes place over several months, and involves a series of clashes and battles. It also unfolds in stages. When Frodo first learns of his journey, Gandalf says to him, "It may be your task to find the Cracks of Doom; but that quest may be for others: I do not know. At any rate you are not ready for that long road yet" (FR, p. 73).

Sam and Frodo appear to be typical pilgrims—a little mad, weak-willed, and very reluctant to endanger themselves or their fellow travelers. For instance, as Frodo considers the journey before him, he says to Gandalf,

> Of course, I have sometimes thought of going away, but I imagined that as a kind of holiday, a series of adventures like Bilbo's or better, ending in peace. But this would mean exile, a flight from

---

[9] Dunne, "Myth and Culture in Theology and Literature," p. 83.

[10] Other great texts—both Western and non-Western—that contain journey motifs include *The Epic of Gilgamesh*, the *Ramayana*, Homer's *Iliad* and *Odyssey*, Virgil's *Aeneid*, *The Song of Roland*, *Tristan*, Bunyan's *Pilgrim's Progress*, Dante's *Divine Comedy*, Chaucer's *Canterbury Tales*, Boccaccio's *Decameron*, Marguerite de Navarre's *Heptameron*, and Shakespeare's *The Tempest*.

danger into danger, drawing it after me . . . But I feel very small, and very uprooted, and well—desperate. The Enemy is so strong and terrible. (FR, p. 69)

These friends need guides in part because they are weak-willed. Tolkien's description of Frodo and Sam is analogous to the medieval pilgrim, Dante, and the fear he experiences as he makes his way through hell with his guide, Virgil. As Dante's trepidation begins to overcome him at various points in the *Inferno*, he faints, incapable of facing the reality before him. Likewise, Frodo struggles against the increasing weight of the Ring, his own self-doubt, and his deep weariness. Historically, philosophers have received aid in their intellectual struggles by teachers and guides. For example, Plato burned his tragedies when he met Socrates. Aristotle joined Plato's Academy and became a teacher in his own right. St. Augustine received spiritual guidance from St. Ambrose. Aquinas studied under Albert the Great. Kant relied upon Hume to "wake him from his dogmatic slumbers." And Jean-Paul Sartre, Hannah Arendt, and Hans-Georg Gadamer contributed to the burgeoning field of existentialism after studying with Martin Heidegger, who himself was deeply indebted to Edmund Husserl.

What would a journey be without a guide (or two)? Tolkien's mythical guide, the one who finds freedom in wandering, is Gandalf. Though Gandalf is often called away from Sam and Frodo to aid in the war effort, he never abandons his hobbit friends, assisting them in both word and deed. Gandalf arranges for Aragorn to serve as a guide to the hobbits. Later, thanks to Gandalf's wise counsel that "Sméagol may yet have "some part to play" (FR, p. 65), Gollum serves as Sam and Frodo's last guide in their almost hopeless Quest to destroy the One Ring.

Pilgrims are different from heroes in the classical sense of the term. According to both ancient mythology and modern epics, heroes are courageous, large in stature, often of divine ancestry or noble birth, sometimes magical, athletic, intelligent, adept at specific skills, and knowledgeable of the arts (often they play musical instruments). Classic Greek examples include Theseus, who with the help of his beloved Ariadne slays the Minotaur who guards the labyrinth in Knossos, and Odysseus, who Homer represents as the noblest and most respected hero for his courage, cunning, and eloquence.

Unlike these heroes, Sam and Frodo experience constant fear and dread; their journey is overshadowed by despair. Like all hobbits, they are small in stature, often mistaken for children. Nor are they of noble ancestry or exceptionally knowledgeable, intelligent, skilled, or athletic. Their strength lies in their devotion, determination, and single-mindedness of purpose. They are not heroes in the classical sense; rather, they exemplify the traits of modern pilgrims. As their journey to Mount Doom approaches its end, the Quest transforms these two reluctant pilgrims into resilient, bold masters whose characters reflect the potency of the Ring. We see this transformation in Sam most clearly in his battle with Shelob. Tolkien writes:

> As if his indomitable spirit had set its potency in motion, the glass [Phial of Galadriel] blazed suddenly like a white torch in his hand. . . . No such terror out of heaven had ever burned in Shelob's face before. . . . She fell back. . . . Sam came on. He was reeling like a drunken man, but he came on. And Shelob, cowered at last, shrunken in defeat, jerked and quivered as she tried to hasten from him. (TT, p. 383)

We see the transformation in Frodo through Sam's eyes when the two companions capture Sméagol: "For a moment it appeared to Sam that his master had grown and Gollum had shrunk: a tall stern shadow, a mighty lord who hid his brightness in grey cloud, and at his feet a little whining dog" (TT, pp. 249–250). Despite their individual growth, these two friends realize their change may be of no consequence as they near the end of their journey to the Cracks of Doom. Sam, in particular, fears that even if they manage to destroy the Ring, they have no hope of escaping Mordor alive:

> But even as hope died in Sam, or seemed to die, it was turned into a new strength. Sam's plain hobbit-face grew stern, almost grim, as the will hardened in him, and he felt through all his limbs a thrill, as if he was turning into some creature of stone and steel that neither despair nor weariness nor endless barren miles could subdue. (RK, p. 225)

Sam and Frodo's strength of character is the source of their authenticity as pilgrims.

Our contemporary concept of "hero" is rooted in the conflicts described in Greek literature, battles between great divinities and god-like humans. It emerged out of our primordial desire for immortality, along with an emergent need for divinity and unity. Despite our affluence and technological advances, the need for extraordinary creatures and events still exists. So why are Sam and Frodo so ordinary? In Plato's *Symposium*, his great dialogue on love, Diotima teaches that profound ideas emerge from one small intellectual spark. Tolkien teaches us the same lesson. The humblest creatures, as small as children, are capable of extraordinary feats.

Now, more than ever, we are realizing that we need ordinary people to be extraordinary. Perhaps Tina Turner's lament in *Thunderdome* is correct—"We don't need another hero." We need people to be all too human and frail. We need Sam and Frodo to be ordinary, not heroic. Tolkien's reluctant pilgrims show us that when ordinary people bind themselves to the good, life can become extraordinary.

16

Happy Endings and Religious Hope: *The Lord of the Rings* as an Epic Fairy Tale

JOHN J. DAVENPORT

On the surface, it seems possible to read Tolkien's tale of hobbits, wizards, and warriors simply as an entertaining adventure. Others regard the work as a Christian allegory. I will argue instead that Tolkien conceived his masterpiece as an epic fairy tale with a kind of religious significance. In particular, Tolkien wanted his story to have a special form of "happy ending" that suggests or echoes the Western religious promise that our struggles to overcome evil are not meaningless, that there will be final justice and a healing of this world. To show this, I will look at Tolkien's theory of the fairy tale and his Arthurian romance model for the happy ending in *The Lord of the Rings*.

Religion and Myth

There has been a long debate among critics about whether *The Lord of the Rings* is fundamentally a religious work. Unlike C.S. Lewis's *Chronicles of Narnia*, Tolkien's book is an epic that involves no obvious Christian allegory and few clear parallels to stories in the Jewish Torah or Christian New Testament. Thus Patricia Spacks writes that for the moral and theological scheme in the work "there are no explicit supernatural sanctions: *The Lord of the Rings* is by no means a Christian work."[1] Indeed

---

[1] Patricia Meyer Spacks, "Power and Meaning in *The Lord of the Rings*," in Neil

many of the symbols, characters, and plot lines in Tolkien's works are closer to sources in Northern European mythology, such as stories of the gods in the Norse *Eddas*, the Finnish *Kalevala*, the Icelandic sagas, and heroic epics such as the Germanic *Lay of the Nibelung* and the Old English *Beowulf*, on which Professor Tolkien was a leading expert in his time.[2] And as Spacks correctly points out, in his famous lecture on *Beowulf*, Tolkien highlights differences between the Christian vision of salvation in an afterlife and the Norse vision of honor won in the heroic struggle to endure against chaos, despite the inevitability of our death: "northern mythology takes a darker view. Its characteristic struggle between man and monster must end ultimately, within Time, in man's defeat."[3]

Moreover, as many critics have recognized, a poignant note of sadness pervades much of Tolkien's work: the motifs of decline, irreversible loss, and the withdrawal of past glory are present throughout *The Lord of the Rings*. We find this not only in the passing of the High Elves, the diminished greatness of Gondor, and the loss of the entwives, but also in reflections on the great struggle at issue in the book. Even after the astounding triumph at Helm's Deep, Théoden, the aged king of the horse-folk of Rohan, still recognizes a reason for sadness:

> "For however the fortune of war shall go, may it not so end that much that was fair and wonderful shall pass for ever out of Middle-earth?"
>
> "It may," said Gandalf. "The evil of Sauron cannot be wholly cured, nor made as if it had not been. But to such days we are doomed." (TT, pp. 168-69)

Yet as Spacks also notes, Tolkien's world shares many similarities with the Christian one, including "the possibility of

---

Isaacs and Rose Zimbardo, eds., *Tolkien and the Critics* (Notre Dame: University of Notre Dame Press, 1968), p. 82.

[2] See J.R.R. Tolkien, "*Beowulf*: The Monsters and the Critics," in Christopher Tolkien, ed., *The Monsters and the Critics and Other Essays* (London: Allen and Unwin, 1983), pp. 5–48. I would argue that Tolkien's work is also deeply inspired by the Arthurian legends and the larger cycle of British national mythology. The very first story Tolkien wrote about his fictional world, "The Fall of Gondolin," has clear links to the Fall of King Arthur.

[3] Spacks, "Power and Meaning in *The Lord of the Rings*," p. 83.

grace."[4] Tolkien's *Silmarillion*, his unfinished prequel to *The Lord of the Rings*, begins with a single supreme God, Ilúvatar, creating from nothing the Ainur, immortal beings similar to archangels and angels in the traditional Christian hierarchy. With their participation, Ilúvatar then creates the physical world, Eä, and all its creatures in a cosmic symphony of divine music. The strife between good and evil begins in this creation story with the fall of the highest of the Ainur, Melkor (who is renamed Morgoth, paralleling Lucifer-Satan), who discovers that the discord he sows into the primordial music in the end only flows into the higher harmony foreseen by Ilúvatar. In the finale of this symphony of creation, "in one chord, deeper than the Abyss, higher than the Firmament, piercing as the light of the eye of Ilúvatar, the Music ceased" (S, p. 17). Here, more clearly than anywhere else in his works, Tolkien gives his world the promise of an ultimate redemption, or what theologians call an *eschatological* end or final judgment and perfection of the world. This promise is echoed at places in *The Lord of the Rings*, for example in Gandalf's memorable response to Denethor after the Steward of Gondor tells the wizard that he has no right to control the affairs of Gondor:

> ". . . the rule of no realm is mine, neither of Gondor nor any other, great or small. But all worthy things that are in peril as the world now stands, those are my care. And for my part, I shall not wholly fail of my task, though Gondor should perish, if anything passes through this night that can still grow fair or bear fruit and flower again in days to come. For I also am a steward. Did you not know?" (RK, p. 16)

The implication is clear enough: just as the Stewards of Gondor are supposed to hold their realm in trust for the lost Númenórean King, should he ever return, so the rightful Owner of the world has entrusted Middle-earth to the care of Gandalf and his fellow wizards (and less directly to the care of the Valar, Ilúvatar's archangelic regents), until He comes to this world Himself.

---

[4] *Ibid.*, p. 86.

But this Owner, Ilúvatar, is barely referenced in *The Lord of the Rings*. Even in *The Silmarillion*, in which the Valar are initially active, Ilúvatar is remote. By the time we reach the Third Age, even the Valar are only vaguely suggested as a power in the Uttermost West beyond the Sea, who sent the wizards to help in the resistance against Sauron. So God and the archangels play virtually no direct role in *The Lord of the Rings*, which focuses on the struggles of mortal beings. In this way, Tolkien's masterpiece is similar to classics of Old English poetry, which focus on our immanent world of time, with all its transitoriness, loss, and courage in the face of mortality. It is not surprising, therefore, that we do not find Tolkien's characters praying to God, or encountering divine figures, or having religious experiences like those recorded in the lives of many saints. As Tolkien explained to his American publisher, the book is set in "a monotheistic world of 'natural theology.' The odd fact that there are no churches, temples, or religious rites and ceremonies, is simply part of the historical climate depicted . . . The 'Third Age' was not a Christian world" (L, p. 220). Thus if a work of literature counts as "religious" only if it examines the nature of God, defends belief in God, or focuses on practices of worship, then *The Lord of the Rings* is not a religious work.

Magic, Fairy Tale Endings, and Eschatology

Nevertheless, *The Lord of the Rings* remains a religious work in quite a different sense. If, as the Danish existentialist Søren Kierkegaard thought, the essence of religious faith lies in embracing the promise of a salvation that we cannot achieve by our own good work alone—a salvation possible only by divine miracle—then Tolkien's work comes closer to this essentially religious attitude than other superficially "religious" works. Tolkien reveals his purpose in an essay titled "On Fairystories,"[5] which explains the deeper idea behind the familiar

---

[5] Reprinted in J.R.R. Tolkien, *The Tolkien Reader* (New York: Ballantine, 1966), pp. 3–73. All references to the essay will be to this edition, but you can also find it in *Tree and Leaf* (London: Allen and Unwin, 1967). In his letters, Tolkien refers frequently to this essay, suggesting its importance to friends and

happy endings we find in classic fairy tales like *Beauty and the Beast, Cinderella,* and *Hansel and Gretel.* In this remarkable essay, Tolkien argues that in their highest form, fairy tales are not, as we have come to think of them, just simplified nursery or old wives stories full of diminutive sprites invented to entertain very young children, but rather a form of serious literary art in which nature appears as a "Perilous Realm," the world of "Faërie." Genuine fairy-stories in this high mode include, for example, the original Greek tale of *Perseus and the Gorgon, The Juniper Tree,* and the medieval tale of *Sir Gawain and the Green Knight.*[6] The central function of magic in such stories is not to perform tricks or spells, but to satisfy "certain primordial human desires," including the desire "to survey the depths of space and time," "to hold communion with other living things," and most importantly, "the realisation, independent of the conceiving mind, of imagined wonder."[7]

Thus, Tolkien argues, it is essential to the genuine fairy tale that its magic be presented as *true* in the secondary world of the story, not explained away as a mere dream, illusion, or product of advanced technology. However, this is not because the magic of Faërie directly represents the divine power of the God who creates the cosmos. As Tolkien explains, the supernatural may play a role in fairy-stories: "Something really 'higher' is occasionally glimpsed in mythology: Divinity, the right to power (as distinct from its possession), the due of worship . . ."[8] But unlike cosmogonic myths of creation, tales of Faërie are not primarily concerned with the Divine or "supernatural." Rather, "fairy-stories as a whole have three faces: the Mystical towards the Supernatural; the Magical towards Nature; and the Mirror of scorn and pity towards Man." The "essential face of Faërie," says Tolkien, "is the middle one, the Magical."[9]

---

relatives, trying to draw critics' attention to it (with little success), and expressing great frustration that the collection in which it first appeared (C.S. Lewis, ed., *Essays Presented to Charles Williams* [New York: Oxford University Press, 1947]) had gone out of print.

[6] *Ibid.,* p. 31.

[7] *Ibid.,* pp. 13–15.

[8] *Ibid.,* p. 25.

[9] *Ibid.,* p. 26.

In other words, what primarily distinguishes tales of Faërie is a certain kind of magic, one that has nothing to do with the alchemist's transmutations, or sorcerer's apprentice tricks, or spells in a Dungeons and Dragons game. The sort of perilous magic native to the world of Faërie, represented in Tolkien's world by High Elves, wizards, dragons, and ents, reveals a face of Nature that is hidden in our ordinary reality. It expresses a living force or spirit in all things, which it is our heart's desire to encounter, and also to employ in creating new reality: "Uncorrupted, it does not seek delusion nor bewitchment and domination; it seeks shared enrichment, partners in making and delight, not slaves."[10] This good will to creative power Tolkien calls "the central desire and aspiration of human Fantasy."[11] In *The Lord of the Rings*, we see this desire for good power personified in Gandalf, and to a lesser extent in Galadriel, who both nevertheless refuse the chance to use the Ring's power to dominate and rob others of their freedom.

But the magic essential to tales of Faërie is not only an expression of the hidden side of nature, its inner glory and living beauty, and of the natural and good human desire to share in this wonder through "sub-creation." For this magic also responds to the innate human desires for what Tolkien calls Recovery, Escape, and Consolation. For Tolkien, Recovery and Escape refer to renewed appreciation of life and the value of nature, and an escape from the alienating delusions of an artificial, mechanized, and increasingly ugly consumerist society. These goals help explain why *The Lord of the Rings* focuses on the comfort and beauty of the Shire and its inhabitants, in contrast not only to Mordor, but also to the ruined Isengard with its hellish underworld of grinding engines.

Finally, we come to Consolation. By this, Tolkien does not mean comforting words, but an answer to the question of whether our efforts, hardships, and suffering have any point, any final significance (the sort of answer Boethius sought in his classic, *The Consolation of Philosophy*). The kind of happy ending that marks genuine fairy stories, in which there is a miraculous reprieve in the midst of impending disaster, hints at an

---

[10] *Ibid.*, p. 53.
[11] *Ibid.*

answer to this ultimate question. Tolkien calls the consolation provided by this unique kind of happy ending a "eucatastrophe," or joyous salvation within apparent catastrophe.

Tolkien proposes the term "eucatastrophe" because, he says, we don't have a word expressing the opposite of "tragedy." He conceives tragedy as the true form and highest function of drama, and eucatastrophe as the true form and highest function of fairy-tale.

> The consolation of fairy-stories, the joy of the happy ending: or more correctly, of the good catastrophe, the sudden joyous 'turn' (for there is no true end to any fairy-tale): this joy, which is one of the things which fairy-stories can produce supremely well, is not essentially 'escapist' or 'fugitive'. In its fairy-tale—or otherworld—setting, it is a sudden and miraculous grace, never to be counted on to recur. It does not deny the existence of *dyscatastrophe*, of sorrow and failure: the possibility of these is necessary to the joy of deliverance; it denies (in the face of much evidence, if you will), universal final defeat, and in so far is *evangelium*, giving a fleeting glimpse of Joy, Joy beyond the walls of the world, poignant as grief.[12]

Tolkien chooses the term "eucatastrophe" to emphasize that the sudden "turning" or unexpected deliverance at the end of a true tale of Faërie must be experienced not as an achievement of triumphant revenge, but rather as a divine gift. The joy produced by such a happy ending requires a surprise, a deliverance that no human effort could have made possible. In a letter to his son, Christopher, Tolkien uses the example of a boy dying of tubercular peritonitis who was taken to the Grotto at Lourdes, but not cured. However, on the train ride home, as he passed within sight of the Grotto again, he was healed. Tolkien writes that this story, "with its apparent sad ending and then its sudden unhoped-for happy ending," gave him that peculiar emotion which comes from eucatastrophe, because it is a "sudden glimpse of the truth . . . a ray of light through the very chinks of the universe about us" (L, pp. 100–01).

The poignant emotion Tolkien finds in this moment in a good fairy tale requires a tragic recognition of the evil and imperfection of our world, or even a Norse-like resignation to the fact that we cannot overcome it by our own power; yet the

---

[12] *Ibid.,* p. 68.

tale rises above this grief in a humanly impossible reprieve that is only made possible by divine grace ("by virtue of the absurd," as Kierkegaard would say). In this sense, Tolkien says, "The Gospels contain a fairy-story, or a story of a larger kind which embraces all the essence of fairy-stories."[13] The resurrection appears as the eucatastrophe of the Gospel story because it is the ultimate reprieve when all appears to be lost. But the eucatastrophic joy of the resurrection involves an eschatological message which is more direct than the hope implied in fairy-tale eucatastrophes. For Christians, the resurrection is the beginning of a new reality that promises eternal life with God in a world to come. In fairy-tale eucatastrophes, such eschatological hope is only indirectly hinted at.

Thus, as Tolkien sees it, the special kind of happy ending we find only in true tales of Faërie gets its power precisely from its veiled eschatological significance: it hints that there is an eternal source of hope beyond all darkness and despair. More simply put, the eucatastrophic turn in the fairy story is a sign or echo of the eschaton, an indirect reference to divine judgment and the coming of a new Kingdom. And the magical appearance of Nature in such tales also intimates something unexpected, namely, that the natural world as we know it is destined for a divine transformation, destined to become part of a new heaven and a new earth.

A good example to explain the notion of eucatastrophe is the medieval tale of *Sir Gawain and the Green Knight,* which Tolkien studied closely and used in creating Frodo. Its central figure, the gigantic Green Knight who challenges Arthur's court, exemplifies what Tolkien called the "essential face" of Faërie, the magical toward nature. As a descendant of the "green man" nature spirit in Celtic mythology, he is a manifestation of a power within living things that cannot be possessed, appropriated, or controlled by human beings, but which nevertheless can act in reciprocity with us. He cannot be killed by natural human power, but he can make perilous bargains.

In brief summary, the story goes as follows.[14] At the New Year's feast in Camelot, the Green Knight comes to dare any of

---

[13] *Ibid.,* p. 71.

[14] See *Sir Gawain and the Green Knight, Pearl, and Sir Orfeo,* translated by J.R.R. Tolkien (London: Allen and Unwin, 1979).

King Arthur's knights to strike him a blow on the neck with his axe, as long as that knight will agree to suffer a similar blow at the Green Chapel one year hence. But when Gawain takes up this challenge, and cuts off the Green Knight's head, the latter picks up his severed head and tells Gawain that he'll see him in a year to complete the bargain! Two days before the appointed tryst, Gawain comes in distress to the house of Sir Bertilak (who is the Green Knight in disguise), and there enters into another perilous bargain: while his host is off hunting, Gawain will stay with his lady in the house, and he and his host will exchange whatever prizes they won at the end of the day. Sir Bertilak's wife (a Green Lady in disguise) then tries to seduce Gawain, testing his honor. With great difficulty Gawain resists the lady's advances, but on the morning before his doom, he accepts her girdle offered as a token of affection—both out of courtesy and because she tells him that its magic power can save him from the axe. He does not pass the girdle to his host, as their bargain required. Later, when the Green Knight comes with terrifying fury to the chapel, Gawain accepts his doom (the resignation that must precede a eucatastrophe). But the Green Knight does not kill Gawain: his first two axe-strokes stop at Gawain's skin, and the third cuts him just enough to cause a permanent scar, as punishment for keeping the girdle. This mark of mortality, similar to Achilles's heel, is the flaw which signals his humanity, his difference from the divine. As Tolkien wrote, "His 'perfection' is made more human and credible, and therefore more appreciable as genuine nobility, by the small flaw."[15]

In the terror of the Green Chapel, Gawain's unexpected reprieve is experienced as astounding grace, utterly unexpected. It is precisely a eucatastrophe in Tolkien's sense. And Gawain is Tolkien's primary model for Frodo. Like Gawain, Frodo accepts the burden and quest that no other knight can undertake. Like Gawain, despite his resolve, Frodo also finally succumbs to temptation and puts on the Ring (just as Gawain put on the girdle). And like Gawain, Frodo ends up with a wound and scar that forever mark his human imperfection. But the Green Knight's test is not primarily a lesson in morality: rather it is an encounter with the divine, as refracted in the perilous Nature of

---

[15] J.R.R. Tolkien, "Sir Gawain and the Green Knight," in *The Monsters and the Critics and Other Essays*, p. 97.

Faërie-magic. What Gawain experiences in the Green Chapel is a foreshadowing or glimpse of salvation at the end of time.

An Epic Fairy Tale

Tolkien's primary goal in *The Lord of the Rings* was to create a fantasy for our time with the same eucatastrophic power that Gawain's fantastic tale had for fifteenth-century Britons, and this is what gives his trilogy its encompassing religious mood. Thus the history of Tolkien's world up to *The Lord of the Rings* is a history with a providential design, unfolding from within towards its transforming end. As Gunnar Urang writes,

> *The Lord of the Rings*, as history, is more than day-to-day on-going history. It is the history of the *end*: it is eschatology. And despite Tolkien's many debts to "Northernness," the shape of this eschatology is not that of Norse mythology but that of the Christian tradition. Tolkien's myth of the end is no Ragnarök [in which all the gods of Valhalla die in the last battle against the forces of chaos]; the twilight is not for any gods but for Sauron and his forces.[16]

This is right, as long as we qualify Urang's statement by noting that even within Tolkien's secondary world, the end of Sauron and his realm is not the ultimate end, but only another crucial turning point, another anticipatory echo of that final greatest and last chord in which the Music of the Ainur ended and was complete.

Understanding Tolkien's conception of fairy tales and their central function sheds much light on *The Lord of the Rings*. Robert Reilly, one of the few commentators to appreciate the importance of Tolkien's essay on Faërie, rightly argues that the "proper genre" of the trilogy is "the fairy story mode as Tolkien conceives it."[17] In explaining his trilogy to W.H. Auden, Tolkien alludes to his essay, "On Fairy-stories," and explains that he sees the modern connection between children and fairy stories as

---

[16] Gunnar Urang, "Tolkien's Fantasy: The Phenomenology of Hope," in Mark Robert Hillegas, ed., *Shadows of the Imagination: The Fantasies of C.S. Lewis, J.R.R. Tolkien, and Charles Williams* (Carbondale: Southern Illinois University Press, 1976), p. 104.

[17] R.J. Reilly, "Tolkien and the Fairy Story," in *Tolkien and the Critics*, p. 129.

"false and accidental," spoiling those stories both in themselves and for children. Tolkien therefore wanted to write a fairy story that was not specifically addressed to children at all, and that utilized "a larger canvass" (L, p. 216).

As the remark indicates, it was part of Tolkien's purpose to write an epic: in scope and depth, *The Lord of the Rings* covers the sort of vast conflict and journey we find in works like Homer's *Odyssey* and Virgil's *Aeneid*. This may seem puzzling, since fairy tales and epics are different genres for Tolkien: epics concern the struggles of heroes against the forces that threaten all life, in the process of which they discover and develop their unique identities (thus epics often involve a descent into an underworld as a figural descent into self or journey of self-discovery).

But as his letters make clear, *The Lord of the Rings* grew directly out of the stories making up *The Silmarillion*: it was a development of the last segments of his encompassing epic narrative. The earlier stories making up *The Silmarillion* were conceived primarily as parts of an epic: its main episodes all concern developments of the self in a hero's quest against what appear to be impossible odds. For example, in the central narrative around which the whole *Silmarillion* was conceived, Beren and Lúthien descend into Morgoth's fortress and succeed, "where all the armies and warriors" of the elves have failed, in retrieving one of the stolen Silmarils (the greatest jewels ever made). As Tolkien emphasizes, their story anticipates Frodo's and Sam's, since it shows that the fortunes of world history "are often turned not by the Lords and Governors, [or] even gods, but by the seemingly unknown and weak" (L, p. 149). So *The Lord of the Rings* acquired the epic form of *The Silmarillion*.

However, although *The Silmarillion* is a work of fantasy, it does not meet all of Tolkien's requirements for a fairy story, since its unfinished sagas contain no true eucatastrophe. Even though the Valar come to overthrow Morgoth, every elven realm is destroyed, and this sorrow is irredeemable. No divine intervention, we feel, could ever make up for the beauty lost in the fall of Gondolin, or give meaning to the destruction of Nargothrond, or explain the tragic deaths of the children of Húrin, or console the endless sorrow of the Fifth Battle (which is perhaps Tolkien's version of the Battle of the Somme, in which he participated). This ultimate battle begins with Fingon, High King of the Noldor, declaring *"Utúlie'n aurë!* The day has come!" (S, p. 190). But it ends with Fingon's death, followed by his friend Húrin's last stand, and his desperate cry, "*Aurë entuluva!* Day shall come again!" (S, p. 195). Húrin's hope can only foreshadow a possible eucatastrophe to come.

By contrast, *The Lord of the Rings* is meant to *combine* the epic quest narrative with the eucatastrophic (or indirectly eschatological) significance of the true faërie tale. One can see why such a combination appealed to Tolkien: no story in the British and Germanic mythologies that he loved so much had perfectly melded these models into a eucatastrophic epic: so this would be a tremendous literary achievement. This synthesis of the epic mode, which tends towards tragedy and sorrow, with the eucatastrophic consolation of the fairy tale, helps explain what several commentators have recognized as the paradoxical "joy-in-sorrow atmosphere [that] pervades the *Rings*" trilogy.[18] For, as Gunnar Urang put it, "'Inside' or 'outside' the story, the main question is whether or not a happy ending is possible; allegorically, whether or not there are, in the battle against evil, any grounds for *hope*."[19] Despite his poignant lament for all the life and beauty lost to evil in our world, Tolkien still means to say that there is hope after all.

Tolkien's Eucatastrophes

Does *The Lord of the Rings* achieve this distinctive goal of crowning an epic quest romance with a eucatastrophe worthy of the greatest fairy stories? I think it comes close, and this helps explain much of the power of this work, which has moved generations of readers. Although there has been some disagreement about it, Tolkien clearly intended the eucatastrophe to come at the end of the chapter "Mount Doom," when Frodo's iron will to achieve his Quest finally falls under the One Ring's power at the very Cracks of Doom, and he puts on the Ring, claiming it for his own. After enduring so much hardship and struggle, and the loss of everything that formerly defined their lives, it seems that Sam and Frodo are destined to fail at the end. The Dark Lord will regain the Ring and triumph, destroying all the beauty

---

[18] Clyde S. Kilby, "Meaning in *The Lord of the Rings*," in *Shadows of the Imagination*, p. 73.

[19] Urang, "Tolkien's Fantasy: The Phenomenology of Hope," p. 103.

that is left in Middle-earth, and Frodo will become another Gollum, Sauron's broken slave.

But then the great "turn" comes: Gollum returns unexpectedly, fights Frodo and bites the finger from Frodo's hand, and then falls into the Cracks of Doom, taking Sauron's Ring with him. Here is the crucial moment of grace, the reprieve unlooked for. Only because Bilbo, Frodo, and Sam have all shown Gollum mercy, has he survived to this moment to bring Sauron down to ruin with him. Yet their mercy and care could not by itself achieve the victory: Fate must answer them. We experience this moment of saving grace through Sam's eyes. He witnesses the tremendous collapse of Barad-dûr, but without any sense of triumph. And then comes perhaps the most poignant moment in the whole text. Sam sees Frodo,

> pale and worn, and yet himself again; and in his eyes there was peace now, neither strain of will, nor madness, nor any fear. His burden was taken away. There was his dear master of the sweet days in the Shire.
> "Master!" cried Sam, and fell upon his knees. In all that ruin of the world for the moment he felt only joy, great joy. The burden was gone. His master had been saved; he was himself again, he was free. (RK, p. 241)

In Sam's joy, which is pure because his unconditional love for Frodo is so selfless, there is more than just a glimpse of *evangelium*. If we have come to love Sam and Frodo while reading their epic story, then at this moment we too will feel the piercing "joy, poignant as grief," which is Tolkien's goal.

In this event, we also see Tolkien's point that a true eucatastrophe is humbling, and thus precisely the opposite of the vengeful spirit of triumph that Nietzsche saw in Christian eschatological hope. Frodo's deliverance is like Sir Gawain's: he is saved, but with a wound that marks the mortal limits he showed when he put on the Ring. And in this respect, he is obviously to be compared to Beren in the *The Silmarillion*. For at the end of his quest to retrieve the Silmarils from Morgoth, Beren loses a hand, just as Frodo loses a finger. The miracle of the outcome astonishes and moves us, but without encouraging any of the spiteful self-righteousness that can mar more conventional "good beats evil" endings. Even if Frodo and Sam had not been rescued by the eagles, and instead had died a more Beowulfian death on Mount Doom after the Ring was destroyed, this would still have counted as a "happy ending" in Tolkien's sense.

Yet while it is the most central to the overall plot, Gollum's final fulfillment of his destiny is not the only moment in *The Lord of the Rings* where we find something like a eucatastrophe, a miraculous restoration beyond any hope that mortal beings could provide by their own power. As Urang suggests, the denouement on Mount Doom is anticipated by a series of unexpected rescues, of "lesser 'happy endings' figuring forth the ultimate triumph," including Frodo's escape at the Ford of Bruinen, Gandalf's return from death, and the victory at Helm's Deep.[20] And the destruction of the Ring is also followed by other eucatastrophic moments as well.

One of these is the moving scene at the end of the seven days that Faramir and Éowyn spend together in the Houses of Healing. As Faramir is falling in love with her, Éowyn remains caught in her grief, for Aragorn, her first love, is away at the final battle before the gates of Mordor. When they see from afar the collapse of Sauron's realm, they do not know for sure what has happened, but Faramir feels it in an upwelling sense of joy and love: "'Éowyn, Éowyn, White Lady of Rohan, in this hour I do not believe that any darkness will endure!' And he stooped and kissed her brow" (RK, pp. 259–260). Still, Éowyn remains torn between Aragorn and Faramir, but finally he confronts her grief directly and asks for her love: "Then the heart of Éowyn changed, or at last she understood it. And suddenly her winter passed, and the sun shone on her. 'I stand in Minas Anor, Tower of the Sun,' she said; 'and behold! the Shadow has departed! I will be a shieldmaiden no longer . . .'" (RK, p. 262). Here the turning is an inner one, like Théoden's reawakening from Wormtongue's spell. But this inward turn towards Faramir is pregnant with that sense of transcendent response, or divine fulfillment of hope, that makes for eucatastrophe. Éowyn's healing, her restoration to her true self, is one with the land's return to health.

We find a similar symbolism after Aragorn is crowned king, and Gandalf takes him up to a "high hallow" on Mount

---

[20] *Ibid.*, p. 105.

Mindolluin, where it is still snowy, to show Aragorn his realm, and to give him hope. In answer to Aragorn's worries, Gandalf says:

> "Turn your face from the green world, and look where all seems barren and cold!". . .
>
> *Then Aragorn turned*, and there was a stony slope behind him running down from the skirts of the snow; and as he looked he was aware that alone there in the waste a growing thing stood. And he climbed to it, and saw that out of the very edge of the snow there sprang a sapling tree no more than three foot high. (RK, p. 270; emphasis added)

Aragorn finds a sapling of Nimloth, the White Tree of Númenor, scion of the tree in Gondolin, which in turn came from a seed of Telperion, the White Tree of Valinor. Its appearance is like a sign from the gods. Here again we find the language of "turning," the unexpected miracle, and with it a profound joy, a sense of fulfillment and completion. However, this is not a separate eucatastrophe, but rather the final piece of the larger "turn" from winter to spring. When the new king replaces the Withered Tree with the new sapling, the glory, hope, and vitality of Gondor are renewed.

The themes we have reviewed are sufficient to explain why Tolkien thought of *The Lord of the Rings* as "a fundamentally religious and Catholic work," even though he intentionally omitted "practically all references to anything like 'religion', to cults or practices, in the imaginary world. For the religious element is absorbed into the story and the symbolism" (L, p. 172). If it were only an epic romance, Tolkien's story would not necessarily have been religious, but as a fairy story for adults, it concludes with an essentially religious message that evil cannot stand forever, that its misappropriation of divine power and right destroys itself in the end. But this does not come about without our participation, our willingness to sacrifice, and our faith (beyond all rational hope) that our mortal efforts will be met with the ultimate response, and day will finally come again.

The Wisdom of the Philosophers

Lao-tzu (born c. 604 B.C.E.)
"Compassion leads to courage."

Buddha (560–480 B.C.E.)
"When a man has pity on all living creatures then only is he noble."

Confucius (c. 551–479 B.C.E.)
"The strength of a nation lies in the integrity of its homes."

Pythagoras (flourished c. 532 B.C.E.)
"What is the most just thing? To sacrifice."

Heraclitus (died c. 510–480 B.C.E.)
"Nothing is permanent except change."

Protagoras (c. 481–411 B.C.E.)
"Man is the measure of all things."

Socrates (470–399 B.C.E.)
"How many things I can do without!"

Plato (428/7–348/7 B.C.E.)
"It is natural for a man who is no fool to be afraid, if he does not know and cannot prove that the soul is immortal."

Diogenes the Cynic (c. 412–323 B.C.E.)
"Of what use is a philosopher who doesn't hurt anybody's feelings?"

Chuang-tzu (c. 399–295 B.C.E.)
"In tranquility he becomes a sage, and in activity he becomes a king."

Aristotle (384–322 B.C.E.)
"The good person is related to his friend as to himself, for his friend is another self."

Mencius (c. 372–289 B.C.E.)
"Humanity subdues inhumanity as water subdues fire."

Epicurus (341–270 B.C.E.)
"Death is nothing to us, since when we are, death has not come, and when death has come, we are not."

Cicero (106–43 B.C.E.)
"There is nothing so absurd but some philosopher has said it."

Lucretius (c. 98–55 B.C.E.)
"It is more useful to watch a man in times of peril, and in adversity to discern what kind of man he is; for then, at last, words of truth are drawn from the depths of his heart, and the mask is torn off, reality remains."

Seneca (c. 4 B.C.E.–65 A.D.)
"Fate leads the willing, and drags along the unwilling."

Epictetus (50–130)
"Do not seek to have events happen as you want them to, but instead want them to happen as they do happen, and your life will go well."

Marcus Aurelius (121–180)
"He who acts unjustly acts unjustly to himself, because he makes himself bad."

Augustine (354–430)
"O love, you ever burn and are never extinguished."

Boethius (c. 480–524)
"Just as knowledge of present things does not impose necessity on the things being done, neither does foreknowledge of future things impose necessity in the things to come."

Anselm (1033–1109)
"You exist so truly, Lord my God, that You cannot even be thought not to exist."

Abu Hamid al-Ghazali (1058–1111)
"I learnt with certainty that it is above all the mystics who walk on the road of God."

Moses Maimonides (1135–1204)
"Know that in every man there is necessarily the faculty of courage."

Thomas Aquinas (1225–1274)
"The love of God is better than the knowledge of God."

Niccolò Machiavelli (1469–1527)
"God is not willing to do everything, and thus take away our free will and that share of glory which belongs to us."

Francis Bacon (1561–1626)
"A little philosophy inclineth man's mind to atheism; but depth in philosophy bringeth men's minds about to religion."

Thomas Hobbes (1588–1679)
"There is no such thing as perpetual tranquillity of mind, while we live here; because life itself is but motion, and can never be without desire, nor without fear."

René Descartes (1596–1650)
"Reading good books is like having a conversation with the most distinguished men of past ages."

Blaise Pascal (1623–1662)
"The heart has its reasons of which reason does not know."

Baruch Spinoza (1632–1677)
"All excellent things are as difficult as they are rare."

John Locke (1632–1704)
"It is enough to justify the fitness of anything to be done by resolving it into "the wisdom of God," who has done it,

though our short views and narrow understandings may utterly incapacitate us to see that wisdom and to judge rightly of it."

Gottfried Leibniz (1646–1716)
"The supreme wisdom, united to a goodness that is no less infinite, cannot but have chosen the best . . . So it may be said that if this were not the best of all possible worlds, God would not have created any."

George Berkeley (1685–1753)
"Truth is the cry of all, but the game of few."

Voltaire (1694–1778)
"If God did not exist, it would be necessary to invent him."

David Hume (1711–1776)
"Be a philosopher; but, amidst all your philosophy, be still a man."

Jean-Jacques Rousseau (1712–1778)
"Let us set down as an incontestable maxim that the first movements of nature are always right. There is no original perversity in the human heart."

Immanuel Kant (1724–1804)
"Two things fill the mind with ever new and increasing admiration and awe, the oftener and more steadily we reflect on them: the starry heavens above and the moral law within."

Jeremy Bentham (1748–1832)
"Nature has placed mankind under the governance of two sovereign masters, *pain* and *pleasure*. It is for them alone to point out what we ought to do, as well as determine what we shall do."

Mary Wollstonecraft (1759–1851)
"How grossly do they insult us who thus advise us only to render ourselves gentle, domestic brutes!"

G.W.F. Hegel (1770–1831)
"We may affirm absolutely that nothing great in the world has been accomplished without passion."

Arthur Schopenhauer (1788–1860)
"In the end everyone stands alone, and the important thing is, who it is that stands alone."

Ralph Waldo Emerson (1803–1882)
"Nothing is more simple than greatness; indeed, to be simple is to be great."

John Stuart Mill (1806–1873)
"If all mankind minus one were of one opinion, and only one person were of the contrary opinion, mankind would be no more justified in silencing that one person than he, if he had the power, would be justified in silencing mankind."

Søren Kierkegaard (1813–1855)
"Without risk there is no faith."

Henry David Thoreau (1813–1862)
"To be a philosopher is not merely to have subtle thoughts, or even to found a school, but to so love wisdom as to live, according to its dictates, a life of simplicity, independence, magnanimity, and trust."

Karl Marx (1818–1883)
"The philosophers have only *interpreted* the world differently, what matters is to *change* it."

Charles Sanders Peirce (1839–1914)
"The opinion which is fated to be ultimately agreed to by all who investigate is what we mean by truth."

William James (1842–1910)
"Believe that life is worth living, and your belief will help create the fact."

Friedrich Nietzsche (1844–1900)
"Live dangerously."

John Dewey (1859–1952)
"We only think when we are confronted by a problem."

Alfred North Whitehead (1861–1947)

"Philosophy begins in wonder. And, at the end, when philosophic thought has done its best, the wonder remains."

Bertrand Russell (1872–1970)

"Hatred has become the rule of life, and injury to others is more desired than benefit to ourselves."

Ludwig Wittgenstein (1889–1951)

"The limits of my language are the limits of my world."

Martin Heidegger (1889–1976)

"You do not get to philosophy by reading many and multifarious philosophical books, nor by torturing yourself with solving the riddles of the universe . . . Philosophy remains latent in every human existence and need not be first added to it from somewhere else."

Jean-Paul Sartre (1905–1980)

"If you love long enough, you'll see that every victory turns into a defeat."

Hannah Arendt (1906–1975)

"The connotation of courage, which we now feel to be an indispensable quality of the hero, is in fact already present in a willingness to act and speak at all, to insert one's self into the world and begin a story of one's own."

Simone de Beauvoir (1908–1986)

"Man is defined as a human being and woman as a female— whenever she behaves as a human being she is said to imitate the male."

Albert Camus (1913–1960)

"The absurd is born of this confrontation between the human need and the unreasonable silence of the world."

The Fellowship of
the Book

GREGORY BASSHAM is Director of the Center for Ethics and Public Life and Chair of the Philosophy Department at King's College, Pennsylvania. He is the author of *Original Intent and the Constitution: A Philosophical Study* (Rowman and Littlefield, 1992) and co-author of *Critical Thinking: A Student's Introduction* (McGraw-Hill, 2002). Greg recently gave a talk to his local Teen Chastity League, entitled "Waiting 2,778 Years for Mr. Right: The Arwen Undómiel Story."

DOUGLAS K. BLOUNT is Associate Professor of Philosophy of Religion at Southwestern Baptist Theological Seminary. He has published articles on philosophical theology and public policy issues. He currently spends his idle hours working on two manuscripts, *Ecce Hobbit* and *Thus Spake Gandalf.* Though he has been known to enjoy a second breakfast on occasion, he is only quite a little fellow in a wide world after all.

ERIC BRONSON heads the Philosophy and History Department at Berkeley College in New York City. Currently, he is editing the forthcoming book, *Baseball and Philosophy* (Open Court, 2004), and co-writing the short film, *Ruckus!* with Dean Ishida (Farouche Films). While Eric appreciates Bilbo's dictum that "Not all those who wander are lost," his own life fails to corroborate that maxim.

B. STEVE CSAKI is Visiting Assistant Professor of Philosophy and Instructor of Japanese at Centre College. He has published articles and presented papers on comparative philosophy, Zen Buddhism, and Taoism. While Steve plays the role of the philosopher farmer, he is haunted by the fact that he is forever too short to play basketball and too tall for the Shire.

John J. Davenport is Assistant Professor of Philosophy at Fordham University. He has published articles on free will, existentialism, moral philosophy, and the philosophy of religion, and recently co-edited the collection, *Kierkegaard After MacIntyre* (Open Court, 1999) with Anthony Rudd. John likes to spend his time in the Ivory Tower of Orthanc peering into his *palantír* to see whether his students are doing their assigned reading.

Bill Davis is Professor of Philosophy and Chair of the Philosophy Department at Covenant College. He has contributed chapters on philosophical theology to *Reason for the Hope Within* (Eerdmans, 1999) and *Beyond the Bounds* (Crossways, 2003), as well as the entry on Thomas Reid for *The Encyclopedia of Empiricism*. Bill's beard and a broad-bladed axe are often found tucked in his belt.

Scott A. Davison earned B.A. and M.A. degrees in philosophy from Ohio State University before completing a second M.A. and a Ph.D. in philosophy from the University of Notre Dame. He is currently an Associate Professor of Philosophy at Morehead State University in Kentucky. Scott's insight into the nature of evil is based not only on philosophical research, but also on extensive "field work" involving the method of "participant observation."

Jorge J.E. Gracia holds the Samuel P. Capen Chair and is SUNY Distinguished Professor of Philosophy at the State University at Buffalo. He is author of twelve books, including *Individuality* (1988), *Philosophy and Its History* (1992), *A Theory of Textuality* (1995), *Texts* (1996), *Metaphysics and Its Task* (1999), *How Can We Know What God Means?* (2000), and *Hispanic/Latino Identity* (2000). He hopes to find the Ring some day and keeps looking for it in and around Niagara Falls.

Thomas Hibbs is Dean of the Honors College and Distinguished Professor of Ethics and Culture at Baylor University. He has published two books on Aquinas, a book on philosophy and pop culture (*Shows about Nothing: Nihilism in Popular Culture*), and is at work on a book on *film noir*. Hibbs's greatest discovery as a young philosophy student was that Guinness comes in pints.

Eric Katz is Professor of Philosophy and Director of the Science, Technology, and Society Program at the New Jersey Institute of Technology. He is the author of *Nature as Subject: Human Obligation and Natural Community* (Rowman and Littlefield, 1997) and the co-editor of three books on environmental ethics and the philosophy of technology. Eric tells his students that professors are never late. They arrive precisely when they mean to.

Joe Kraus is Assistant Professor of English at King's College. He is the co-author of *An Accidental Anarchist* (Academy Chicago, 2001), and has published several articles on ethnic literature and history, particularly on the figure of the gangster. After he looked into Galadriel's mirror, he realized that he desperately needed a shave.

Andrew Light is Assistant Professor of Environmental Philosophy at New York University, and Research Fellow at the Institute for Environment, Philosophy and Public Policy at Lancaster University, England. He is the author of *Reel Arguments: Film, Philosophy, and Social Criticism* (Westview, 2003), and has edited or co-edited thirteen books on environmental ethics, philosophy of technology, and aesthetics, including *Technology and the Good Life?* (University of Chicago Press, 2000), *The Aesthetics of Everyday Life* (Seven Bridges, 2003), and *Moral and Political Reasoning in Environmental Practice* (MIT Press, 2003). Andrew has been known to shout, "Begone, foul dwimmerlaik, lord of carrion!" at committee meetings.

Jennifer L. McMahon is Assistant Professor of Philosophy and Chair of the Philosophy Program at Centre College. She has published articles on Sartre, Eastern philosophy, and aesthetics. Claiming to be a descendent of the Rohirrim, Jennifer epitomizes Sartre's notion of bad faith when she attributes her tendency to amass horses to a genetic predisposition.

Alison Milbank is Assistant Professor of English at the University of Virginia and author of *Daughters of the House: Modes of the Gothic in Victorian Fiction* (Palgrave Macmillan, 1992) and *Dante and the Victorians* (Manchester University Press, 1999); she has also edited two novels by Ann Radcliffe. She is currently completing book-length studies on *Gothic, Sacrifice, and the Modern* and *Tolkien and Christianity*. Alison was born in the Shire and left by the firth of Lune to find her way to Valinor, but ended up in America instead.

Theodore Schick, Jr. is Professor of Philosophy at Muhlenberg College and co-author (with Lewis Vaughn) of *How to Think about Weird Things* (McGraw-Hill, third edition 2003), and *Doing Philosophy* (McGraw-Hill, second edition 2002). His most recent book is *Readings in the Philosophy of Science: from Positivism to Postmodernism* (McGraw-Hill, 1999). He trims his toe hairs to hobbit length.

Aeon J. Skoble is Assistant Professor of Philosophy at Bridgewater State College. He is co-editor of the anthology *Political Philosophy: Essential Selections* (Prentice-Hall, 1999), co-editor of *The Simpsons and Philosophy* (Open Court, 2001), and co-editor of the forthcoming *Woody Allen and Philosophy* (Open Court, 2004). He writes on moral, political, and social theory for both scholarly and lay journals, and is editor of the annual journal *Reason Papers*. Aeon plans to live to the ripe old age of eleven-one and then vanish.

J. Lenore Wright is Assistant Director of the Baylor Interdisciplinary Core and an affiliated faculty member of the Philosophy Department at Baylor University. Her research interests include aesthetics and art criticism, philosophy and popular culture, and film theory. Her most recent publications are "Socrates at the Cinema: Using Film in the Philosophy Classroom," co-authored with Anne-Marie Bowery, in *Teaching Philosophy* (March 2003) and "The Wonder of Barbie: Female Representation in Popular Culture," in *Essays in Philosophy* (January 2003). Lenore regularly feels the Eye of Sauron upon her and has recurrent nightmares about Ringwraiths and orcs. Her husband has heard her mumbling in her sleep, "my precious, my precious tenure."

The Wizard's Index

abnegation, 98
Ackerman, Diane, 58
Adam and Eve, 103, 104n. 6
Adams, Douglas, 133
Adimantus, 7
Aeneid, The (Virgil), 179, 213–14
afterlife. *See* immortality, in *The Lord of the Rings*
Ainur, 74, 206, 213
Albert the Great, 201
Al-Ghazali, 132
alienation, 37
Alighieri, Dante. *See* Dante Alighieri
allegory, in *The Lord of the Rings*, 21–22, 80–81, 151, 193, 204
Aman, 34, 42, 44, 124, 126, 132–34
Ambrose, St., 195, 201
Amon Hen, 11, 16
Anduin, 141–42
Apology (Plato), 128
Aquinas, Thomas, 132
Aragorn, 5, 11, 15, 55, 61, 68, 73, 112, 130, 137, 146, 147, 171, 176, 177, 186, 187, 198, 201
  and Arwen, 35, 82, 123–25, 135–36
  contrasted with Boromir, 115–16
  death of, 136
  as King Elessar, 145, 147, 198
  and the Ring, 115–16
  and the sapling of Nimloth, 217–18
Arda, 124
Arendt, Hannah, 77, 79–80, 201
Ariadne, 201
Aristotle, 62, 110–16, 118, 132, 201

on friendship, 54, 70
on happiness, 63–64, 126
on tragedy, 99
on virtue, 110ff.
Arthurian legends, 205n. 2
Arwen, 35, 42, 54, 82, 123–25, 126, 134–36
Asimov, Isaac, 21, 25
Atani, 74
atomic bomb, and the Ring, 25
Auden, W.H., 213
Augustine, St., 53, 58, 102, 103, 107, 108, 131, 174, 194–95, 201
Aule, 154n. 4
Aurelius, Marcus, 53

Bagginses. *See* Bilbo; Frodo
Baldur, 40
Balin, 152
Balrog, 96, 130, 143, 177, 198
Barad-dûr, 18, 54, 70, 216
Barrow-downs, 156
Barrow-wights, 15, 95
Beare, Rhona, 2
beauty, 56–57, 91
Beauty and the Beast (fairy tale), 208
beer, in *The Lord of the Rings*, 49, 55
Bentham, Jeremy, 117
Beowulf, 40, 41, 80, 205
Beren, 214, 216
Berman, Marshall, 139–140, 146
Bert (troll), 89
Bertilak, Sir, 211–12